Chemistry in Balance

A M Hughes

**Head of Chemistry,
Tavistock School**

Bell & Hyman

Published in 1985 by
BELL & HYMAN LIMITED
Denmark House
37–39 Queen Elizabeth Street
London SE1 2QB

ISBN 0 7135 2671 8

Printed and bound in Great Britain
at The Bath Press, Avon

Contents

Introduction

Ever since the first caveman burnt wood to keep warm, chemistry has affected our lives. Nowadays, chemistry is involved in making our food, our medicines, our clothes and our transport. Without the work of chemists there would be no radios, televisions, computers, satellites, detergents, plastics, pesticides, bombs, missiles or industrial pollution. Chemistry is a very important subject. Its influence on your life is almost certainly going to increase. You cannot ignore it.

This book aims to introduce you to chemistry as simply as possible. Each chapter deals with an important topic in chemistry. By working through these topics you should get some idea of the way in which chemists think. You should realise some of their achievements and recognise some of their problems.

I hope that you will enjoy working with this book and I hope you find it helpful for your school chemistry course.

Safety statement

It is not intended that pupils should attempt any of the experiments described in this book, without first obtaining permission and any necessary guidance from their teacher. It is assumed that any experiment with a potential hazard (e.g. burning hydrogen in air) or using potentially hazardous chemicals (eg sodium, potassium, concentrated acids etc.) will be demonstrated by the teacher.

Teachers may find the following publications useful:
1. *Hazards in the chemical laboratory* edited by G. D. Muir published by The Chemical Society.
2. *Hazardous Chemicals: A manual for Schools and Colleges* by Scottish Schools Science Equipment Research Centre published by Oliver and Boyd.
3. *Cleapse HAZCARDS* published by CLEAPSE development group.
4. *Safety in Science Laboratories* Department of Education and Science.

A M Hughes

1 What are things made of?

Think of hard substances like diamond or steel. Think of soft substances like foam rubber or putty. Think of liquids that pour easily, like water, and liquids that hardly pour at all, like treacle. Think of a jelly wobbling on a plate. Imagine what would happen if you hit each of these with a hammer. They would behave very differently.

There are so many different things—with so many different properties; it is hardly surprising that we ask "What are things made of?" This has been asked for thousands of years. Many suggestions have been made to answer it. Gradually scientists have come to believe that all things are made up of tiny particles. No scientist has ever seen one of these particles, they are far too small for that, but many simple experiments suggest that matter *must* be made up of particles.

1.1 Some evidence for particles

There are some simple experiments that make scientists think all things are made of particles.

1. *Mixing nitrogen dioxide and air*

Nitrogen dioxide is a brown gas and so it can clearly be seen. It is about 1½ times more dense (heavier) than air. If the apparatus in Fig. 1.1 was left for about 15 minutes, we might expect the results shown in Fig. 1.2.

If you try these experiments you will find that the nitrogen dioxide and the air mix completely in both experiment 1 and experiment 2. This is shown in Fig. 1.3.

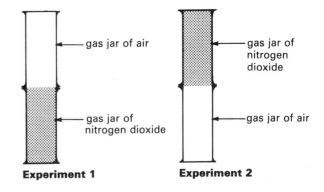

gas jar of air

gas jar of nitrogen dioxide

gas jar of nitrogen dioxide

gas jar of air

Experiment 1

Experiment 2

Fig 1.1

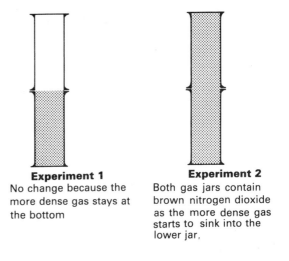

Experiment 1
No change because the more dense gas stays at the bottom

Experiment 2
Both gas jars contain brown nitrogen dioxide as the more dense gas starts to sink into the lower jar.

Fig 1.2

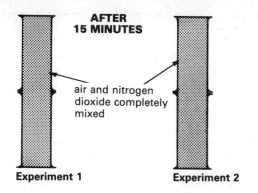

AFTER 15 MINUTES

air and nitrogen dioxide completely mixed

Experiment 1   Experiment 2

Fig 1.3

It may seem difficult to explain this unexpected result. However, if the gases are made up of *tiny particles, moving in all directions*, they will mix. The fact that nitrogen dioxide particles are heavier than air particles does not stop them mixing.

2. Smoke cell experiment

If the light from the lamp is focused by the lens into the empty glass box, it passes straight through (see Fig. 1.4). No light will enter the microscope. The person at A would just see a dark background. If the box is filled with smoke some of the light will be reflected by the smoke particles into the microscope.

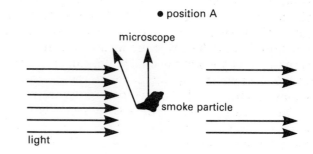

• position A

microscope

light

smoke particle

Fig 1.5 A smoke particle scattering light

At A specks of light reflected from the smoke particles are seen against a dark background. Each speck represents a smoke particle (see Fig 1.5).

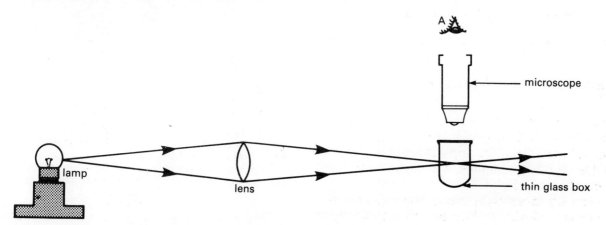

A

microscope

lamp

lens

thin glass box

Fig 1.4

3

If you try this experiment you will see that the specks of light are always moving in random directions. If you plotted the movement of *one* smoke particle it would be like that shown in Fig 1.6.

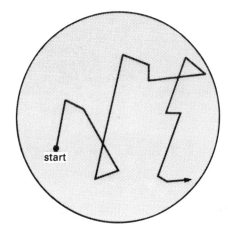

Fig 1.6

The smoke particles move in straight lines. They change direction suddenly and for no apparent reason.

The explanation is that the smoke particles are being hit by other particles that are too small to be seen. Therefore the air in the glass box must be made up of tiny particles. These air particles must be moving and hitting the smoke particles.

If the experiment is repeated using pollen grains in water, the pollen grains move in a similar way to the smoke particles. So, water must also be made up of tiny, moving particles.

1.2 Solids, liquids and gases

Matter is almost certainly made up of tiny particles, but matter is peculiar stuff. Many substances can be solids, liquids or gases at different temperatures. Solid, liquid and gas are known as the three *states of matter.*

These states have some very different properties. Think of water as an example. Ice is hard and brittle and can be cut into different shapes. Water flows and has a shape which depends on the shape of its container. It cannot be compressed much. Steam, like water, has no shape. It completely fills any container and is easily compressed.

These differences can be explained in terms of particles.

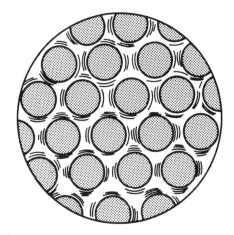

Fig 1.7 Solid

In any solid the particles are close together. In crystals they are packed in a regular pattern. The particles are anchored about fixed positions. They can only vibrate about these fixed positions. The vibrations become stronger as the temperature increases. Particles in a solid are strongly attracted to each other.

are free to move. The particles move so fast that there is little attraction between particles. The particles travel faster as the temperature increases.

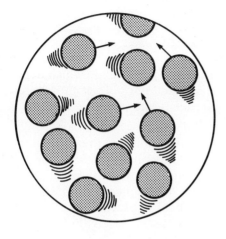

Fig 1.8 Liquid

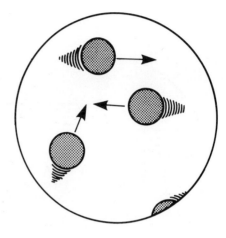

Fig 1.9 Gas

In liquids the particles are close together. They are free to move within the liquid, but are attracted to the other liquid particles. The particles move faster as the temperature increases.

In gases the particles are usually far apart. They

Table 1 shows the important differences between solids, liquids and gases. You should now be able to understand how these differences in properties can be explained by using the idea of particles.

Solids	Liquids	Gases
Have high density	Have high density	Have low density
Cannot be compressed	Cannot be compressed	Easily compressed
Have fixed shape	No fixed shape	No fixed shape
Can be cut with difficulty	Easily entered	Very easily entered

Table 1

1.3 Changes of state

Whether a substance is a solid, a liquid or a gas depends on temperature. We say water is a liquid because that is how it exists at room temperature. However, every day in kitchens water is changed from one state to another. Can you think where and when in your kitchen these changes take place?

We give names to these changes of state. These names are shown in Table 2.

Change of state			Name of change
Solid	$\longrightarrow$	Liquid	Melting
Solid	$\longrightarrow$	Gas	Sublimation
Liquid	$\longrightarrow$	Gas	Evaporation
Liquid	$\longrightarrow$	Solid	Freezing
Gas	$\longrightarrow$	Liquid	Condensation
Gas	$\longrightarrow$	Solid	Sublimation

Table 2

Let us look at the tiny particles of a substance when these changes take place (see Fig 1.10).

Melting/Freezing

When a solid melts, the particles vibrate so strongly that they break away and become liquid particles. The solid becomes smaller and smaller and more and more liquid is formed.

When a liquid freezes, liquid particles move so slowly that they stick together when they collide. Solid crystals are formed. More and more liquid particles stick onto the crystals until all the liquid has frozen.

At the melting point of the substance, freezing and melting take place at the same rate. Solid particles become liquid particles at the same rate as liquid particles become solid particles. If an ice cube sits in a beaker of water at 0°C it will not get bigger or smaller, but it might change its shape.

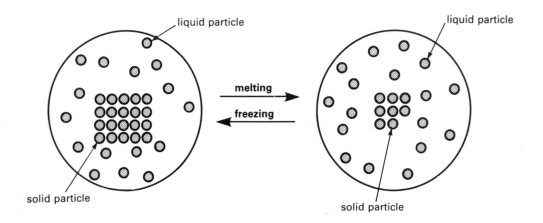

Fig 1.10 Melting and freezing

Evaporation/Condensation

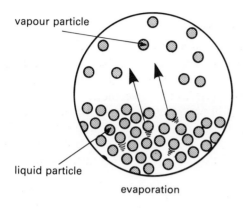

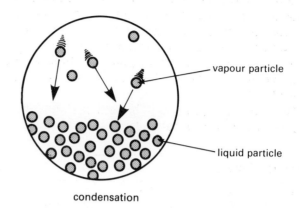

Fig 1.11 Evaporation and condensation

In the liquid state the particles move around but are attracted to other particles. Some have enough energy to break away and become gas particles.

In the gas state the particles are free to move. When gas particles collide with liquid particles they are attracted to them. Some bounce off, others become liquid particles.

Evaporation takes place when particles leave the liquid state *faster* than they join it from the gas state. A muddy puddle dries up because once water particles have found enough energy to escape from the liquid state they are blown away. They are unlikely to be captured by the water in that puddle again.

Condensation takes place when particles leave the liquid state *slower* than they join it from the gas state. As the temperature is lowered particles travel slower. Particles in the liquid state find it more difficult to escape. Particles in the gas state are more likely to be captured if they collide with a liquid.

Sublimation

A solid can change directly to a gas, missing out the liquid state. This means particles break off the solid with enough energy to exist as gas particles (see page 8). This is not as unusual as you might expect. Think of mothballs or any other solid that smells. Particles must escape from the solid and become gas particles or you could not smell them.

A gas particle can also slow down enough to become a solid particle without going through the liquid state. This is why freezer compartments of fridges 'ice up'. Water vapour particles collide with the very cold surface and change directly into solid particles.

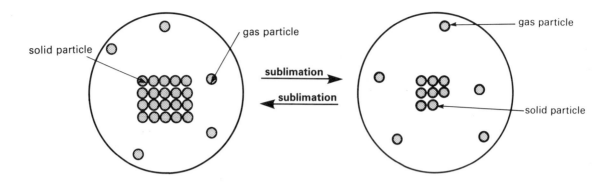

Fig 1.12 Sublimation

1.4 Dissolving

Where does the sugar go when you stir it into a cup of tea? The whole drink becomes sweet so the sugar must go everywhere. Is this more evidence that matter is made up of small particles? We can easily explain the process of dissolving using the idea of tiny particles.

Particles of the liquid (*solvent*) collide with particles of the substance being dissolved (*solute*). When they collide, they attract each other. Solvent particles pull off solute particles from the solid solute. The solvent particles surround the solute particles. This stops them rejoining. As the solvent particles move, the solute particles spread through the solution.

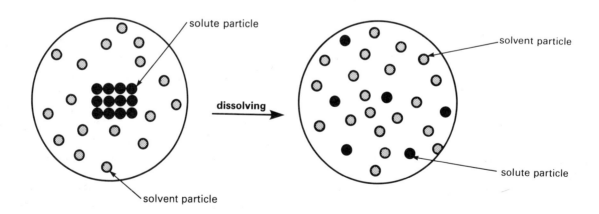

Fig 1.13 Dissolving

8

1.5 Diffusion

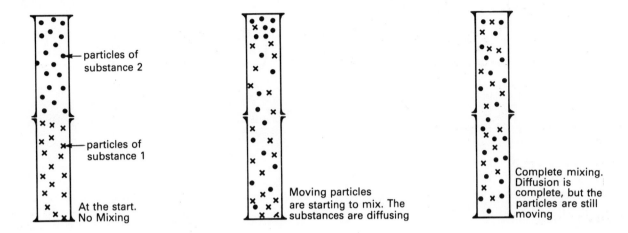

particles of substance 2

particles of substance 1

At the start. No Mixing

Moving particles are starting to mix. The substances are diffusing

Complete mixing. Diffusion is complete, but the particles are still moving

Fig 1.14

When two substances mix without help the process is called *diffusion*. We have already said diffusion is difficult to explain unless the idea of small particles is used. Fig 1.14 shows how we believe diffusion takes place.

Gases diffuse faster than liquids because there are greater spaces between the particles in gases. Mixing is therefore easier.

We should be grateful that gases diffuse quickly:

1. Unpleasant smells quickly disappear.
2. Gas leaks at home or school can often be quickly detected before any dangerous build up takes place.
3. If no diffusion took place in the earth's atmosphere, the most dense gas might sink to ground level. The oxygen band might well be out of our reach.

1.6 Are particles the answer?

On page 1 we asked "What are things made of?". Tiny, moving particles is an answer, but certainly not the full one. When scientists decided that matter was made up of tiny particles they could explain a number of observations like melting and dissolving, which could not be explained before.

But many other questions then had to be asked: Questions like "How big are the particles?", "How heavy are they?", "Why do they attract each other?", "How can particles of one substance be changed into particles of another substance?".

Partly by wanting to know the answer to these questions and by wanting to make better use of the Earth's resources, the science of chemistry has developed.

Questions

1. BOILING, CONDENSATION, DISSOLVING, DIFFUSION, EVAPORATION, FREEZING, MELTING, SUBLIMATION.

Choose from the list, the word which best describes the process taking place in each of the following.
For example Clothes drying on a clothes line—evaporation.

a Water forming on a kitchen window while food is being cooked
b Water changing to ice
c Sugar is stirred into a cup of tea
d Molten metal solidifies in a mould
e The smell of a 'stink bomb' gradually disappears
f A small puddle gradually dries up in warm weather
g Water changes to steam at 100°C
h Iodine changes from a solid to a gas without becoming a liquid
i Ice forms from water vapour on the freezer compartment of a fridge
j Bubbles of ethanol vapour form in liquid ethanol

2. A solid compound X was heated steadily for 20 minutes. Its temperature varied as shown in the graph

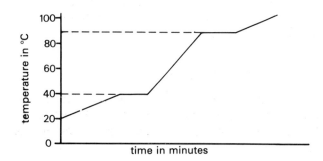

a At what temperature did X melt?
b What is the boiling point of X?
c What is the highest temperature at which X can exist as a solid?
d Would you expect X to be a solid, a liquid, or a gas at the following temperatures: (i) 25°C, (ii) 50°C, (iii) 100°C?
e At what temperature does X exist as a solid *and* as a liquid?

3. Draw diagrams to show what happens in terms of particles when:

a Sugar dissolves in water
b Ice melts
c Water freezes

4.
a Name 2 ways in which:
   (i) a liquid differs from a solid
   (ii) a liquid differs from a gas
   (iii) a gas differs from a solid
b Draw simple diagrams to show how the particles are arranged in
(i) solids (ii) liquids (iii) gases
c Are the attractive forces between particles greatest in solids, liquids or gases?

5. Explain the following in terms of particles:
a Gases are easily compressed
b Solids need large forces in order to bend or break them
c 1 litre of ice weighs approximately 1000 g whereas 1 litre of water vapour weighs about 0·75 g

6. Suppose the pupils in your school are particles.
List the times of the day when these particles are arranged like:
a particles in a gas   **c** particles in a solid
b particles in a liquid

2 Pure substances and mixtures

	PURE SALT	ROCK SALT
Appearance	Pure white crystals	White crystalline solid with grey or brown streaks
Taste	Normal salty taste	Salty taste with earthy taste added
Effect of adding to water	Colourless solution forms	Cloudy solution forms. It may be grey or brown. A grey or brown solid slowly settles
Adding barium chloride solution to a solution	No reaction	A white precipitate *may* form
Adding silver nitrate solution to a solution	A white precipitate forms	A white precipitate forms

Table 1

Chemists need pure substances. If a substance is pure it always has the same properties. It will always react in the same way. This is not so with an impure substance. Its properties can vary.

Table 1 compares pure salt (sodium chloride) with rock salt. Rock salt is sodium chloride as it is found in underground deposits.

From **Table 1** you can see that the properties and reactions of the pure salt are always the same. The properties of the impure salt depend on the type of impurity present and on its concentration.

Nearly all pure substances that chemists use have gone through two stages: they have been separated from a mixture and have been tested to find out how pure they are.

2.1 Separating mixtures

If we want to separate two substances in a mixture, we must find some difference between them. We can then use this difference in the method of separation that we choose.

1. Using differences in particle size

In a mixture of sand and water, the water particles are very small and will pass through a filter paper.

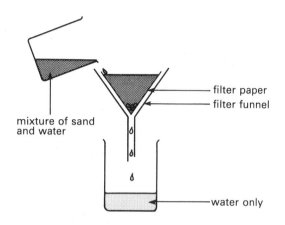

mixture of sand and water

filter paper

filter funnel

water only

Fig 2.1 Apparatus for filtration

The sand particles are much larger and will not pass through. We can therefore separate sand and water by filtration.

The *liquid* that passes through the filter paper is known as the *filtrate*.

The *solid* that stays on the filter paper is known as the *residue*.

The filter paper is a very fine sieve. Its holes are smaller than sand particles but bigger than water particles. Filtration or sieving is often used as a method of separation. It can separate crystals from the solutions in which they were made; it can remove dust from air; it can even be used to grade apples into different sizes. How many different uses of filtration can you think of in your home?

2. Using differences in boiling point

Suppose you wanted to get pure water from salt water. Filtration would be no use, since dissolved salt particles are about the same size as water particles. Another difference in property must be used. Sodium chloride melts at 806°C and water boils at 100°C. This difference can be used and the mixture separated by *distillation* (see Fig 2.2).

In the distillation flask the water is changed into water vapour. This passes into the condenser, where it is cooled and changes back into water. The condenser is sloped so that the pure water formed runs away from the distillation flask into the collecting dish.

If we wish to separate two liquids with similar boiling points (eg: ethanol, boiling point 80°C, and water, boiling point 100°C) by distillation, *fractional distillation* must be used.

The fractionating column is a long tube packed with glass beads. These give a large surface area for evaporation and condensation. The thermometer bulb is level with the condenser so that the boiling point of the liquid being collected is measured. The liquid with the lowest boiling point is collected first. When no more passes into the condenser, the collection dish is changed and the flask is heated more strongly to collect a substance with a higher boiling point. In this way the original liquid mixture is divided up into a number of *fractions* in separate collection dishes.

One of the major uses of fractional distillation is in refining crude oil. In industrial separations using fractional distillation, it would be very inefficient if the collecting vessel and the heat supply had to be changed often.

You can see how industry uses fractional distillation when refining crude oil on page 115.

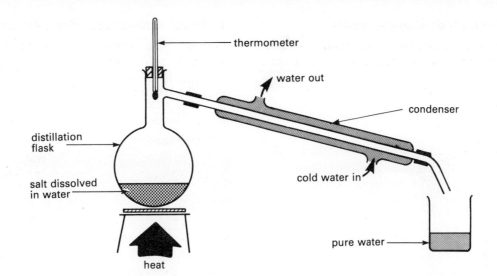

Fig 2.2

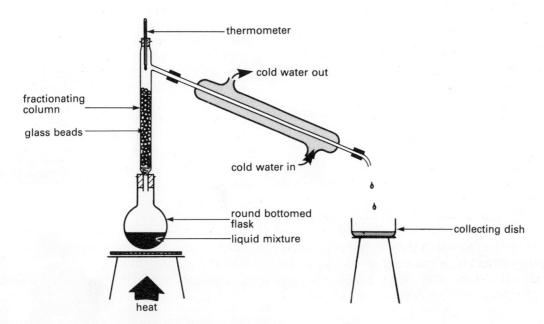

Fig 2.3 Laboratory apparatus for fractional distillation

3. Separating substances that sublime

Some substances—such as iodine, do not usually melt or boil when heated. These substances *sublime* (change directly from a solid to a gas). This property can be used to separate substances that sublime from those that don't, by a process very similar to distillation (see Fig 2.4).

When the mixture is heated, the substance that sublimes changes to a gas. This rises up the tube until it reaches the test tube that is water cooled. On the surface of the water cooled test tube the substance changes back from a gas into a solid.

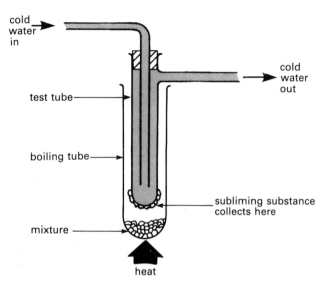

Fig 2.4 Separating by subliming

4. Using differences in solubility

If one substance is soluble in water and another is insoluble, they can easily be separated from a mixture as shown in Fig 2.5:

If the two substances are both soluble in water they can still be separated, if they dissolve to different extents. The separation process is known as *fractional crystallisation*.

Suppose you wanted to purify a sample of potassium nitrate with a potassium chloride impurity. You could use the method shown in Fig 2.6.

Stir mixture with water to dissolve the soluble substance

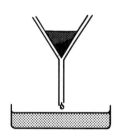

Filter off the insoluble substance

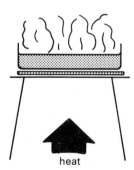

Evaporate the water to leave the soluble substance

Fig 2.5

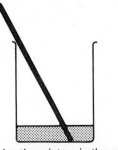

Dissolve the mixture in the *minimum* amount of hot water. The solution is now saturated with potassium nitrate, but not with potassium chloride

Cool the solution. Potassium nitrate crystals form. Potassium chloride stays dissolved

Filter off the potassium nitrate crystals

Fig 2.6

Chromatography

Chromatography is a very useful technique. It can be used to separate tiny quantities of very similar substances.

A small spot of the mixture in solution is placed on the filter paper strip and the end of the strip is dipped into the solvent. As the solvent soaks up the filter paper, it pulls the substances to be separated along with it. The more soluble a substance is in the solvent, the more it will keep up with the solvent as it soaks up the paper. This separates the mixture. Fig 2.8 shows what is seen when three dyes are separated.

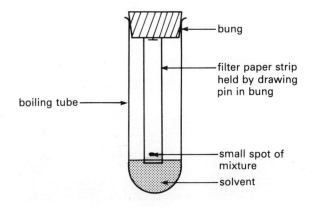

Fig 2.7 Apparatus for simple paper chromatography

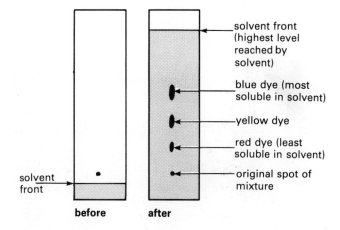

Fig 2.8

The separate spots of dye can then be cut out and the dyes washed into solution using suitable solvents.

Chromatography can be used to find out what flavourings have been added to food, or even to prove that a sample of engine oil has come from a particular car.

Using liquids that don't mix

Liquids that don't mix are known as *immiscible* liquids. Oily liquids such as ethoxyethane or methyl benzene are immiscible with water.

A liquid like ethoxyethane can be used to separate a single substance from a solution of the substance and its impurity in water. The substance to be separated is usually far more soluble in the ethoxyethane than are its impurities. In the laboratory the separation is carried out using a separating funnel.

The separating funnel is shaken to mix the layers well. The liquids are then allowed to settle. The aqueous (water) layer and the ethoxyethane layer are run into separate containers. The ethoxyethane is then allowed to evaporate in a safe place, leaving the separated substance behind.

5. Using differences in density

There are two ways of using these differences to separate mixtures of solids. Both are used to concentrate metal ores.

(i) Using oils

The ore is crushed. It is then stirred into an oil which has a very carefully controlled density. The useless rock (gangue) floats on the surface of the oil and the more dense mineral sinks. The two can then be separated.

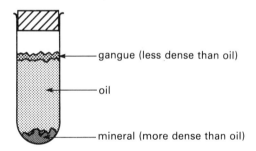

Fig 2.10

(ii) By agitating

If the crushed ore is placed in water and the water is agitated, different layers form. The most dense material falls to the bottom.

There are many methods which can be used to separate mixtures. All the methods require that

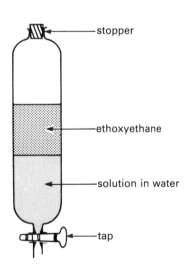

Fig 2.9 Using a separating funnel

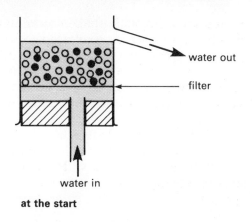
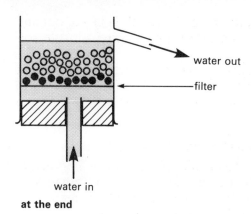

at the start   at the end

Fig 2.11 Separating by agitating

substances to be separated, should have some differences in their properties. The methods differ in their efficiency and use.

Chromatography is very efficient, but it can only be used on a small scale. In the concentration of metal ores, the same efficiency is not needed, but the method must work on a large scale. Some methods such as filtration or fractional distillation can be adapted to work on a large or small scale.

2.2 Knowing it's pure

Once a substance has been purified it must be tested to prove that it is pure. It is worth considering some of the properties of pure substances.

Properties of pure substances

1. It will look pure. *Example*: A white substance cannot be pure if it has black specks in it.
2. It will have a fixed melting point and boiling point. *Example*: Water melts at 0°C and boils at 100°C at atmospheric pressure.

3. It will all melt at one temperature.
4. It cannot be separated into anything simpler by methods such as filtration, distillation, chromatography, crystallisation or fractional distillation. *Example:* A pure red dye only gives one spot on a chromatogram. A mixture of red dyes gives several.

By investigating one or more of these properties, we can find out if a substance is pure.

A method often used is to measure the melting point of the substance (see page 18).

A small sample of the substance is placed in a very thin tube. This is strapped to a thermometer with the sample level with the bulb of the thermometer. The thermometer and sample are placed in an oil bath and the oil *slowly* heated. The sample in the thin tube is watched carefully and the temperature at which it melts is noted.

If the substance is pure it completely melts at one temperature. If it is impure it melts over a temperature range.

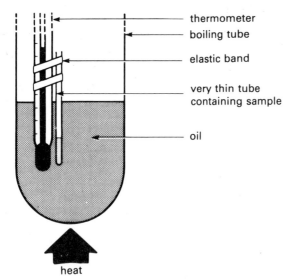

thermometer
boiling tube
elastic band
very thin tube containing sample
oil

heat

Fig 2.12 Small scale apparatus for measuring melting point

2.3 Elements and compounds

We have seen that pure substances cannot be simplified by methods such as filtration, distillation, crystallisation or chromatography. However, some pure substances can be broken down into simpler substances by stronger methods such as heating or using electricity.

Pure substances can be divided into two groups:

1. Compounds: These are pure substances that can be broken down into simpler substances by chemical methods. This is the main group of pure substances.

Sodium chloride, copper (II) sulphate crystals and carbon dioxide gas are common compounds used in laboratories.

2. Elements: These are pure substances that *cannot* be broken down into anything simpler by any chemical method. Just over one hundred elements exist.

Elements are very important as they are the basic substances from which everything else is made. Carbon, oxygen, hydrogen, nitrogen, iron, aluminium, tin and copper are examples of common elements. Many elements cannot be found free in nature, because they react with other elements to form compounds. Elements can react with each other in so many different ways that millions of different compounds exist.

Chemists have to decide whether substances are elements, compounds or mixtures. They also have to give reasons for their choice. Here are a few examples:

1. *Air:* Air is a mixture for the following reasons:

a Its composition changes. Town air often contains more polluting gases than country air. Also, the oxygen and carbon dioxide content of the air vary slightly.

b It has the properties of all the pure substances it contains. Air turns lime water milky. This is a property of carbon dioxide. It will blacken hot copper. This is a property of oxygen.

c It can be separated into different pure substances by physical means. Liquid air can be fractionally distilled to give oxygen and nitrogen.

d It can be made by mixing its components.

2. *Sodium chloride.* Sodium chloride is a compound for the following reasons:

a Its composition does *not* change. Any pure sample contains 39·3% of sodium, by weight.

b It cannot be broken down by any physical method.

c It can be broken down into simpler substances by chemical methods. If electricity is passed through molten sodium chloride, sodium and chlorine are formed.

d It can only be made from other material by a chemical change. *Example:* sodium burns in chlorine to form sodium chloride.

3. *Copper*. Copper is an element for the following reasons:

a Its composition does not change.
b It cannot be broken down into anything simpler by any chemical method.
c In all its chemical reactions it *combines* with other elements.

2.4 Chemical change

It is easy to see that a mixture can be made just by mixing two or more substances. We have all mixed paints or made a cup of coffee by stirring coffee powder into hot water.

It is not as simple to understand that a compound must be made by a chemical change. What is a chemical change? How do we recognise one?

Chemical changes are happening everywhere, all the time. As you read this your hair is growing, food is being cooked somewhere nearby, iron is rusting, cars are burning petrol. All these are very different processes, but they are all chemical changes.

The following list should help you recognise a chemical change.

1. In a chemical change new substances are always formed.
2. In a chemical change the starting substances cannot be reformed by methods such as chromatography, distillation, filtration.
3. In chemical changes heat is usually produced or absorbed. There is a temperature change. If heat is produced the temperature increases and the change is said to be *exothermic*. If heat is absorbed from the surroundings the temperature decreases and the change is said to be *endothermic*.
4. During a chemical change there is often a visible change. *Example:* The mixture may fizz, there may be a colour change, a precipitate may form.

Questions

1. CHROMATOGRAPHY, CRYSTALLISATION, DISTILLATION, FRACTIONAL DISTILLATION, FILTRATION.

Choose from the above techniques the one most suitable for the following separations.

a Getting pure water from sea water
b Getting salt crystals from salt water
c Removing the dust from air
d Separating black ink into its individual dyes
e Getting turpentine from turpentine contaminated with paint
f Getting pure water from a cup of tea

2. Your young brother has mixed the pepper and the salt in the kitchen. Assume that the only properties of pepper that you know are
(i) it has a strong smell (ii) it is insoluble in water
Describe how you would produce pure salt and pure pepper from the mixture.

3. Iodine sublimes when it is heated. Describe how you would obtain pure iodine from a mixture of iodine and sand. Include a fully labelled diagram of the apparatus you would use.

4. Decide whether each of the following is a pure substance or a mixture:

a coal	**b** copper	**c** milk
d iron	**e** sugar	**f** steel
g brass	**h** salt	**i** pepper
j air.		

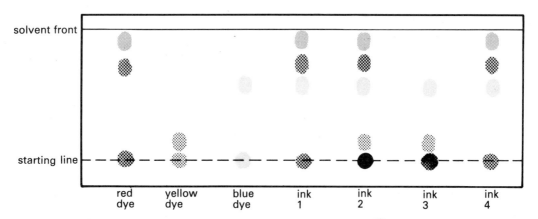

red dye	yellow dye	blue dye	ink 1	ink 2	ink 3	ink 4

5. The diagram shows the chromatogram produced by 3 dyes and 4 different inks

a Which dye is not a pure substance?

b What colour would you expect ink 1 to be?

c Which ink is green?

d Which 2 inks are identical?

e Which dye would you expect to be least soluble in the solvent used? Give a reason for your answer.

6. The table gives information about 4 *pure* substances

a Explain why substance A must be an element. What element could it be?

b Explain why substance B must be a compound. What compound could it be?

c Decide whether C and D are elements or compounds. Give a reason for your choice in each case.

7. In which of the following is a chemical change taking place:

a toasting bread   **b** melting ice

c boiling potatoes   **d** buttering bread

e dissolving sugar in water   **f** burning coal

g boiling water   **h** frying an egg

8. In each of the following experiments decide whether or not a chemical change is taking place. Give as many reasons as you can for your answers.

a A green powder was dropped into a colourless liquid. The mixture fizzed violently and a clear blue solution was formed.

b A colourless liquid turned litmus paper red. When another colourless liquid was added to it, there was no visible change, but the temperature increased by 12°C. The colourless solution formed turned litmus paper blue.

Name of substance	Appearance	Effect of heating substance in air
A	Black powder	Burns, when red hot, forming carbon dioxide only
B	Colourless gas	Burns with a blue flame forming carbon dioxide and water
C	Green powder	Turns to a black powder and forms carbon dioxide gas
D	Colourless gas	Burns with a blue flame forming water only

Table 1

c White needle shaped crystals were dropped into water. They dissolved to form a colourless solution. When the solution was left to evaporate, white needle shaped crystals were formed.

d Two colourless solutions were mixed in a test tube. The mixture immediately turned cloudy. A white solid slowly settled to the bottom of the test tube.

9. ◯ represents atoms of element A and

● represents atoms of element B.

Decide whether each of the following boxes contains an element, a compound or a mixture.

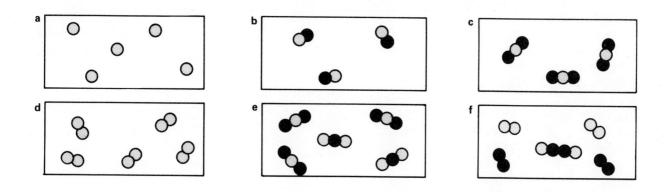

3 Atoms — the simplest particles

Elements are the simplest substances, from which all other substances are made. We also know that scientists believe that all matter is made up of tiny particles, but what are these particles like? The smallest particle of an element that can exist is known as an *atom*.

Atoms are very, very small. They have a diameter of about one ten millionth of a centimetre. Look at a one centimetre length on your ruler. Try to imagine ten million particles fitting into that space.

Atoms are far too small to be seen, so scientists have had to imagine a model of the atom. As scientists get more information about atoms, they gradually improve their model.

At first it was thought that atoms were hard balls, like tiny billiard balls. Later it was found that atoms could be broken down by strong electric fields into charged particles. Later still, experiments suggested that atoms were not solid, but contained large empty spaces. These and other discoveries led to the model of the atom that we accept today.

3.1 Structure of the atom

Atoms are now thought to be made up of three different particles; protons, neutrons and electrons. Each atom is made up of two regions; the nucleus and the shells (Fig 3.1).

The nucleus: The nucleus is extremely small. It is about one ten thousandth of the diameter of the atom. To get some idea of this size, imagine an atom in which the nucleus was the same size as you. This atom would have a diameter of about ten miles.

The nucleus contains *protons* that are positively charged and *neutrons* that are uncharged. Nearly all the mass of an atom is due to the protons and neutrons. Therefore the nucleus is very dense.

The shells: The shells contain negatively charged *electrons*. These spin round the nucleus like planets round the sun. Electrons are very light, even compared with protons and neutrons. 1840 electrons weigh the same as 1 proton.

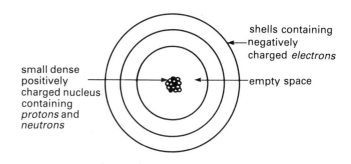

Fig 3.1 The atom

Name of particle	relative mass	relative charge
Proton	1	+1
Neutron	1	0
Electron	almost 0	−1

Table 1

Table 1 shows some of the properties of protons, neutrons and electrons.

You can see from **Table 1** that protons and electrons have the same charge, but this charge is opposite in sign. Since atoms are electrically neutral, they must *contain equal numbers of protons and electrons*. You should also see that the mass of an atom depends mainly on the number of protons and neutrons it contains.

We need to define two terms to help us describe the structure of atoms of different elements.

1. *Atomic number:* The atomic number of an element is the number of protons in the nucleus of an atom of that element. Each element has a different atomic number.

2. *Mass number:* The mass number is the sum of the number of protons and neutrons in the nucleus of an atom. It tells us approximately how heavy that atom is.

A carbon atom that contains 6 protons and 6 neutrons has a mass number of 12. A sodium atom that contains 11 protons and 12 neutrons has a mass number of 23.

3.2 Isotopes

For many years it was thought that all atoms of the same element were identical. It was eventually realised that atoms of the same element could have a different mass. This is because they contain different numbers of neutrons in their nuclei.

Isotopes are atoms of the same element having different mass numbers. They therefore have different masses. All isotopes of the same element have the same chemical properties.

Chlorine is an element which has isotopes. All chlorine atoms have an atomic number of 17. This means that all chlorine atoms contain 17 protons and 17 electrons. The two main isotopes of chlorine have mass numbers of 35 and 37. Therefore:

The isotope of mass number 35 must contain $35 - 17 = 18$ neutrons.

The isotope of mass number 37 must contain $37 - 17 = 20$ neutrons.

Chemists use a shorthand form to describe the isotopes of elements. They write the mass number and the atomic number before the symbol for the element.

$$^{\text{mass number}}_{\text{atomic number}} \text{SYMBOL}$$

The isotopes of chlorine are therefore written as $^{35}_{17}\text{Cl}$ and $^{37}_{17}\text{Cl}$.

3.3 Relative atomic mass

The mass number of an isotope tells us approximately how heavy an atom of that isotope is. However, there is a more accurate scale which is used to measure the masses of atoms. This is the relative atomic mass scale. The isotope of carbon of mass number 12 ($^{12}_{6}\text{C}$) is taken as the standard on this scale.

It is given a relative atomic mass of 12. The masses of all other atoms are compared with this. If an atom were twice as heavy as an atom of $^{12}_{6}\text{C}$, it would have a relative atomic mass of $2 \times 12 = 24$. If the atoms were 5 times as heavy it would be $5 \times 12 = 60$.

Most elements have isotopes and most samples of an element contain a mixture of isotopes. The relative atomic mass scale allows for this. The following example shows how.

A normal sample of chlorine contains $\frac{3}{4}$ of the $^{35}_{17}\text{Cl}$ isotope and $\frac{1}{4}$ of the $^{37}_{17}\text{Cl}$ isotope.
The relative atomic mass of chlorine is therefore:
$(\frac{3}{4} \times 35) + (\frac{1}{4} \times 37) = 35 \cdot 5$.

A table showing the relative atomic masses of the elements is given at the end of the book.

3.4 What about the electrons?

You might say "Electrons are so small, they can't have much effect on the properties of an atom." Nothing could be further from the truth. Chemists believe that electrons control the chemical properties of substances. Different substances have different chemical properties because they have different numbers of electrons and because the electrons are arranged differently in the shells.

Fig 3.2 A hydrogen atom

Hydrogen is the lightest element. It has the simplest atoms. Hydrogen has an atomic number of 1 and therefore only one electron. This electron goes into the shell nearest the nucleus. This is known as the first shell.

The first shell can hold a maximum of two electrons, so in the lithium atom (atomic number 3) one electron has to go into the second shell.

Fig 3.3 A lithium atom

The second shell can hold a maximum of eight electrons. This means that sodium with an atomic number of eleven is the first element to have electrons in the third shell.

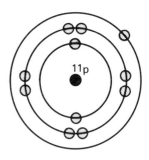

Fig 3.4 A sodium atom

Diagrams showing the arrangement of electrons in an atom uses a lot of space. Chemists use a shorthand form. This just shows the number of electrons in each shell without drawing the shells.

Hydrogen has an electron arrangement 1.
Lithium has an electron arrangement 2.1.
Sodium has an electron arrangement 2.8.1.

Table 2 shows the electron arrangement of elements with atomic numbers 1–20.

Some elements are very similar to others. Sodium, potassium, and lithium have very similar chemical reactions. Notice that they each have one electron in their outermost shell.

Chlorine and fluorine have very similar chemical reactions. Notice that they both have seven electrons in their outermost shell. Chlorine and fluorine are very different from lithium, sodium, or potassium. It seems likely that the electrons in the outermost shell are the ones mainly responsible for chemical properties.

Name of element	Chemical symbol	Atomic number	Electron arrangement
Hydrogen	H	1	1
Helium	He	2	2
Lithium	Li	3	2.1
Beryllium	Be	4	2.2
Boron	B	5	2.3
Carbon	C	6	2.4
Nitrogen	N	7	2.5
Oxygen	O	8	2.6
Fluorine	F	9	2.7
Neon	Ne	10	2.8
Sodium	Na	11	2.8.1
Magnesium	Mg	12	2.8.2
Aluminium	Al	13	2.8.3
Silicon	Si	14	2.8.4
Phosphorus	P	15	2.8.5
Sulphur	S	16	2.8.6
Chlorine	Cl	17	2.8.7
Argon	Ar	18	2.8.8
Potassium	K	19	2.8.8.1
Calcium	Ca	20	2.8.8.2

Table 2

The outermost shell electrons are known as *valence* electrons. Sodium, lithium and potassium each have one valence electron. Chlorine and fluorine each have seven valence electrons.

Scientists now have a very detailed model of the atom. This has slowly developed over the past hundred years. It will continue to develop. One day we might find out more about the structure of the nucleus. Perhaps protons, neutrons and electrons themselves can be broken down. Scientists will continue to make their model as accurate as possible, using all the information they can find.

Questions

1. ELECTRONS, ION, ISOTOPE, PROTONS, NEUTRONS, NUCLEUS. Choose words from the above list to complete the following passage. Each word can be used once, more than once, or not at all.

   All atoms are made up of a small, dense (1) ＿＿ surrounded by shells containing (2) ＿＿. Most atoms contain three different particles: protons, (3) ＿＿ and electrons. (4) ＿＿ are positively charged, (5) ＿＿ are negatively charged and (6) ＿＿ are uncharged. The lightest of these particles are the (7) ＿＿. All atoms of the same element contain the same number of (8) ＿＿ and (9) ＿＿. Atoms of the same element with different numbers of (10)＿＿ are known as isotopes.

2. Look up what is meant by atomic number and mass number, then copy and complete the Table.

Name of element	Atomic number	Mass number	Number of protons	Number of neutrons
sulphur	16	32		
chlorine			17	18
iron	26			30
sodium		23	11	
bromine		80		45
oxygen	8			8
aluminium		27	13	
magnesium	12	24		

3. Draw diagrams to show the structures of the atoms represented by:

   a $^{12}_{6}\text{C}$ **b** $^{23}_{11}\text{Na}$ **c** $^{35}_{17}\text{Cl}$ **d** $^{1}_{1}\text{H}$

4. Copy and complete the Table.

Name of element	Mass number	Number of protons	Number of neutrons	Number of electrons	Electron arrangement
hydrogen	1				
carbon			6		2.4
sulphur	32	16			
oxygen		8	8		
potassium			20		2.8.8.1
nitrogen	14			7	
argon	40	18			
helium		2	2		

5. Use the information shown in the Table to answer the following questions.

Name of particle	Number of protons	Number of neutrons	Number of electrons
A	17	18	17
B	11	12	10
C	10	10	10
D	8	8	10
E	17	20	17
F	12	12	12
G	16	16	16

a Which particle has more protons than electrons?

b Which particle has more electrons than protons?

c Which is the heaviest particle?

d Which is the lightest particle?

e Name 2 particles that are neutral atoms.

f Which of the particles is an atom with 2 electrons in its outermost shell?

g Which of the particles is a neutral atom with 6 electrons in its outermost shell?

h Which of the particles is negatively charged?

i Which of the particles is positively charged?

j Which of the particles are isotopes of the same element?

4 Sorting out the elements

Imagine the animals boarding Noah's ark two by two. Noah had quite a job on his hands. He couldn't put the foxes and the rabbits together, or the lions with the antelopes. If everything was to survive the animals had to be in well chosen groups. *Noah had to be organised.*

In some ways chemists in the 19th century had a similar problem. Over 60 elements had been discovered. Many of their compounds had been prepared. There was a mountain of information, but this was not organised. The elements had to be grouped in some way so that similarities between elements could be noted; patterns and trends could be observed. Only if chemists managed to organise their facts could the study of chemistry advance.

4.1 Metals and non metals

If you were asked to divide elements into groups, what groups would you choose? You might divide them into solids, liquids and gases. How useful would this be? One of the earliest attempts to group the elements was to divide them into metals and non metals.

Many metals have physical and chemical properties in common. The same applies to non metals. Physical properties are properties such as melting point, density and appearance. They do not involve any chemical reactions. The chemical properties of a substance are the chemical reactions of that substance.

Table 1 shows how the properties of metals and non metals differ.

Table 1

PROPERTIES OF METALS	PROPERTIES OF NON METALS
Physical properties	
1. Can be bent and hammered without breaking	1. Are brittle (easily broken) when solid
2. Are good conductors of electricity	2. Are poor conductors of electricity
3. Are good conductors of heat	3. Are poor conductors of heat
4. Usually have a high melting point	4. Usually have a low melting point
5. Usually have high densities	5. Usually have low densities
6. Have a metallic lustre(shine)	6. Do not have a metallic lustre(shine)
Chemical properties	
7. React with oxygen to form basic oxides. (These neutralise acids)	7. React with oxygen to form acidic oxides. (These neutralise alkalis)
8. Form chlorides that do not react with water	8. Form chlorides which often react with water
9. Metal chlorides conduct electricity when molten	9. Non metal chlorides do not conduct electricity when molten

This is a useful start at grouping the information. If you were told that a new element Devonium was a metal you would know a lot about it before you even saw a lump of it.

Unfortunately the metal/non metal grouping is not completely reliable, as there are some exceptions. Can you think of a metal element that melts below room temperature? Can you think of a non metal element that is a good conductor of electricity? Can you think of a metal element that is less dense than water? These elements do exist. You can use the data page at the back of the book (page 186) to identify them.

The greatest disadvantage of the metal/non metal grouping is that it only divides the elements into two groups. Chemists had to find a way of dividing the metals and non metals into smaller groups.

4.2 The Periodic Table of the elements

The modern Periodic Table greatly improves on the metal/non metal grouping of the elements. In the Periodic Table, elements are arranged in order of increasing atomic number. Elements with similar chemical properties are found in the same vertical columns.

In Chapter 3 we saw the first 20 elements listed in order of increasing atomic number. We can get some idea about how the Periodic Table was obtained by looking at these elements again.

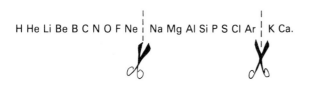

Suppose we cut the list every time we come to an element similar to one of lower atomic number. We might cut at the positions shown because lithium (Li), sodium (Na) and potassium (K) are very similar elements. If we take the strips formed by cutting the list of elements, we can arrange them so that similar elements are in vertical columns. We get

H He Li Be B C N O F Ne
      Na Mg Al Si P S Cl Ar
      K Ca

By this method the first 20 elements are arranged as they are in the modern Periodic Table.

The first thing to realise about the Periodic Table is that it divides the elements into metals and non metals. You can see this by looking at the full Periodic Table on page 31 or by looking at the outline of the Periodic Table in Fig 4.1.

The elements to the left of the steps are metals. Those to the right are non metals. There are many more metals than non metals.

The Periodic Table also divides the elements up into horizontal rows and vertical columns. *The horizontal rows are called periods. The vertical columns are called groups.*

Periods

As we move from left to right along any period there is a gradual change from metal to non metal. A large number of trends and patterns in the physical and chemical properties of elements can be detected as we move across a period. Use the data page to plot a graph of density of element against its atomic number. Do this for the first twenty elements. Is there any pattern in the way the densities of elements vary across a period?

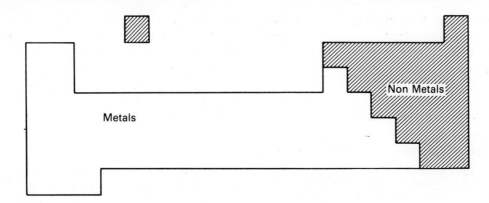

Fig 4.1 The Periodic Table

Groups

From Fig 4.2, you will see that most of the groups in the Periodic Table are numbered. Elements in the same group have the same number of valence electrons (outer shell electrons). The number of valence electrons in an atom of an element is equal to its group number.

Carbon (C) is in group 4. It has 4 valence electrons.
Chlorine (Cl) is in group 7. It has 7 valence electrons.
Sodium (Na) is in group 1. It has only 1 valence electron.

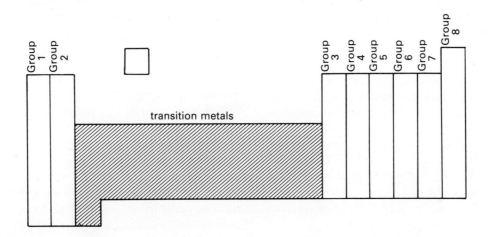

Fig 4.2 The groups of the Periodic Table

Because the elements in the same group have the same number of valence electrons, they also have very similar chemical properties.

Note: Helium is an exception in group 8. It has 2 valence electrons, whereas the other elements in this group have 8.

If you look at Fig 4.2 you will see that there are elements placed between group 2 and group 3. These are known as the *transition elements.* They all have 2 valence electrons. They therefore have a number of chemical properties in common.

4.3 Using the Periodic Table

To see just how useful the Periodic Table is to chemists, we must look at certain parts of the table in detail.

1. *The transition metals:* These have the following properties in common:

a they are strong, high melting point metals,
b they are dense metals,
c they form coloured (non white) compounds,
d they form insoluble oxides, hydroxides and carbonates,
e they make good catalysts (see Chapter 18),
f transition metal compounds can be oxidising or reducing agents (see Chapter 11).

Suppose that a chemist was told that an element was a transition metal. He would know that it had the general properties of a *metal* and the special properties of a *transition metal*. He would have learnt a great deal about the element very easily.

Suppose you were given a metal carbonate and asked to find out what metal it contained. If it dissolved in water you would know that it couldn't be a transition metal carbonate. They are all insoluble. This simple experiment would get rid of a large number of possible metals. It would make your problem much easier.

2. *The Alkali metals*

The elements in group 1 of the Periodic Table are known as the alkali metals. You may have seen samples of lithium, sodium and potassium in the laboratory. You are very unlikely to see samples of rubidium, caesium or francium. However, because the elements in a group are similar, it should be possible to predict the properties of rubidium, caesium and francium.

The alkali metals have the following properties in common:

a they are soft metals that can be cut with a knife,
b they are less dense than water,
c they are stored under oil because they react with air and water,
d they form alkaline solutions when they react with water,
e all alkali metal compounds dissolve in water,
f each of the alkali metals can be prepared by passing electricity through its molten chloride.

The group 1 metals are similar, but they are not identical.

This can be seen by reacting lithium, sodium and potassium with water. All three react to form an alkaline solution and hydrogen gas is produced. However, they do not all react at the same rate. Lithium reacts fairly slowly. Sodium reacts faster and enough heat is produced to melt the sodium. Potassium reacts even faster. Enough heat is produced to melt the potassium and to set fire to the hydrogen gas as it is formed.

You should see from this evidence that the group 1 metals become more reactive going down the group. They become more reactive with increasing atomic number. The element francium, at the bottom of the group, must be very, very reactive.

Perhaps now you realise why you are unlikely to see a sample of francium. If you were given a

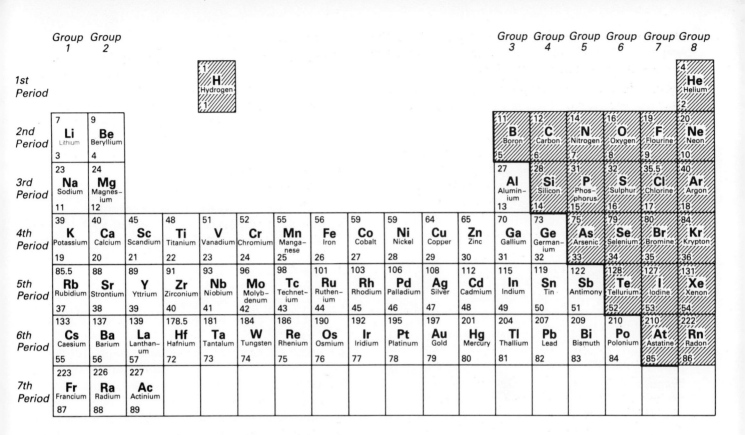

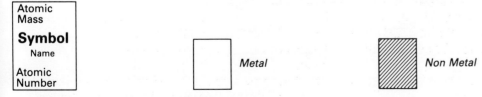

Fig 4.3 The periodic table of the elements

sample of francium, I'm sure you would keep it well away from water.

3. *The noble gases*

The noble gases are helium, neon, argon, xenon, krypton and radon. They are found in group 8 of the Periodic Table.

The noble gases are very unreactive and very few compounds of the noble gases have ever been prepared. The noble gases are the only elements that exist as single atoms. This means that their atoms must be very stable.

Since the chemical properties of an element depend on the arrangement of electrons in its atoms, the noble gases must have a very stable electron arrangement. The properties of the noble gases have greatly helped chemists to understand how atoms of other elements react together to form compounds.

The Periodic Table allows similar elements to be grouped. It allows patterns and trends to be seen. It makes chemistry a much easier subject to study, because it organises the facts. As you work through this book you should often look at the Periodic Table. In this way you will realise many of the patterns and trends that exist.

Questions

1. The diagram below shows an outline of the Periodic Table with 10 elements in position. You are to use the letters given for each element to answer the following.

   Example: Name 1 metal element.   Answer R

   a name 2 elements in the same group
   b name 2 elements in the same period
   c which element is in group 1 of the Periodic Table?
   d name 2 transition metals
   e name 2 noble gases
   f name 2 non metal elements
   g name an element in group 7 of the Periodic Table
   h which element has the highest atomic number?
   i which element would be stored under oil?
   j name an element that exists as individual atoms
   k name an element with a coloured (non white) oxide

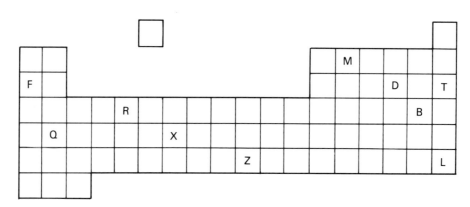

2. A new element Devonium has been discovered. It is a soft element which is easily cut with a knife. It reacts violently with water forming hydrogen gas and leaving an alkaline solution. It is a very good conductor of electricity.

a Is Devonium a metal or a non metal? Give a reason for your answer.
b How would you store a sample of Devonium?
c Name an element similar to Devonium.
d In which group of the Periodic Table would you expect to find Devonium?
e How many electrons would you expect there to be in the outermost shell of a Devonium atom?
f Would you be surprised if you found a lump of Devonium on a river bank? Explain your answer.

3. Use a copy of the Periodic Table to identify the following elements from the information provided.

Element A It has an atomic number of 16.
Element B It has an atomic mass of 64.
Element C It has an electron arrangement 2.8.1.
Element D It is the least dense element in group 5.
Element E Atoms of element E contain 18 electrons.
Element F It has the symbol W.

4. List all the reasons why you think copper is a metal.
5. List all the reasons why you think carbon is a non metal.

5 The way in which atoms combine

When two balls collide, they bounce apart and go their separate ways. When two magnets collide there is a strong chance that they will stick together and move off together. When two atoms collide, they can either stick together, or bounce apart. They either combine or they don't.

The only substances that exist as individual atoms are the noble gases (helium, neon, argon, xenon, krypton and radon). All other substances exist as groups or clusters of atoms stuck together.

In the element hydrogen, pairs of atoms stick together.

In the element sulphur, groups of 8 atoms stick together.

In the element carbon, millions of atoms stick together.

When *atoms* of *different* elements stick together a *compound* is formed.

5.1 Why do atoms combine?

The chemical properties of an element depend on the arrangement of electrons in the atoms of that element. The noble gases are very stable because they have a very stable arrangement of electrons. If two atoms of a noble gas collide, they will not combine. They will bounce apart. However, the atoms of all other elements have less stable electron arrangements. They can combine when they collide. When atoms combine they try to become more stable. They try to get the stable electron arrangement of a noble gas.

5.2 How do atoms combine?

Atoms can obtain a more stable electron arrangement in a number of different ways.

1. *Electron transfer*

Sodium has an atomic number of 11. A sodium atom therefore has 11 protons and 11 electrons. The protons are in the nucleus and the electrons are in shells around the nucleus as shown in Fig 5.1.

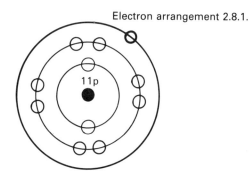

Electron arrangement 2.8.1.

11p

Fig 5.1 The sodium atom

The sodium atom gets the stable arrangement of a neon atom (2.8) by losing its outermost electron.

34

When this happens it is left with 11 protons (11+ charges), but only 10 electrons (10− charges). It is no longer a neutral atom. It becomes positively charged. The sodium *atom* changes into a sodium *ion* (1+ charge).
An ion is a charged atom or group of atoms.

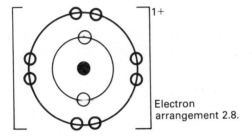

Electron arrangement 2.8.

Fig 5.2 The sodium ion

Chlorine has an atomic number of 17. The chlorine atom therefore has 17 protons and 17 electrons as shown in Fig 5.3.

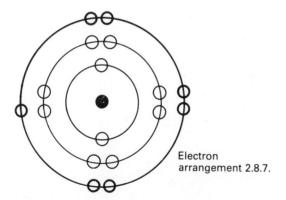

Electron arrangement 2.8.7.

Fig 5.3 The chlorine atom

The chlorine atom gets a stable electron arrangement by finding one more electron for its outermost shell. When this happens it gets the stable electron arrangement of an argon atom (2.8.8). The chlorine atom is left with 17 protons (17+ charges) and 18 electrons (18− charges). It becomes a negatively charged ion (1− charge). The ion formed when a chlorine atom gains an electron is known as the *chloride* ion.

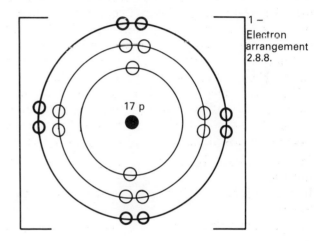

17 p

1 −
Electron arrangement 2.8.8.

Fig 5.4 The chloride ion

The sodium atom needs to lose an electron to become stable. The chlorine atom needs to gain an electron to become stable. If a sodium atom collides with a chlorine atom it is possible for both atoms to become stable at the same time. This is shown in Fig 5.5 (page 36).

By sodium giving its outermost electron to the chlorine atom, both atoms get a stable electron arrangement. The compound sodium chloride is formed. Sodium chloride is made up of ions. It is known as an *ionic compound*.

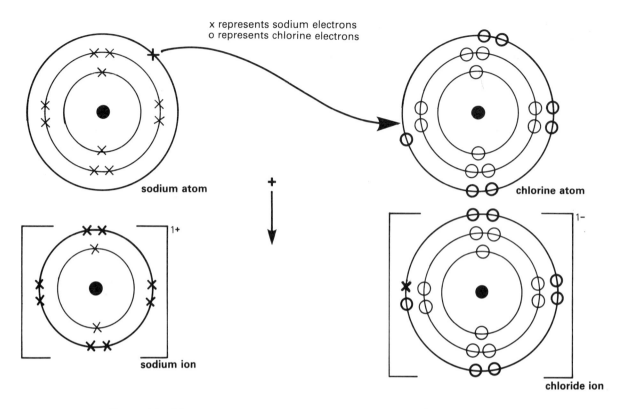

x represents sodium electrons
o represents chlorine electrons

sodium atom

chlorine atom

sodium ion

chloride ion

Fig 5.5 Forming sodium chloride

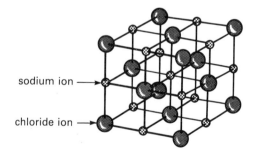

sodium ion →

chloride ion →

Fig 5.6 The structure of sodium chloride

Since sodium ions and chloride ions are oppositely charged, they attract each other. As the ions stick together a crystal of sodium chloride is built up as shown in Fig 5.6.

The attractive forces that hold the ions together in an ionic solid are known as *ionic bonds* (electrovalent bonds).

Magnesium oxide is another substance that is formed by *transferring electrons*.

Magnesium (atomic number 12) has 12 protons and 12 electrons. It has the electron arrangement 2.8.2. To form a stable electron arrangement it must lose 2 electrons.

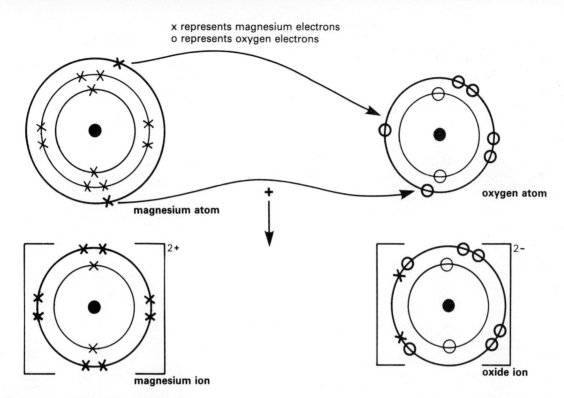

x represents magnesium electrons
o represents oxygen electrons

magnesium atom

oxygen atom

+

magnesium ion 2+

oxide ion 2-

Fig 5.7 Forming magnesium oxide

Oxygen (atomic number 8) has 8 protons and 8 electrons. It has an electron arrangement 2.6. It needs to gain 2 electrons to get a stable electron arrangement.

By electron transfer, magnesium atoms form magnesium ions and oxygen atoms form oxide ions. This is shown in Fig. 5.7 below.

You should note that the ions in magnesium oxide have double the charge of the ions in sodium chloride.

2. Electron sharing

Some atoms get a stable electron arrangement by sharing electrons. Consider hydrogen: a single hydrogen atom has just one electron. This is unstable. If the shells of two hydrogen atoms overlap, it is possible for electrons to be shared. This is shown in Fig 5.8.

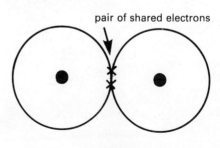

pair of shared electrons

Fig 5.8

If the pair of shared electrons is held where the shells overlap, each hydrogen atom can consider that it has *two* electrons in its shell. Each atom therefore has the stable electron arrangement of a helium atom. The shared pair of electrons is known as a *covalent bond*. Covalent bonds hold atoms together very strongly.

By sharing electrons the two hydrogen atoms form a hydrogen *molecule*. A molecule is a group of atoms held together by covalent bonds. Molecules are neutral. They are not charged like ions. A substance that is made up of molecules is known as a covalent substance.

Many non metal elements exist as molecules. Chlorine is another example (see Fig 5.9 below).

Many compounds are also formed by sharing electrons. Methane (CH_4) is an example. In methane the electron shells of the hydrogen atoms overlap with the outer shell of the carbon atom, and 4 pairs of electrons are shared. Four covalent bonds are formed. By forming these bonds each hydrogen atom gets 2 electrons in its electron shell. Each gets the stable electron arrangement of a helium atom. Carbon atoms get 8 electrons in their outer shells. They get the stable electron arrangement of neon atoms (2.8). This is shown in Fig 5.10 above.

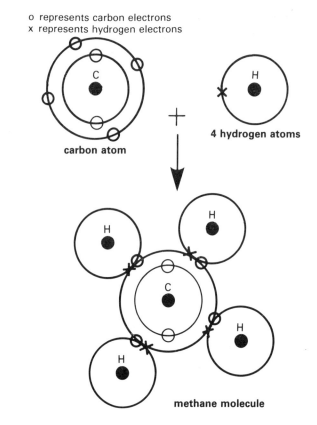

o represents carbon electrons
x represents hydrogen electrons

carbon atom

4 hydrogen atoms

methane molecule

Fig 5.10 Forming methane

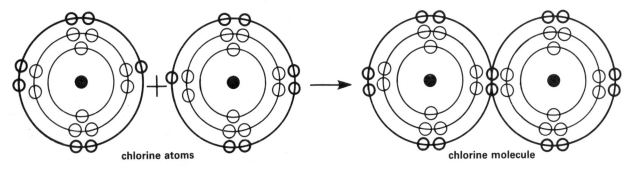

chlorine atoms

chlorine molecule

Fig 5.9 Forming chlorine molecules

When a covalent compound is formed, only the valence electrons are involved in forming covalent bonds. Because of this we can simplify the picture of a methane molecule to that shown in Fig 5.11.

$$
\begin{array}{c}
\text{H} \\
\text{x o} \\
\text{H} \; \overset{\text{o}}{\underset{\text{x}}{}} \; \text{C} \; \overset{\text{x}}{\underset{\text{o}}{}} \; \text{H} \\
\text{o x} \\
\text{H}
\end{array}
$$

Fig 5.11

In Fig 5.11 the shells are left out and only the electrons that form covalent bonds are shown. The picture of the methane molecule can be shown even more simply by showing each covalent bond as a line, instead of as a pair of electrons.

The picture of the methane molecule then becomes:

$$
\begin{array}{c}
\text{H} \\
| \\
\text{H} - \text{C} - \text{H} \\
| \\
\text{H}
\end{array}
$$

Fig 5.12

A line is often used to represent a covalent bond when chemists want to show the structure of a molecule as simply as possible.

Example:

$$
\begin{array}{c}
\text{O} \\
\diagup \quad \diagdown \\
\text{H} \qquad \text{H}
\end{array}
$$
is water

$$
\begin{array}{c}
\text{H} \qquad \text{H} \\
| \qquad | \\
\text{H} - \text{C} - \text{C} - \text{H} \\
| \qquad | \\
\text{H} \qquad \text{H}
\end{array}
$$
is ethane

$$
\text{O} = \text{C} = \text{O}
$$
is carbon dioxide

3. Metallic bonding

Metals are usually dense, high melting point solids. This means that the metal atoms must be packed closely together and there must be strong attractive forces between the atoms.

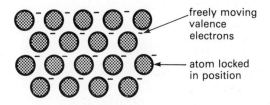

freely moving valence electrons

atom locked in position

Fig 5.13 The structure of metals

In metals each atoms is held in a fixed position, but the valence electrons of each atom are free to move throughout the whole of the metal structure. Scientists believe that these free moving electrons hold the metal atoms strongly together.

5.3 Types of structure

Atoms can stick together by forming ions, by sharing electrons, or by giving electrons to a central pool, as in metals. In each case, only the valence electrons are involved. Because of the different types of bonding that can exist, matter can occur in one of five different structures:

1. Ionic giant structures

These are structures formed by ionic substances such as sodium chloride. A large number of ions pack together in a regular pattern to form a crystal structure.

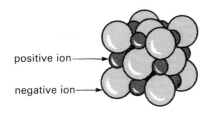

positive ion

negative ion

Fig 5.14 Ionic giant structure

2. Metal giant structures

These structures are found in metals. Large numbers of atoms pack together closely in a regular pattern to form a crystal structure.

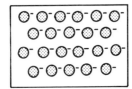

Fig 5.15 Metal giant structure

3. Covalent giant structures

These are found in substances such as diamond, graphite and quartz. Large numbers of atoms stick together by forming covalent bonds to give a very strong crystal structure.

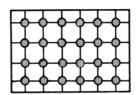

Fig 5.16 Covalent giant structure

4. Molecular structures

In these structures a definite number of atoms are held together by covalent bonds to form molecules. The number of atoms per molecule is usually fairly small. In water molecules there are three atoms per molecule. In butane molecules there are 14 atoms per molecule. The atoms within any molecule are very tightly held, but the attractive forces between different molecules are usually weak. Most covalent compounds are molecular structures.

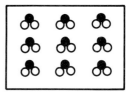

Fig 5.17 Molecular structure

5. Atomic structures

These are substances that exist as individual atoms. Only the noble gases can exist as atomic structures.

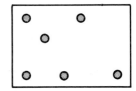

Fig 5.18 Atomic structure

5.4 The effect of bonding on properties

Compounds that are formed in different ways have different properties. Ionic compounds have different properties from covalent compounds.

Properties of ionic compounds

1. They are crystalline solids	Positive and negative ions attract each other. They build up into a regular crystal structure.
2. Have high melting points and boiling points	When an ionic substance melts each ion is free to move. A lot of energy (heat) is needed to overcome the attractive forces between ions.
3. Are usually soluble in water	Water molecules attract the ions. The water molecules separate the ions and keep them apart.
4. Conduct electricity when molten or dissolved in water	If charged particles can move, electricity can flow. When ionic substances are molten or dissolved the ions are free to move.

Properties of covalent compounds

1. Usually have low melting points and boiling points—so they are often gases or liquids	The atoms within a molecule are strongly held together, but there are only weak attractive forces between molecules. The molecules are easily separated.
2. They do not conduct electricity	Molecules are neutral. Charged particles are needed to conduct electricity.
3. Do not usually dissolve in water	Water molecules cannot attract the molecules of the covalent substance strongly enough to separate them.

5.5 Bonding and the Periodic Table

The Periodic Table can act as a useful guide to the type of compounds that elements form.

Metals form ionic compounds in which the metal atom has been changed to a metal ion. Metal ions are positively charged. The number of charges on the metal ion is equal to the group number of that element.

Sodium is in group 1. It forms the ion Na^{1+}.

Aluminium is in group 3. It forms the ion Al^{3+}.

Non metal elements form ionic compounds and covalent compounds. When a non metal element reacts with a metal it forms an ionic compound. In these compounds the non metal atom is changed to a negative ion. When a non metal element reacts with another non metal element it forms a covalent compound.

Questions

1. Sodium atoms contain 11 electrons, chlorine atoms contain 17 electrons.

a Draw diagrams to show the arrangement of electrons in:
(i) a sodium atom, (ii) a chlorine atom.

b Draw a diagram to show the arrangement of electrons, and the type of bonding in sodium chloride.

2. Nitrogen atoms contain 7 electrons.

a Draw a diagram to show the arrangement of electrons in a nitrogen atom.

b Draw a diagram to show the arrangement of electrons and the type of bonding in ammonia (NH_3).

3. Draw diagrams to show the arrangement of electrons in the following particles. Look up the atomic number of each element on the data page.

a a magnesium atom
b a sodium ion (Na^+)
c an oxide ion (O^{2-})
d a carbon atom
e a hydrogen molecule.

4. ARGON, ALUMINIUM, DIAMOND, MAGNESIUM OXIDE, METHANE, SODIUM CHLORIDE, WATER.
From the above list choose:

a 2 ionic substances
b 2 substances that exist as molecules
c a substance that exists as a covalent giant structure
d a substance that exists as individual atoms
e a substance that conducts electricity when solid
f the substance with the highest melting point
g the substance with the lowest boiling point.

5. A hydrogen atom contains only 1 electron. An oxygen atom contains 8 electrons. Draw a diagram to show the arrangement of electrons in a water molecule.

6. Find the element strontium in your Periodic Table.

a is it a metal or a non metal?
b which group of the Periodic Table is it in?
c how many electrons are there in its outermost shell?
d will it gain or lose electrons to form a stable electron arrangement?
e will strontium chloride be ionic or covalent? Give a reason for your answer.

7. You are given 2 white crystalline solids. One is ionic, the other is covalent. Describe the tests you would perform to find out which was which.

8.

Name of element	Electron arrangement
A	2.8.2.
B	2.8.4.
C	2.8.6.
D	2.8.8.

a In which groups of the Periodic Table would you find each element?
b which element will form a 2+ ion?
c which element will form a 2− ion?
d which element does not form any compounds?
e which 2 elements react to form a covalent compound?
f which 2 elements react to form an ionic compound?

9. Substance A has a melting point of 804°C. It dissolves in water to form a colourless solution.

This solution conducts electricity.

Substance B has a melting point of 1728°C. It is insoluble in water. It does not conduct electricity.

Substance C has a melting point of 1083°C. It is a good conductor of electricity at room temperature.

Substance D melts at −117°C and boils at 78°C. It dissolves in water to form a colourless solution. This solution does not conduct electricity.

Use this information to answer the following questions:

a which substance could be a metal element?
b only one of the substances smells—which one?
c which one of the substances is an ionic solid?
d which one of the substances is made up of molecules?
e which one of the substances is a covalent giant structure?

10. The diagram shows the arrangement of electrons in a methane molecule.

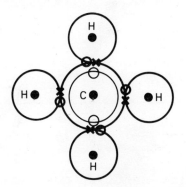

a how many electrons are there in a carbon atom?

b how many atoms are there in a methane molecule?
c how many covalent bonds are there in a methane molecule?
d how many electrons are 'shared' in a methane molecule?
e is a methane molecule, positively charged, negatively charged or neutral?

43

6 The language of chemistry

A language is a way of passing information from one person to another. Chemistry has its own language. It is used by chemists to describe chemicals and chemical change as neatly as possible. Many languages such as English, French and German have a common alphabet. The same letters are used to make different words. Other languages such as Chinese and Arabic have their own alphabet. Like Chinese and Arabic, the language of chemistry has its own unique letters which make up the chemical alphabet.

6.1 The chemical alphabet

The simplest chemicals that exist are the elements. Each element is given a shorthand form, known as its *chemical symbol.* These symbols are the letters of the chemistry alphabet. Table 1 shows the symbols of some common elements.

In Table 1, many elements have a symbol which is the first, or first two letters of its name. *Example:* sulphur (S); calcium (Ca). Some elements have symbols which are totally different from the name. *Example:* sodium (Na); Iron (Fe). The reason for this is that when these elements were given their symbols in the late 18th or 19th century they were known by different latin names.

Before we can use the language of chemistry we must learn at least some of the alphabet. One way of learning the chemical symbols for various elements is by spelling words using the chemical symbols.

Name of element	Symbol
aluminium	Al
argon	Ar
arsenic	As
bromine	Br
calcium	Ca
carbon	C
chlorine	Cl
copper	Cu
iron	Fe
hydrogen	H
iodine	I
lead	Pb
lithium	Li
magnesium	Mg
nickel	Ni
nitrogen	N
oxygen	O
phosphorus	P
potassium	K
silicon	Si
sodium	Na
sulphur	S
uranium	U
zinc	Zn

Table 1

Example: The word CLASP can be spelt using the elements chlorine, arsenic and phosphorus. (ClAsP). What chemical elements are needed to spell the following words: CAP, PALS, HOOK, SHOCK, BRUSH, POLISH, CLOCK?

44

The Periodic Table gives the chemical symbols for each element. Use the Periodic Table to see how many words you can think of, which can be spelt using chemical symbols, in 10 minutes. What is the longest word that can be spelt using chemical symbols?

6.2 Formulae from symbols

The chemical symbols give chemists a shorthand way of describing atoms of different elements. To a chemist, 4H means 4 hydrogen atoms and 6Al means 6 aluminium atoms. We know that it is unusual for atoms to exist by themselves. They have a strong tendency to stick together. When atoms of different elements stick together compounds are formed. The language of chemistry has to be able to describe these compounds using chemical symbols. This description of the compound is known as the *formula* of the compound.

The compound water is made up of molecules. Each molecule of water contains 2 hydrogen atoms and one oxygen atom. We could write the formula of water as H2O1, where this means 2 hydrogen atoms and one oxygen atom. However this is confusing, (could it be 201 hydrogen atoms?). In order to make it less confusing we lower the numbers so that the formula can be written H_2O_1.

It seems pointless writing 1 every time 1 atom of an element is present; so the formula can be simplified to H_2O. If there is no number after the symbol for an element in a formula, this means that there is only 1 atom of that element in each *formula unit*.

Do you remember that there are two types of compounds: covalent and ionic? In covalent compounds the *formula unit* is the molecule.

Therefore, the formula describes how many atoms of each type there are in one molecule of the compound. In ionic compounds no molecules exist. The compound is made up of ions. Therefore in ionic compounds the *formula unit* is the simplest cluster of ions that is electrically neutral.

Sodium chloride is made up of ions Na^{1+} and Cl^{1-}. The formula of sodium chloride is NaCl.

Magnesium chloride is made up of ions Mg^{2+} and Cl^{1-}. The formula of magnesium chloride must be $MgCl_2$.

The formula of a substance gives information about its 'make up' in a very convenient way.

Chlorine is a covalent gas. It is made up of molecules. In each molecule 2 chlorine atoms are stuck together. The formula of a chlorine molecule is Cl_2. If these two chlorine atoms were not stuck together they would be described differently ie 2Cl.

Chlorine is a very simple substance.

TNT is an example of a more complicated compound. TNT is a covalent compound with formula $C_7H_5N_3O_6$. Each TNT molecule must contain 7 carbon atoms, 5 hydrogen atoms, 3 nitrogen atoms and 6 oxygen atoms.

6.3 Writing formulae

For many years the chemical formulae of all compounds were found by experiment. For complicated substances like TNT experimental methods are still needed. However, the formulae of many simple compounds can be written directly from the name of the compound, using the idea of *valency*.

Valency can be thought of as a *number* which is given to an element or a group of elements. It allows the formulae of compounds to be written directly from their names.

VALENCY

POSITIVE			NEGATIVE		
1+	2+	3+	1−	2−	3−
Li *Lithium* Na *Sodium* K *Potassium* Ag *Silver* H *Hydrogen* NH_4 *Ammonium*	Mg *Magnesium* Ca *Calcium* Ba *Barium* Fe *Iron* (II) Ni *Nickel* Cu *Copper* (II) Zn *Zinc* Pb *Lead*	Fe *Iron* (III) Al *Aluminium*	OH *Hydroxide* Cl *Chloride* Br *Bromide* I *Iodide* NO_3 *Nitrate* NO_2 *Nitrite* HCO_3 *Hydrogen carbonate*	O *Oxide* S *Sulphide* SO_3 *Sulphite* SO_4 *Sulphate* CO_3 *Carbonate*	

Table 2

Certain rules apply in writing formulae. These rules are:

1. The sum of the positive valencies must equal the sum of the negative valencies.

2. If any group, which contains more than 1 element, occurs more than once in a formula, it must be bracketed.

Example: The formula of calcium nitrate must be written as $Ca(NO_3)_2$ and not as $CaNO_{32}$.

The following examples show how the idea of valency can be used to write the formulae of compounds.

a. *Magnesium oxide*
Magnesium   Oxide
Mg   2+   O   2−
The positive and negative valencies balance.
Therefore the formula is MgO.

b. *Potassium oxide*
Potassium   Oxide
K   1+   O   2−
K   1+
   $\overline{2+}$ $\overline{2-}$
Two potassium atoms are needed for the positive and negative valencies to balance.
Therefore the formula is K_2O.

c. *Aluminium oxide*
Aluminium   Oxide
Al   3+   O   2−
Al   3+   O   2−
           O   2−
   $\overline{6+}$ $\overline{6-}$
Two aluminium atoms and three oxygen atoms are needed to balance the valencies.
Therefore the formula is Al_2O_3.

46

d. *Calcium hydroxide*

Calcium		Hydroxide	
Ca	2+	OH	1−
		OH	1−
	2+		2−

One calcium atom needs two hydroxide groups for the valencies to balance.

Therefore the formula is $Ca(OH)_2$.

The bracket is needed because the 2 applies to both the oxygen and hydrogen atoms in the hydroxide group.

6.4 Chemical equations

Possibly the most important job of the language of chemistry is to describe chemical reactions or chemical changes. It does this with chemical equations.

Magnesium burns brightly in oxygen to form magnesium oxide. This change can be written as a *word equation*.

magnesium + oxygen → magnesium oxide

The → means *reacts to form*.

If we replace the names of the chemicals with their formulae we get:

$$Mg + O_2 \rightarrow MgO$$

This is a chemical equation for the reaction between magnesium and oxygen.

Looking at this equation it looks as if one oxygen atom disappeared as the reaction took place. There are 2 oxygen atoms on the left hand side of the equation and only 1 on the right hand side. This is impossible as *atoms cannot be created or destroyed in any chemical reaction*.

The chemical equation needs to be altered in some way. It needs to be *balanced*. The correct equation for the reaction between magnesium and oxygen is

$$2Mg + O_2 \rightarrow 2MgO$$

A balanced equation must contain the same number of atoms of each element on both sides of the arrow. Equations are balanced by placing numbers *in front* of the formulae of the substances in the equation.

Example 1.

Unbalanced
$$CH_4 + O_2 \rightarrow CO_2 + H_2O$$
Balanced
$$CH_4 + 2O_2 \rightarrow CO_2 + 2H_2O$$

Example 2.

Unbalanced
$$Mg + HCl \rightarrow MgCl_2 + H_2 \uparrow$$
Balanced
$$Mg + 2HCl \rightarrow MgCl_2 + H_2 \uparrow$$

Example 3.

Unbalanced
$$AgNO_3 + MgCl_2 \rightarrow AgCl \downarrow + Mg(NO_3)_2$$
Balanced
$$2AgNO_3 + MgCl_2 \rightarrow 2AgCl \downarrow + Mg(NO_3)_2$$

In the examples some upward and downward pointing arrows appeared. An upward arrow shows that the substance was formed as a gas. In the second example hydrogen gas was formed.

A downward arrow shows that a substance is formed as a *precipitate*. A precipitate is a *solid* formed in a chemical reaction on mixing two solutions. In the third example silver chloride is formed as a precipitate.

Reversible reactions

In some chemical reactions the products of the reaction react together to reform the starting substances. These reactions are known as *reversible reactions*.

The reaction between nitrogen and hydrogen to form ammonia is an example of a reversible reaction.

nitrogen + hydrogen $\rightleftharpoons$ ammonia

$$N_2 + 3H_2 \rightleftharpoons 2NH_3$$

Because the reaction is reversible it is impossible to change all the nitrogen and hydrogen into ammonia.

The $\rightleftharpoons$ sign in the equation tells us that the reaction is reversible. The equations for all reversible reactions have the $\rightleftharpoons$ sign instead of the arrow ($\rightarrow$).

Questions

1. Write the formulae of the following compounds. You are told the number of atoms of each type in a formula unit of the compound. *Example:* Compound A (1 carbon atom, 2 oxygen atoms) formula = CO_2.

   compound B (1 magnesium atom, 2 chlorine atoms)
   compound C (1 nitrogen atom, 3 hydrogen atoms)
   compound D (1 sodium atom, 1 chlorine atom)
   compound E (2 hydrogen atoms, 2 oxygen atoms)
   compound F (3 carbon atoms, 6 hydrogen atoms, 1 oxygen atom)
   compound G (1 magnesium atom, 1 sulphur atom, 4 oxygen atoms)
   compound H (1 calcium atom, 1 carbon atom, 3 oxygen atoms)

2. Use your valency table to write the formulae of the following compounds:

   a magnesium oxide   b hydrogen nitrate
   c calcium carbonate   d hydrogen chloride
   e iron (II) hydroxide   f ammonium carbonate
   g potassium sulphate   h sodium chloride
   i sodium sulphide   j sodium sulphate
   k copper (II) nitrate   l copper (II) sulphate
   m lead carbonate   n lead nitrate
   o zinc hydroxide   p zinc chloride
   q calcium chloride   r silver nitrate
   s hydrogen sulphate   t barium chloride

3. Find out the common names of:

   a hydrogen chloride solution
   b hydrogen nitrate solution
   c hydrogen sulphate solution

4. How many atoms are there in each of the following formulae units?

   a SO_2 b Pb_3O_4 c $CuSO_4$
   d N_2 e ZnO f $(NH_4)_2SO_4$
   g CH_4 h NO_2 i CO
   j C_4H_{10}

5. Write the names of the compounds which have the following formulae:

   a $MgCl_2$ b $AgNO_3$ c $ZnSO_4$
   d Al_2O_3 e $CaCO_3$ f NH_4Cl
   g $NaOH$ h $CuSO_4$ i FeS
   j Na_2SO_3

6. Balance the following equations:

   a $Mg + O_2 \rightarrow MgO$
   b $CO + O_2 \rightarrow CO_2$
   c $Fe_2O_3 + H_2 \rightarrow Fe + H_2O$
   d $Na_2CO_3 + HCl \rightarrow NaCl + H_2O + CO_2 \uparrow$

e $FeCl_2 + Cl_2 \rightarrow FeCl_3$
f $Na + H_2O \rightarrow NaOH + H_2 \uparrow$
g $AgNO_3 + CaCl_2 \rightarrow AgCl \downarrow + Ca(NO_3)_2$
h $NaNO_3 \rightarrow NaNO_2 + O_2 \uparrow$
i $C_2H_6 + O_2 \rightarrow CO_2 + H_2O$
j $H_2 + Cl_2 \rightarrow HCl$

7. Write balanced equations for the following reactions:

a zinc + oxygen(O_2) $\rightarrow$ zinc oxide
b lead nitrate + sodium chloride $\rightarrow$ lead chloride$\downarrow$ + sodium nitrate
c magnesium + sulphuric acid(H_2SO_4) $\rightarrow$ magnesium + hydrogen (H_2)$\uparrow$
                                          sulphate
d copper (II) + sulphuric $\rightarrow$ copper (II) + carbon(CO_2)$\uparrow$ + water
    carbonate   acid   sulphate   dioxide
e copper (II) + sodium $\rightarrow$ copper (II)$\downarrow$ + sodium
    sulphate   hydroxide   hydroxide   sulphate
f zinc   + hydrochloric $\rightarrow$ zinc   + water
    oxide   acid (HCl)   chloride
g iron + sulphur $\rightarrow$ iron (II) sulphide
h zinc + copper (II) chloride $\rightarrow$ zinc chloride + copper$\downarrow$
i ammonium + calcium $\rightarrow$ calcium   + ammonia(NH_3)$\uparrow$ + water
    chloride   hydroxide   chloride
j calcium   + carbon $\rightarrow$ calcium   + water
    hydroxide   dioxide   carbonate$\downarrow$

7 The mole

7.1 Recipe work

Suppose you wanted to make a sandwich cake, you might use a recipe like this:

110 g (4 oz) self raising flour
110 g (4 oz) butter
110 g (4 oz) caster sugar
2 eggs
Oven temperature 190°C

Grease two 7″ sandwich tins and line each one with greased greaseproof paper. Sift the flour into a large bowl. Add the other ingredients and beat for two minutes. Bake in the centre of the oven for 25–30 minutes.

The recipe tells you which ingredients to use; how much to use and how to treat the ingredients. By mentioning the size of the baking tins it even tells you approximately how much cake to expect. All this information is needed if you are to bake the cake properly.

Chemists also use recipes to prepare new substances. One of the problems facing a chemist when making up a recipe is: "How much of each ingredient (*reagent*) do I need to use?" Suppose you wanted to prepare 100 g of copper (II) sulphate crystals starting from copper (II) oxide. What is the smallest amount of copper (II) oxide that you could use? Is it 12·5 g, 32 g, 67 g, 100 g or 160 g?

Guessing the amount of a substance needed for a chemical reaction can be very difficult. Chemists need to be able to work out how much of each substance they need. In this chapter you are going to find out how to do this.

7.2 Formula mass

In Chapter 3 you saw that chemists could work out how heavy atoms of each element are by comparing them with 1 atom of carbon ($^{12}_{6}C$). This gave us the relative atomic mass scale. On this scale, carbon (the standard) is given an atomic mass of 12. The idea of atomic mass (or relative atomic mass to be more accurate) has been extended to compounds. You will remember that compounds can exist as molecules or groups of ions.

Chemists have compared the mass of 1 formula unit of a compound with 1 atom of carbon. In this way each substance can be given a formula mass.

The formula mass of any compound can be worked out by adding together the atomic masses of each atom in the formula unit.

Example 1. Sodium chloride

Formula NaCl
Atomic masses Na = 23, Cl = 35·5.
Formula mass = 23 + 35·5 = 58·5.

Example 2. Water
Formula H_2O. There are 2 hydrogen atoms and 1 oxygen atom.
Atomic masses H = 1, O = 16.
Formula mass = 2 × 1 + 16 = 18.

Example **3.** Sulphuric acid
Formula H_2SO_4. There are 2 hydrogen atoms, 1 sulphur atom and 4 oxygen atoms.
Atomic masses H = 1, S = 32, O = 16.
Formula mass $= 2 \times 1 + 32 + 4 \times 16$
$\qquad\qquad = 2 \quad + 32 + 64 = 98.$

Example **4.** Ammonium sulphate
Formula $(NH_4)_2SO_4$. Allowing for the brackets there are 2 nitrogen atoms, $2 \times 4 = 8$ hydrogen atoms, 1 sulphur atom and 4 oxygen atoms.
Atomic masses N = 14, H = 1, S = 32, O = 16.
Formula mass
$= 2 \times 14 + 8 \times 1 + 32 + 4 \times 16$
$- 28 \quad + 8 \quad + 32 + 64 = 132.$

For COVALENT SUBSTANCES the formula unit is a *molecule*. For these substances the FORMULA MASS is known as the *molecular mass*.

7.3 The mole

Chemists, like cooks, weigh out their ingredients. Chemists cannot count out the number of atoms they want to use in a reaction. For these reasons chemists needed to know how heavy each atom was in grammes. They have found out that 12 g of carbon ($^{12}_{6}C$) contains six hundred thousand million million million atoms. This enormous number is known as Avogadro's number. To make life simple, we will call this number N.

Consider the three substances shown in Table 1.

Name of substance	Type of formula unit	Formula mass
carbon	atom	12
magnesium	atom	24
water	molecule	18

Table 1

N atoms of carbon weigh 12 g.
N atoms of magnesium weigh 24 g, because each atom of magnesium is twice as heavy as a carbon atom.
N molecules of water weigh 18 g, because each water molecule is $1\frac{1}{2}$ times as heavy as a carbon atom.

Once Avogadro's number had been calculated, chemists were able to work out the number of particles present in any amount of a substance.

Chemists then defined the mole:
A mole is the amount of a substance that contains N formula units of that substance.

So, 1 mole of carbon atoms weighs 12 g
$\qquad$ 1 mole of magnesium atoms weighs 24 g
$\qquad$ 1 mole of water molecules weighs 18 g.

1 mole of any substance weighs its formula mass in grammes.

Example: Calcium carbonate.
Formula: $CaCO_3$
There is 1 calcium atom, 1 carbon atom and 3 oxygen atoms
Formula mass $= 40 + 12 + 3 \times 16$
$\qquad\qquad\quad = 40 + 12 + 48 = 100$
So, 1 mole of calcium carbonate weighs 100 g

Let us now see how chemists are able to use the idea of the mole.

7.4 Equation calculations

Consider burning magnesium in oxygen to form magnesium oxide. The balanced equation for the reaction tells us that 2 atoms of magnesium react with 1 molecule of oxygen to form 2 formula units of magnesium oxide.

Magnesium + oxygen → magnesium oxide
2 Mg + O_2 → 2 MgO
2 atoms 1 molecule 2 formula units

Multiply by N

$2N$ atoms N molecules $2N$ formula units

This is the same as

2 moles 1 mole 2 moles

This means

2×24 g 2×16 g $2 \times 24 + 2 \times 16$ g
48 g 32 g 80 g

ie 48 g of magnesium react with 32 g of oxygen to form 80 g of magnesium oxide.

The balanced equation tells us how many particles of each substance react. It also tells us how many moles of each substance react. We therefore know what mass of each substance reacts. This means chemists can calculate the amount of each substance they need for a recipe. There is no need to guess.

We can now think of a chemical equation as showing the number of moles of each substance reacting.

iron + sulphur → iron (II) sulphide
Fe + S → FeS
1 mole 1 mole 1 mole

copper (II) + sulphuric → copper (II) + water
oxide acid sulphate
CuO + H_2SO_4 → $CuSO_4$ + H_2O
1 mole 1 mole 1 mole 1 mole

aluminium + oxygen → aluminium oxide
4Al + $3O_2$ → $2Al_2O_3$
4 moles 3 moles 2 moles

Now consider some simple calculations involving equations:

1. How much calcium carbonate would you have to heat to make 14 g of calcium oxide?

The balanced equation for the reaction is:

$CaCO_3$ → CaO + $CO_2\uparrow$
1 mole 1 mole 1 mole

1 mole of calcium carbonate → 1 mole of calcium oxide

1 mole of $CaCO_3$ = 40 + 12 + 3 × 16 = 100 g
1 mole of CaO = 40 + 16 = 56 g

Therefore

100 g $CaCO_3$ → 56 g CaO

$\frac{100}{56}$ g of $CaCO_3$ → $\frac{56}{56}$ g of CaO = 1 g of CaO

$\frac{100 \times \cancel{14}^{1}}{\cancel{56}}$ g of $CaCO_3$ → 14 g of CaO

25 g of $CaCO_3$ → 14 g of CaO

So 25 g of calcium carbonate are needed.

2. How much oxygen is needed to completely burn 32 g of methane?

The balanced equation for the reaction is:

CH_4 + $2O_2$ → CO_2 + $2H_2O$
1 mole 2 moles 1 mole 2 moles

1 mole of methane reacts with 2 moles of oxygen
1 mole of methane (CH_4) = 12 + 4 × 1 = 16 g
1 mole of oxygen (O_2) = 16 + 16 = 32 g

So 16 g of CH_4 react with 64 g of oxygen

$\frac{16}{16}$ = 1 g of CH_4 react with $\frac{64}{16}$ = 4 g of oxygen

32 g of CH_4 react with 4 × 32 = 128 g of oxygen

So 128 g of oxygen are needed.

7.5 Calculating formulae

We can use the idea of moles to calculate the formula of a substance from experimental results. The formula calculated is the simplest possible formula for that compound. It is known as the empirical formula of the substance.

Example 1: A compound is formed by 32 g of sulphur reacting with 32 g of oxygen. What is the formula of the compound formed? ($S = 32$, $O = 16$)

1 mole of sulphur atoms = 32 g
1 mole of oxygen atoms = 16 g

The experimental results tell us that:

1 mole of sulphur atoms react with 2 moles of oxygen atoms
N atoms of sulphur react with $2N$ atoms of oxygen.
1 atom of sulphur reacts with 2 atoms of oxygen
So, the formula of the compound must be SO_2.

Example 2: 3 g of carbon react with 8 g of oxygen to form a compound. What is the formula of this compound? ($C = 12$, $O = 16$.)

3 g of carbon $= \frac{3}{12}$ moles $= \frac{1}{4}$ mole of carbon atoms

8 g of oxygen $= \frac{8}{16} = \frac{1}{2}$ mole of oxygen atoms

$\frac{1}{4}$ mole of carbon atoms react with $\frac{1}{2}$ mole of oxygen atoms

$4 \times \frac{1}{4} = 1$ mole of carbon atoms react with
$4 \times \frac{1}{2} = 2$ moles of oxygen atoms

N atoms of carbon react with $2N$ atoms of oxygen
1 atom of carbon reacts with 2 atoms of oxygen
So, the formula of the compound formed must be CO_2.

Questions

For these questions look up the data page for any relative atomic masses that you need.

1. Calculate the formula mass of the following:
   a CO_2 b $CaCO_3$ c FeS
   d $CuSO_4$ e C_6H_{12} f H_2O
   g $Ca(OH)_2$ h O_2 i $(NH_4)_2SO_4$
   j Na_2O

2. Calculate the mass of 1 mole of the following:
   a Cl_2 b SO_2 c Na_2CO_3
   d CuO e $Zn(NO_3)_2$ f $CaCl_2$
   g $MgCO_3$ h MnO_2 i C_2H_6
   j $C_2H_4O_2$

3. Calculate the mass of 2 moles of the following:
   a oxygen atoms   b argon atoms
   c bromine atoms   d copper atoms
   e carbon atoms

4. Calculate the mass of 2 moles of the following:
   a sodium chloride   b sodium hydroxide
   c sodium carbonate d sodium nitrate
   e sodium sulphate

5. $2Pb(NO_3)_2 \xrightarrow{\text{heat}} 2PbO + 4NO_2\uparrow + O_2\uparrow$

   Use the above equation to answer the following questions:
   a How many moles of lead nitrate have to be heated to make 4 moles of nitrogen dioxide?
   b If 4 moles of lead nitrate are heated how many moles of oxygen gas will be formed?
   c If 10 moles of lead oxide are formed how many moles of oxygen gas will be formed at the same time?
   d Calculate the mass of: (i) 1 mole of oxygen gas, (ii) 4 moles of nitrogen dioxide gas
   e If 18·4 g of nitrogen dioxide are formed in this reaction what mass of oxygen is also formed?

6. $2KHCO_3 \xrightarrow{heat} K_2CO_3 + CO_2\uparrow + H_2O\uparrow$

a Calculate the formula mass of each of the following:
(i) potassium hydrogen carbonate
(ii) potassium carbonate
(iii) carbon dioxide
(iv) water

b What mass of potassium carbonate is obtained by heating 50 g of potassium hydrogen carbonate?

c How much potassium hydrogen carbonate must be heated to form 11 g of carbon dioxide?

7. copper (II) $\rightarrow$ anhydrous + water
sulphate   copper (II)
crystals   sulphate
$CuSO_4.5H_2O \rightarrow CuSO_4 + 5H_2O$

a Calculate the formula mass of:
(i) copper (II) sulphate crystals
(ii) anhydrous copper (II) sulphate
(iii) water

b What mass of water is formed when 1 mole of copper (II) sulphate crystals are heated?

c What mass of water is formed when 1000 g of copper (II) sulphate crystals are heated?

d What mass of copper (II) sulphate crystals must be heated to form 32 g of anhydrous copper (II) sulphate?

e What is the percentage by mass of water in copper (II) sulphate crystals?

8. $Fe + CuSO_4 \rightarrow FeSO_4 + Cu\downarrow$

a Calculate the mass of 1 mole of each of the following:
(i) Fe, (ii) Cu, (iii) $CuSO_4$, (iv) $FeSO_4$

b How much iron is needed to form 8 g of copper?

c What mass of iron (II) sulphate is formed from 28 g of iron?

d What mass of copper (II) sulphate is needed to react with 14 g of iron?

e What mass of iron (II) sulphate can be made from 16 g of copper (II) sulphate?

9.

a Calculate the mass of 1 mole of calcium carbonate.

b What mass of oxygen is there in 1 mole of calcium carbonate?

c What is the percentage (by mass) of oxygen in calcium carbonate?

10. In each of the following calculate the formula of the compound formed when:

a 24 g of carbon react with 32 g of oxygen
b 46 g of sodium react with 16 g of oxygen
c 12 g of magnesium react with 80 g of bromine
d 6 g of carbon react with 2 g of hydrogen
e 10 g of hydrogen react with 80 g of oxygen
f 24 g of sulphur react with 36 g of oxygen

8 Water

Water is funny stuff. Imagine a visit to a Water Shop.

"Good morning, Can I help you?"

"Yes, I would like a bottle of water, please."

"What type would you like?"

"What have you got?"

"Well, there is sea water, rain water, river water, pond water, ditch water, tap water, or distilled water, in large bottles. We do have a few small bottles of soda water, tonic water, Vichy water and rose water.

Did you want hard or soft water?"

"HELP!"

We use the word water in a number of ways. We use it to describe a pure substance with chemical formula H_2O. We also use it to describe the impure forms that we meet daily. These impure forms are known as *natural water*.

8.1 Natural water

There is an awful lot of water about. Four fifths of the Earth's surface is covered with it. Most of this is sea water.

Sea water is very salty. In fact, every 100 g of sea water has just under 3 g of sodium chloride dissolved in it. It also contains sizeable amounts of calcium, magnesium and potassium compounds. These substances got there by rocks dissolving, and rivers carrying the dissolved rocks down to the sea.

At its best, sea water is a perfectly clear, colourless liquid. Animals and plants live in it, because it dissolves air and allows sunlight to pass through it.

Man has always thought that since the sea is so large, he could use it as a dumping ground. Nothing that he could do could have any real effect on the sea. Unfortunately this is not true. The Mediterranean sea is showing serious signs of pollution. It cannot cope with the sewage and industrial waste being poured into it. Hopefully, man will realise his mistake before it is too late.

Rain water is the purest form of natural water, but even this can be far from pure. As rain falls it dissolves gases in the air and picks up dust. Rain water in some industrial areas is quite highly acidic. This is because it dissolves polluting gases such as sulphur dioxide, nitrogen dioxide and hydrogen sulphide. Acidic rain water is largely responsible for the decay of old buildings.

Surface water is the type of natural water most important to man. It is rain water that flows over the Earth and then passes into streams and rivers. We usually get water for our homes from this source. The water in streams and rivers is known as *fresh water*. This means that it is not salty. It certainly does not mean that it is perfectly fresh and clean. Fresh water contains dissolved substances, together with bacteria and mud. It is not usually safe to drink. It needs to be carefully treated before it comes into our homes.

In the past, many of our rivers have been heavily polluted. Some became dead rivers; unable to support life. Some were better suited to developing photographs than swimming. The main causes of this pollution were oil, detergents and heavy metal compounds from industry, together with sewage, and fertilisers washed from the land. Fortunately, there are now stricter pollution laws and most rivers are far cleaner than they were 20 years ago.

8.2 The water cycle

Have you ever listened to people moaning about the weather during a wet spell? They say things like:

"Oh dear, Its still tipping it down"
or "There can't be much more rain up there."
or "Will it never stop raining?"

Sadly for the moaners it will never stop raining. It might stop for a day or two, possibly a week or even a month, but eventually the rain will return. The *water cycle* makes sure of this.

The sun shines and the wind blows. This causes water to evaporate. It evaporates from the seas, lakes, rivers, ditches and puddles. Water vapour passes into the atmosphere and rises. As it rises it cools; it cools so much that it condenses into tiny droplets of water, forming clouds. The clouds grow. They eventually become unstable and the water falls as rain. The rain forms puddles, fills ditches and flows along rivers into lakes and into the sea.

The sun still shines and the wind still blows and so it goes on. Water is constantly being changed into water vapour and water vapour is constantly being changed into water. The natural waters of the Earth are constantly being distilled.

We should be grateful for the water cycle. It gives us a constant supply of fresh water for cooking, washing, for industry and agriculture. Life wouldn't be nearly as easy if all water was in the sea.

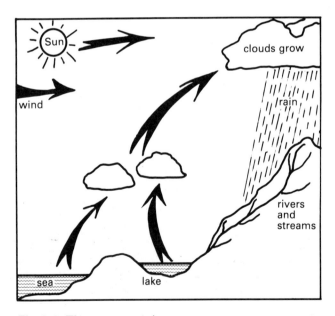

Fig 8.1 The water cycle

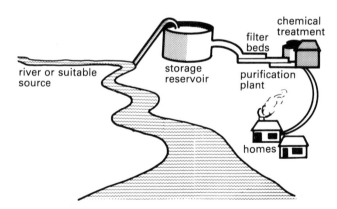

Fig 8.2 Water for our homes

8.3 Water for our homes

When we turn on a tap we get as much clean water as we need. We don't expect tap water to be muddy and we certainly don't expect it to be harmful to drink. There are 10 Regional Water Authorities in England and Wales. They provide enough water of the right quality.

The first thing a Water Authority has to do is to choose a suitable source. It must check that the rivers and streams it wants to use do not contain dissolved harmful substances, like arsenic or heavy metal compounds.

Often, water is pumped from streams and rivers into *storage reservoirs*. While the water is in these reservoirs much of the mud settles and some bacteria are killed by sunlight. The water is then filtered through sand a number of times. This removes the remaining mud and most of the bacteria. The water is finally sterilised with chlorine gas before it is supplied to our homes. Chlorine kills any bacteria that are left in the water.

Tap water is not pure. It contains a number of dissolved substances. The important thing is that it is safe to drink.

8.4 Hard and soft water

Tap water in London is not the same as tap water in Plymouth. You could hardly expect it to be. The water passes over different types of rocks in each area. It dissolves different substances. We describe our water supplies as *hard* or *soft*. Most water in the London area is hard. Most water in the Plymouth area is soft.

Hard water is water that contains dissolved calcium and magnesium compounds. The greater the concentration of these compounds, the harder the water gets. **Soft water has little or no calcium or magnesium compounds dissolved in it.**

Properties of hard water

The difference between hard and soft water can clearly be seen when washing with soap. Hard water does not easily form a lather with soap. Instead, the calcium and magnesium compounds react with the soap to form an insoluble scum. Only when they have all been removed as scum can a lather form. Hard water wastes soap. Also the scum particles can wear the fibres of fabrics.

Types of hard water

There are two types of hardness of water:

1. *Temporary hardness* which can be removed by boiling.
2. *Permanent hardness* which cannot be removed by boiling.

Temporary hardness is caused by calcium hydrogen carbonate and magnesium hydrogen carbonate. When rain water, containing dissolved carbon dioxide, passes over limestone or dolomite type rocks these soluble hydrogen carbonates are formed.

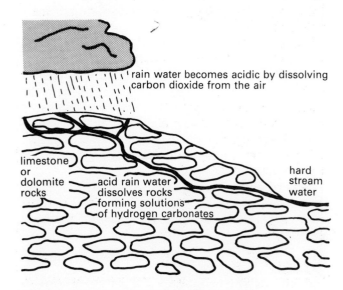

rain water becomes acidic by dissolving carbon dioxide from the air

limestone or dolomite rocks

acid rain water dissolves rocks forming solutions of hydrogen carbonates

hard stream water

Fig 8.3 Forming temporary hard water

limestone + rainwater → temporary hard water

$$CaCO_3 + CO_2 + H_2O → Ca(HCO_3)_2$$

The hydrogen carbonates that cause temporary hardness of water break down on heating to form insoluble carbonates.

calcium hydrogen carbonate → calcium carbonate ↓ + carbon dioxide ↑ + water

$$Ca(HCO_3)_2 → CaCO_3 ↓ + CO_2 ↑ + H_2O$$

The insoluble carbonates formed are the fur or scale which is sometimes found in kettles or boilers in hard water areas. The scale in boilers can be a nuisance. It stops heat getting through to the water, so more fuel is needed. It also means the boiler has to be descaled from time to time. This can be expensive.

Permanent hardness is caused by the sulphates and chlorides of calcium and magnesium. It is unaffected by heating and is therefore as good as soft water in kettles or boilers, *but* it does form a scum with soap.

It is wrong to think that hard water is in all ways inferior to soft water. If a detergent is used for washing, instead of a soap, hard water is just as good as soft water. Hard water can provide the calcium our bodies need for teeth and bones. It often tastes better and certainly makes better beer. Some people believe that people living in soft water areas have a greater chance of suffering from heart disease.

Nevertheless, hard water is often softened. At least some of the dissolved calcium and magnesium compounds are removed. Several methods are used.

1. *The washing soda method*

Sodium carbonate crystals are often known as washing soda. Washing soda softens water be-cause it removes calcium and magnesium ions as insoluble carbonates.

calcium hydrogen carbonate + sodium carbonate → calcium carbonate ↓ + sodium hydrogen carbonate

$$Ca(HCO_3)_2 + Na_2CO_3 → CaCO_3 ↓ + 2NaHCO_3$$

Sometimes the sodium carbonate crystals are coloured and some scent is added. They are then known as bath salts.

2. *Ion exchange methods*

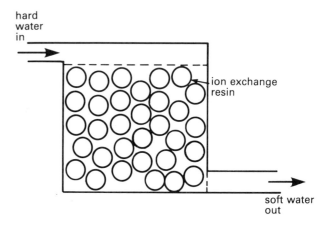

hard water in

ion exchange resin

soft water out

Fig 8.4

Man made resins can be used to purify water. As the hard water is passed over these resins, calcium and magnesium ions become attached to the resin. They are replaced in the water by sodium ions or hydrogen ions from the resin. In this way the water is softened.

Extremely pure water known as *deionised water* can be made by using a resin which exchanges hydrogen ions for metal ions and hydroxide ions for the negative ions, like sulphate or chloride.

3. *The lime method*

Lime (calcium hydroxide) has been widely used to

remove *temporary hardness*. It reacts with the hydrogen carbonates to form insoluble carbonates:

calcium + calcium → calcium↓ + water
hydrogen hydroxide carbonate
carbonate (lime)

$$Ca(HCO_3)_2 + Ca(OH)_2 \rightarrow 2CaCO_3\downarrow + 2H_2O$$

Care must be taken with this method. If too much lime is added the water becomes hard again.

8.5 Waste water

In our homes we mess up the nice clean water that the Water Authorities provide. We pull out plugs, drain washing machines and flush toilets and all our waste water disappears. It doesn't really disappear. It usually enters a sewer system. It is on its way to the Sewage Treatment Works.

When the raw sewage first arrives at the treatment works it is very coarsely filtered. It is then pumped into large tanks where the solids settle out. The solid *sludge* is then passed into huge containers known as *digestors*. These are kept warm (about 30°C). In them the solid waste breaks down to form safe chemicals and methane gas is produced. This gas is used to power the treatment works. After 20–30 days in the digestor the treated sludge is removed and dried. It can then be dumped. It may even be possible to use it as a garden fertiliser.

The liquid part of the sewage also has to be treated, before the water is allowed to pass into rivers or into the sea. The waste matter in the water has to be changed by micro-organisms into safe chemicals.

Two different methods are used:

1. The water is sprinkled through rotating pipes onto beds of stones. On these stones the micro-organisms grow as a slime.

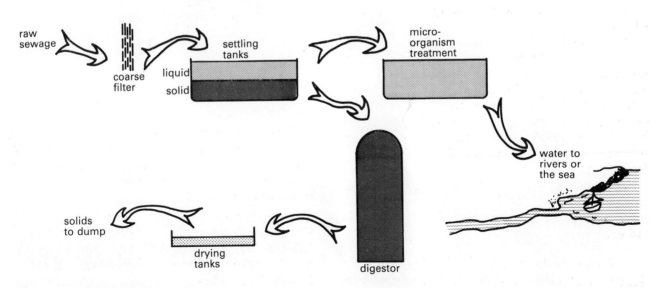

Fig 8.5 Treating sewage

As the water trickles over the stones the micro-organisms react with the waste matter in the water.

2. A supply of micro-organisms is added to a tank of liquid sewage and air is blown through the mixture for 6–12 hours. The micro-organisms are then allowed to settle and then the safe water is run off.

8.6 Water—the chemical

To a chemist, water is a covalent compound of hydrogen and oxygen. We can make water in the laboratory by burning hydrogen and allowing the flame to touch a cold surface.

hydrogen + oxygen → water
$$2H_2 + O_2 \rightarrow 2H_2O$$

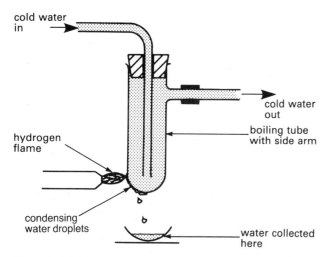

Fig 8.6 Making water

The liquid collected can be shown to be water by using either anhydrous copper (II) sulphate or anhydrous cobalt chloride.

Water turns anhydrous copper (II) sulphate from *white* to *blue*.
Water turns anhydrous cobalt chloride from *blue* to *pink*.

These chemicals can be used as a test for water, but they do not tell us if the water is pure. Distilled water, sea water, even a cup of tea will turn anhydrous cobalt chloride from blue to pink.

Pure water has a number of characteristic properties:
1. It melts at 0°C and boils at 100°C.
2. It has a density of 1 g/cm^3 at 4°C.
3. It is a very poor conductor of electricity.

Tap water is pure enough for many jobs, but sometimes extra pure water is needed. Extra pure water is needed to top up car batteries and for making solutions in laboratories. This extra pure water can be made either by distilling tap water or by passing tap water through an ion exchange resin. You have most likely seen bottles labelled *distilled water* or *deionised water* in your school.

8.7 Water as a solvent

The most remarkable thing about water is that it can dissolve so many different substances. It is a very good *solvent*. A solvent is a liquid that can dissolve substances (*solutes*) to form *solutions*.

solvent + solute → solution

Dissolving gases

Most gases dissolve in water to form solutions. Some gases like ammonia or hydrogen chloride are very soluble in water. 1 cm^3 of water will dissolve over 600 cm^3 of ammonia at room temperature. These very soluble gases change chemically as they dissolve in water.

ammonia + water $\rightleftharpoons$ ammonium ions + hydroxide ions

$$NH_3 + H_2O \rightleftharpoons NH_4^+ + OH^-$$

Most of the common gases are far less soluble in water. 1000 cm^3 of water will dissolve only 6 cm^3 of oxygen at room temperature. These less soluble gases do not change when they dissolve in water. The gas molecules are just held in the water structure.

The amount of a gas that can be dissolved in water decreases as the water gets hotter. We say that *the solubility of all gases decreases as the temperature increases.* You can see this every time a kettle boils. When the temperature of the water is about 60°C (too hot to touch) lots of air bubbles can be seen in the water. As it is heated more the kettle becomes quite noisy as air bubbles escape. Just before the water boils the kettle becomes quiet; all the air has been removed. The boiling noise then starts.

A sample of the air dissolved in water can be collected in the laboratory using the apparatus shown in Fig 8.7.

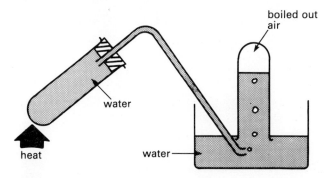

Fig 8.7 Collecting air from water

The air which can be boiled out from water is different from normal air. It contains a higher proportion of oxygen. It will relight a glowing splint.

Dissolving solids

If you have ever tried making a cup of tea or coffee, using cold water you will know that solids dissolve better in *hot* water. We say that *the solubility of solids increases with increasing temperature.*

The solubility of a solid in water is the number of grammes of that solid which can be dissolved in 100 g of water.

It is the mass of solid that is needed to form a saturated solution with 100 g of water.

A saturated solution is one which cannot dissolve any more of the solute at that temperature.

Potassium nitrate has a solubility of 31·6 g per 100 g water at 20°C. It has a solubility of 110 g per 100 g water at 60°C.

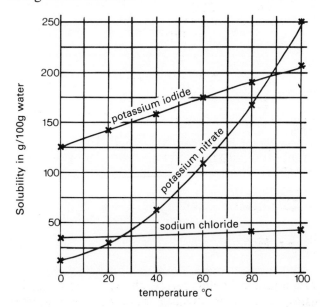

Fig 8.8

61

Figure 8.8 shows how the solubility of different solids varies with temperature.

These graphs are known as *solubility curves*. Solubility curves provide much information. Let us consider the solubility curve of potassium nitrate in detail. It is shown in Fig. 8.9.

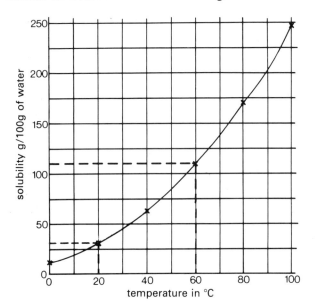

Fig 8.9

The curve tells us:
1. At room temperature (20°C) 31·6 g of potassium nitrate are needed to saturate 100 g of water.
2. At 60°C 110 g of potassium nitrate are needed to saturate 100 g of water.
3. If a solution containing 110 g of potassium nitrate in 100 g of water is cooled from 80°C:
a crystals of potassium nitrate will first form at 60°C
b more and more crystals will form as it is cooled further
c when the solution has cooled to 20°C, 110 − 31·6 = 78·4 g of crystals will be formed.

8.8 Hidden water

Many substances contain hidden water. The substances are perfectly dry but contain water which is chemically held. This chemically held water is known as *water of crystallisation*. Copper (II) sulphate crystals and sodium carbonate crystals are examples of substances with water of crystallisation.

Copper (II) sulphate crystals have the formula $CuSO_4.5H_2O$. Each formula unit of copper (II) sulphate has 5 water molecules stuck onto it. Sodium carbonate crystals have the formula $Na_2CO_3.1OH_2O$.

Substances that contain this water of crystallisation are known as *hydrated* substances. When they are heated they lose their water. They are then known as *anhydrous* substances.

| hydrated copper (II) sulphate | → | anhydrous copper (II) sulphate | + water |

$$CuSO_4.5H_2O \rightarrow CuSO_4 + 5H_2O$$

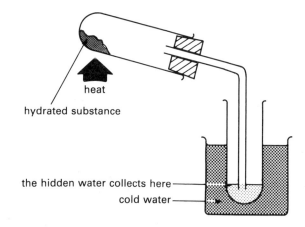

Fig 8.10 Collecting hidden water

It is possible to collect some of the water hidden in hydrated substances by using the apparatus shown in Fig 8.10.

How would you find out if the water collected is pure water?

Questions

1. AMMONIA, ANHYDROUS COPPER (II) SULPHATE, CARBON DIOXIDE, SODIUM CHLORIDE, OXYGEN, MAGNESIUM SULPHATE CRYSTALS.

   Choose from the above list:

   a a substance used to test for water
   b the substance that makes rainwater acidic
   c a substance that is more soluble in cold water than in hot water
   d a substance that is more soluble in hot water than it is in cold water
   e a substance which loses water on heating
   f a substance that causes hardness of water
   g a substance found in sea water but not in fresh water

2. 'A water molecule in the river Thames at Oxford may be drunk several times before it reaches London'. Explain how this is possible.

3. Imagine that you are stranded on a small island. Every day is warm and sunny. Every night is cold. It never rains on the island so there are no streams or rivers. How would you manage to produce enough drinking water to live?

4.
   a Name 3 ways in which rivers become polluted.
   b Name 2 ways in which you could tell that a stretch of river was heavily polluted.
   c Carefully describe the stages by which normal river water is changed into drinking water.

5. Suggest reasons why caves are found in limestone rocks but never in granite rocks.

6. Suppose you were given 2 samples of tap water, one hard, the other soft:

   a how would you find out which sample was hard water?
   b how would you find out if it was temporary or permanent hard water?
   c name 2 substances that dissolve in water making it hard.
   d give 1 advantage of hard water over soft water.
   e give 2 advantages of soft water over hard water.
   f how would you soften temporary hard water so that it could be used in an industrial boiler?

7. You find an unlabelled bottle containing a colourless liquid in the laboratory:

   a how would you show that the liquid contains some water?
   b how would you show that the liquid contains no dissolved solids?
   c how would you show that the liquid was pure water?

8.

Temperature (°C)	0	20	40	60	80	100
Solubility of substance C (g/100 g of water)		10	14	25	42	63	92

Plot a graph of solubility of substance C against temperature with temperature as the horizontal axis. From your graph calculate:

a the solubility of substance C at: (i) 30°C (ii) 50°C
b the temperature at which the solubility of substance C is 50 g/100 g of water

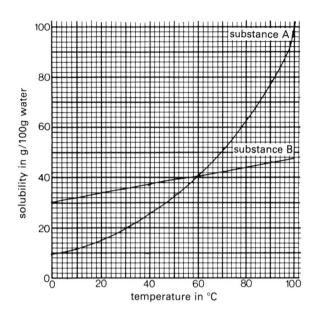

9. Use the graph provided to answer the following questions:

a What is the solubility of substance A at (i) 20°C (ii) 80°C?

b At what temperature do substances A and B have the same solubility?

c At 40°C what is the solubility of (i) substance A (ii) substance B?

d How much of substance A could be dissolved in 200 g of water at 100°C?

e How much of substance B could be dissolved in 50 g of water at 0°C?

9 Acids, alkalis and salts

9.1 Recognising acid and alkalis

When we first think of acids we think of liquids with a sour taste that burn the skin. When we first think of alkalis we think of liquids that neutralise acids and make our skin feel soapy. It would be silly to decide whether a substance was an acid or an alkali by tasting it, or pouring it on your hand. Chemists have had to find a different method.

Chemists find out if a substance is an acid or an alkali by adding an indicator to a solution of the substance.

An indicator is a substance which has one colour in acidic solutions and another colour in alkaline solutions.

The following table shows some common indicators:

Name of indicator	Colour in acid solution	Colour in alkaline solution
Litmus	Red	Blue
Phenolphthalein	Colourless	Red
Methyl orange	Red	Yellow
Screened methyl orange	Red	Green

Table 1

Litmus is the most common indicator.

These indicators tell us if a solution is acidic or alkaline, but they do not tell us how acidic or how alkaline the solution is.

pH scale

This is a number scale used to describe how acidic or how alkaline a solution is.

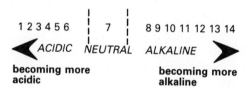

The pH of solutions is usually measured by using Universal indicator. (This is a mixture of indicators). It has different colours in solutions of different pH.

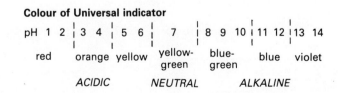

9.2 Acids

The following table gives information about some common acids:

Name of acid	Chemical formula	Where can it be found?	State at room temperature (when pure)
Hydrochloric	HCl	In your stomach	Gas
Sulphuric	H_2SO_4	In car batteries	Liquid
Nitric	HNO_3	Formed in atmosphere during thunderstorms	Liquid
Ethanoic(acetic)	$H_4C_2O_2$	In vinegar	Liquid
Citric	$H_8C_6O_7$	In lemon juice	Solid
Tannic	$H_{52}C_{76}O_{46}$	In tea	Solid

Table 2

The table tells us that:
1. Acids contain hydrogen.
2. Acids can be solids, liquids or gases.

Properties of acids

Note Acids only show these properties if water is present.

PROPERTY	EXCEPTION
1. Have a sour taste.	
2. Turn litmus red.	
3. Turn Universal indicator red, orange or yellow.	
4. Produce carbon dioxide from carbonates.	Sometimes the reaction stops after a short while.
5. Produce hydrogen gas with most metals.	Nitric acid does not. Unreactive metals like Cu, Ag do not react.
6. Dissolve in water to form solutions which conduct electricity.	

Table 3

9.3 Alkalis

The following table will give you some information about common alkalis:

Name of alkali	Formula	State at room temperature (when pure)
Sodium hydroxide	NaOH	Solid
Potassium hydroxide	KOH	Solid
Calcium hydroxide	$Ca(OH)_2$	Solid
Barium hydroxide	$Ba(OH)_2$	Solid
Ammonia	NH_3(NH_4OH in water)	Gas

Table 4

With the exception of ammonia, all alkalis are metal hydroxides. The metals which form alkalis are in groups 1 and 2 of the Periodic Table.

Properties of alkalis

Note Alkalis only show these properties if water is present.

PROPERTY	EXCEPTION
1. Have a soapy feel.	
2. Turn litmus blue.	
3. Turn Universal indicator blue-green, blue or violet.	
4. Produce hydrogen gas with aluminium.	Only strong alkalis do this.
5. Dissolve in water forming conducting solutions.	
6. React with acids forming a salt and water only.	

Table 5

Explanation of acidity

By studying a large number of acids and alkalis chemists have been able to find out why acids have properties in common and why alkalis have properties in common.

Acids

OBSERVATION	DEDUCTION
1. Acids do not show acidic properties when pure or when dissolved in solvents other than water.	**1.** Water must play an important part in acidity.
2. Acids do not conduct electricity when pure or dissolved in solvents other than water.	**2.** Acids are covalent substances.
3. Water is a poor conductor of electricity.	**3.** Water is a covalent substance.
4. All acids conduct electricity when dissolved in water.	**4.** Acids must form ions when dissolved in water.
5. All solutions of acids in water produce hydrogen gas at the negative electrode when electricity is passed through the solution.	**5.** All acidic solutions must contain *positive* hydrogen ions.

From this type of reasoning, we can say that acids are substances that produce H^+ ions when added to water.
So, acidity is caused by the H^+ ion in water.

Alkalis

OBSERVATION	DEDUCTION
1. Pure alkalis do not show alkaline properties, but solutions of alkalis dissolved in water do.	**1.** Water plays an important part in alkaline behaviour.
2. All solutions of alkalis in water conduct electricity.	**2.** Alkaline solutions must contain ions. An ion must cause alkaline behaviour.

Table 7

It can be shown that all alkaline solutions contain hydroxide ions(OH^-). *So, alkaline behaviour is caused by the OH^- ion in water.*

Neutralisation

When an acid is neutralised by an alkali, the hydrogen ions react with hydroxide ions to form water molecules.

$$H^+ + OH^- \rightarrow H_2O$$

When an acidic solution is neutralised its pH increases until it reaches 7. Any solution of pH = 7 is neutral.

Strong and weak acids

We have said that when an acid dissolves in water, the acid molecules change into ions. *Example:* $HCl \rightarrow H^+ + Cl^-$

With some acids not all the molecules change into ions.

In a *strong* acid *all* the molecules change into ions when dissolved in water.

Example: hydrochloric acid, sulphuric acid

In a *weak* acid only some of the molecules change into ions when the acid is dissolved in water.

Example: ethanoic acid, citric acid.

Strong and weak alkalis

A *strong* alkali is *completely* ionised when dissolved in water.

Example: NaOH.

A *weak* alkali is only *partly* ionised when dissolved in water.

Example: ammonia.

9.4 Salts

Salts are ionic substances. They contain the positive ions of a metal (or ammonium ions) and the negative ions formed when an acid dissolves in water (see Table 8).

We can make salts in the laboratory in a number of ways.

METHODS OF MAKING SALTS

A. Methods which use acids

1. *By reacting a metal with an acid* (see page 70)

Many metals react with acids to produce salts and hydrogen gas:

Example

METAL	+	ACID	→	SALT	+	HYDROGEN ↑
zinc	+	sulphuric acid	→	zinc sulphate	+	hydrogen ↑
Zn	+	H_2SO_4	→	$ZnSO_4$	+	H_2 ↑

Name of salt	Formula	Positive ion	Negative ion
magnesium sulphate	$MgSO_4$	Mg^{2+}	SO_4^{2-}
copper (II) chloride	$CuCl_2$	Cu^{2+}	Cl^{1-}
lead chloride	$PbCl_2$	Pb^{2+}	Cl^{1-}
ammonium nitrate	NH_4NO_3	NH_4^{1+}	NO_3^{1-}

Table 8

Method

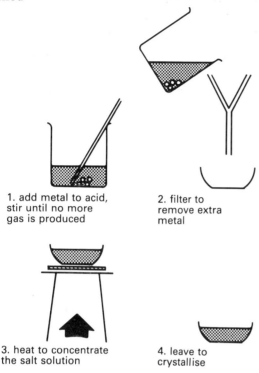

1. add metal to acid, stir until no more gas is produced

2. filter to remove extra metal

3. heat to concentrate the salt solution

4. leave to crystallise

Fig 9.1

When not to use this method

1. If the metal in the salt is very reactive eg sodium.
2. If the metal does not react with an acid (ie very unreactive metals such as copper or silver).
3. If the salt does not dissolve in water.

2. *By reacting a metal carbonate with an acid*

Metal carbonates react with acids to form a salt, carbon dioxide gas and water:

Method

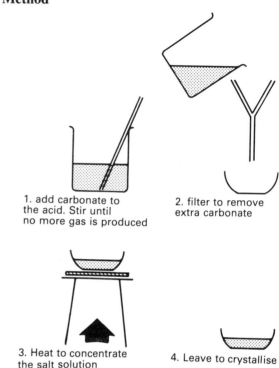

1. add carbonate to the acid. Stir until no more gas is produced

2. filter to remove extra carbonate

3. Heat to concentrate the salt solution

4. Leave to crystallise

Fig 9.2

When not to use this method

1. If the salt does not dissolve in water.
2. If the carbonate *does* dissolve in water.

Example: CARBONATE + ACID → SALT + CARBON DIOXIDE ↑ + WATER
copper (II) + sulphuric → copper (II) + carbon dioxide ↑ + water
carbonate   acid   sulphate
$CuCO_3$ + H_2SO_4 → $CuSO_4$ + $CO_2 \uparrow$ + H_2O

3. By reacting a base with an acid.

A base is a substance that reacts with an acid to form a salt and water only. They are usually metal oxides or metal hydroxides.

All metal oxides and hydroxides are bases. An alkali is a base that dissolves in water.

a For bases that do not dissolve in water

Example:

ACID	+	BASE	→	SALT	+	WATER
sulphuric acid	+	copper (II) oxide	→	copper (II) sulphate	+	water
H_2SO_4	+	CuO	→	$CuSO_4$	+	H_2O

Method

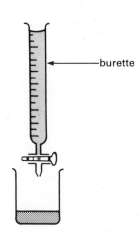

1. Add base to warm acid until no more will react. Stir all the time

2. Filter to remove extra base

3. Heat to concentrate the salt solution

4. Leave to crystallise

Fig 9.3

When not to use this method

1. If the base is an alkali.
2. If the salt is insoluble in water.

b Reaction on an alkali (soluble base) and an acid

Example:

Sodium hydroxide	+	Hydrochloric acid	→	Sodium chloride	+	Water
NaOH	+	HCl	→	NaCl	+	H_2O

Method

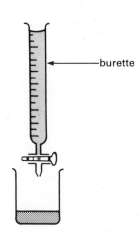

—burette

Fig 9.4

1. Fill a burette with acid up to the zero mark. (Bottom of curve of liquid should be level with the zero mark—see diagram).
2. Use a pipette to place 20 cm³ of alkali in the beaker.
3. Add 2 drops of indicator to the alkali.
4. Run acid from the burette into the alkali solution until the solution is *just* acidic. The indicator shows this point.
5. Note the volume of acid added.
6. Repeat the experiment using the same volumes of acid and alkali but no indicator.
7. Heat the solution formed in **6.** to concentrate it.
8. Leave to crystallise.

B. Methods not needing acids

1. *Precipitation method*

Method

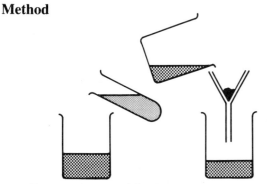

1. To a solution containing lead ions add a solution containing chloride ions until no more precipitate forms

2. Filter to remove the precipitate

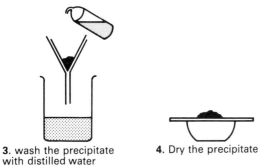

3. wash the precipitate with distilled water

4. Dry the precipitate

Fig 9.5

This is used only to prepare salts which do not dissolve in water. The salt is formed as a precipitate:

Example:

| lead | + | sodium | → | lead | + | sodium |
| nitrate | | chloride | | chloride ↓ | | nitrate |

$$Pb(NO_3)_2 + 2NaCl \rightarrow PbCl_2\downarrow + 2NaNO_3$$

The following table gives information about the solubility of salts and bases.

TYPE OF COMPOUND	SOLUBILITY
CARBONATE	All INSOLUBLE *except* sodium, potassium and ammonium
CHLORIDE	All SOLUBLE *except* silver and lead.
HYDROXIDE (and OXIDE)	All INSOLUBLE *except* sodium, potassium and ammonium.
NITRATE	All soluble.
SULPHATE	All soluble *except* barium, calcium and lead.

Table 9

Water of crystallisation

Many salts contain water of crystallisation. This is water which is held within the crystal structure. It can be removed by heating the crystals. Only salts that are soluble in water can have water of crystallisation.

Salts with water of crystallisation:
$MgSO_4.7H_2O$
$CuSO_4.5H_2O$

Salts without water of crystallisation:
$NaCl$ (soluble)
$PbCl_2$ (insoluble)

Terms used to describe salts

1. ANHYDROUS: anhydrous salts have *no* water of crystallisation.

2. HYDRATED: hydrated salts have water of crystallisation.

3. DELIQUESCENT: a deliquescent salt absorbs water vapour from the atmosphere, and dissolves in this water to form a solution. Metal nitrates are deliquescent.

CHOOSING A METHOD OF PREPARING A SALT

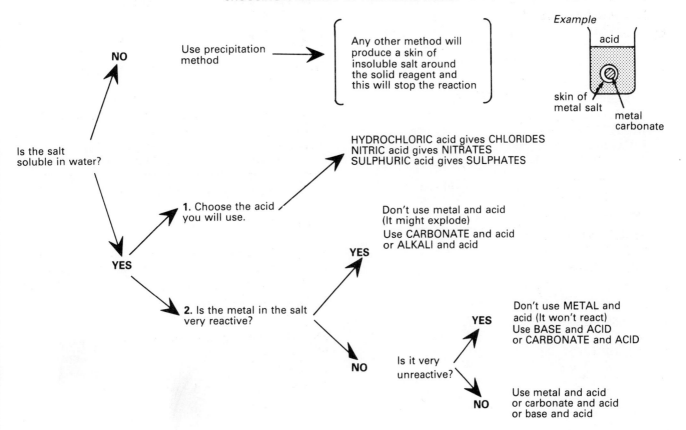

HYDROCHLORIC acid gives CHLORIDES
NITRIC acid gives NITRATES
SULPHURIC acid gives SULPHATES

Don't use metal and acid
(It might explode)
Use CARBONATE and acid
or ALKALI and acid

Don't use METAL and
acid (It won't react)
Use BASE and ACID
or CARBONATE and ACID

Use metal and acid
or carbonate and acid
or base and acid

4. HYGROSCOPIC: a hygroscopic salt absorbs water vapour from the atmosphere, but not enough to make it dissolve. Common salt (NaCl) is hygroscopic.

5. EFFLORESCENT: an efflorescent salt is a hydrated salt which loses some or all of its water of crystallisation when left in air. Washing soda ($Na_2CO_3 \cdot 1OH_2O$) is efflorescent.

Questions

1. The following table shows the pH of a number of aqueous solutions:

SOLUTION	A	B	C	D	E
pH	10	4	2	7	8

a

(i) Which solution is the most acidic?

(ii) Which solution is the most alkaline?
(iii) Which solution is neutral?
(iv) Which solution could be sugar solution?
(v) Which solution could be vinegar?

b Which of the following *could* give a neutral solution on mixing?
   (i) A + B
   (ii) C + D
   (iii) B + D
   (iv) C + E
   (v) A + B + C + D + E

2. AQUEOUS AMMONIA, CITRIC ACID, COPPER, COPPER (II) CARBONATE, COPPER (II) OXIDE, HYDROCHLORIC ACID, MAGNESIUM, SODIUM HYDROXIDE.

Choose from the above list:

a an alkali
b a base which is not an alkali
c a substance that produces carbon dioxide gas when added to dilute sulphuric acid
d a mixture
e a strong acid
f a weak acid
g a substance which produces hydrogen gas when added to dilute sulphuric acid
h a substance that reacts with acids to form salt and water only
i a weak alkali
j a substance found in lemons

3. ACIDIC, ALKALINE, ANHYDROUS, CARBONATE, DELIQUESCENT, EFFLORESCENT, HYDROGEN, HYDROXIDE, INDICATOR, NEUTRAL, PRECIPITATE.

Choose from the above list the word needed to complete the following:

a When copper nitrate crystals are left on a watch glass in the laboratory they turn to a blue solution. This is because copper nitrate crystals are _____ .

b Any solution with a pH less than 7 must be _____ .

c Any solution with a pH greater than 7 must be _____ .

d An acidic solution must contain an excess of (i) _____ ions over (ii) _____ ions.

e Salts which lose water on heating are said to be _____ .

f When washing soda crystals ($Na_2CO_3.1OH_2O$) are left in an open laboratory they lose weight and become powdery. This is because washing soda crystals are _____ .

g A solution of sodium chloride in water is _____ .

h A substance that has different colours in acidic and alkaline solutions is known as an _____ .

i A solid formed on mixing 2 solutions is known as a _____ .

4. The following are methods of preparing salts:
   (i) metal + acid   (ii) alkali + acid
   (iii) base + acid   (iv) carbonate + acid
   (v) precipitation

Which of these methods would you use to prepare the following salts:

a copper (II) sulphate ( )
b magnesium sulphate
c lead chloride
d sodium chloride
e zinc nitrate
f calcium carbonate
g silver chloride
h zinc chloride
i potassium sulphate
j lead nitrate

5. What 2 chemicals would you use to make each of the following salts?

a copper (II) sulphate
b magnesium chloride
c lead sulphate (insoluble)
d sodium nitrate
e copper (II) carbonate (insoluble)

6. Complete the following word equations and then, if you can, change them into balanced symbol equations:
a zinc + hydrochloric acid →
b lead carbonate + nitric acid →
c sodium hydroxide + sulphuric acid →
d copper (II) oxide + hydrochloric acid →
e silver nitrate + sodium chloride →
f magnesium + sulphuric acid →
g potassium carbonate + nitric acid →
h lead nitrate + sodium sulphate →

7. Describe in detail how you would prepare *pure, dry* crystals of magnesium sulphate ($MgSO_4.7H_2O$) starting from magnesium oxide.

8.
a Describe 3 different tests that you could perform to show that a solution was acidic.

b Describe 2 different tests that you could perform to show that a solution was alkaline.

9. Name the reagents you would use to carry out the reactions A–E:

10. The waste water from a factory was found to be acidic. In a test, 5 litres of the waste water needed 1 g of lime (calcium hydroxide) to neutralise it. The factory puts 100 000 litres of waste water into a local river every hour. This water *must* be neutral.
a How much lime will be needed to neutralise the waste water every hour?
b How much lime will be used each day? (Assume that the factory works 24 hours every day).
c Suggest a way in which the lime could be added to the water.

11. A solution containing 0.1 mol/dm^3 of hydrochloric acid has a pH of 1.
A solution containing 0.1 mol/dm^3 of ethanoic acid has a pH of 3. What explanation can you suggest for this difference?

CuO
copper oxide
(solid)
⟶ A ⟶
Cu(NO$_3$)2
copper nitrate
(solution)
⟶ B ⟶
CuCO$_3$
copper carbonate
(insoluble solid)

C ↓

CuSO$_4$
copper sulphate
(solution)
← E ←
Cu(OH)$_2$
copper hydroxide
(insoluble solid)
← D ←
CuCl$_2$
copper chloride
(solution)

10 The air and oxygen

10.1 Air: What's in it?

Air is a mixture. It is a most important mixture. Without it, life as we know it could not exist. Table 1 shows what normal air contains.

Name of substance	Percentage in air
nitrogen	78%
oxygen	20%
carbon dioxide	0·03%
noble gases	1% (mainly argon)
water vapour	variable (often about 1%)
polluting gases	variable

Table 1

Because air is a mixture, the percentage of each gas varies from time to time and from place to place.

Nitrogen

The largest part of air is nitrogen. It is an unreactive element. It can react with oxygen during thunderstorms to form nitrogen dioxide and this can dissolve in rain water to form nitric acid. However, thunderstorms don't happen that often. Most of the time the nitrogen in the air shows no sign of reacting.

Oxygen

Oxygen is the most active part of the air. We need oxygen for breathing and for burning all fuels.

Carbon dioxide

Only a small fraction of the air is carbon dioxide, but it is a very important part. It is needed by plants to make food.

Noble gases

These are helium, neon, argon, xenon, krypton and radon. They are very unreactive but they are very useful to man once they have been separated from the air.

Helium is used in helium/oxygen mixtures for diving. It is much better than compressed air for deep diving; there is less chance of the 'bends'.

Neon is used to fill some lamp bulbs and advertising strip lights.

Argon is the most plentiful of the noble gases in air. It is used to fill light bulbs. Do you know why light bulbs cannot be filled with air?

Water vapour

The water vapour in the air varies from time to time. Imagine the air in your kitchen. It contains far more water vapour when food is being prepared than at other times.

Polluting gases

These are the harmful gases in the atmosphere. They get there mainly by man's activity. Table 2 shows some of the common polluting gases which are found in air.

Name of polluting gas	How it gets into the atmosphere	Harmful properties
sulphur dioxide	by burning fuels.	poisonous to man. Acidic, attacks buildings and railings.
nitrogen dioxide	from car exhausts. Produced by some industries.	poisonous to man. Acidic.
carbon monoxide	from car exhausts.	poisonous to man.

Table 2

10.2 Getting chemicals from air

Air is a convenient source of important gases needed by industry. These gases are obtained by the fractional distillation of liquid air. There are a number of stages in this process.

1. The air is filtered to remove dust.
2. Carbon dioxide is removed by passing the air through sodium hydroxide solution:

carbon + sodium → sodium + water
dioxide   hydroxide   carbonate

$$CO_2 + 2NaOH \rightarrow Na_2CO_3 + H_2O$$

3. Water vapour is removed using a drying agent like silica gel.
4. The air is compressed to about 200 atmospheres and then cooled with liquid nitrogen.
5. The cooled compressed air is then allowed to expand suddenly. This sudden expansion cools the air even more.
6. By repeating the cycle of compression, cooling and expansion, liquid air is eventually formed.
7. Finally, the liquid air is fractionally distilled. Pure nitrogen, oxygen and argon can be obtained.
   This process is shown in Fig 10.1.

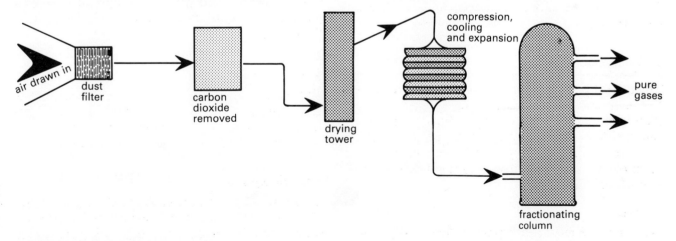

Fig 10.1 Getting gases from air

Once these gases have been separated from air, they are sold either as gases in cylinders, or as liquids. Enormous quantities of nitrogen and oxygen are used by industry each year.

10.3 Oxygen—the V.I.P.

Oxygen is a very important element. We need it for breathing. When we breathe we draw air into our lungs. In our lungs red blood cells pick up oxygen. They can do this because they contain the substance *haemoglobin*. Haemoglobin reacts with oxygen to form a substance called *oxyhaemoglobin*.

HAEMOGLOBIN + OXYGEN
$$\rightleftharpoons \text{OXYHAEMOGLOBIN}$$

The red blood cells then travel around the body. At various parts of the body oxyhaemoglobin gives up its oxygen. This oxygen then burns digested food and gives us energy. Most of the oxygen we breathe in is changed into carbon dioxide and water in our bodies. The air we breathe out is therefore different to the air we breathe in

Air breathed in	Air breathed out
20% oxygen	16% oxygen
0·03% carbon dioxide	4% carbon dioxide

Table 3

From Table 3 you can see that our lungs are not very efficient. They only use about $\frac{1}{4}$ of the oxygen we breathe in. When people are ill sometimes their lungs work even less efficiently. We give these people extra oxygen from cylinders, so that their bodies can more easily get the oxygen they need.

You can find out the percentage of oxygen in the air in your school laboratory by using the apparatus shown in Fig 10.2.

Draw 100 cm³ of air into syringe A through the three way tap. Turn the three way tap so that the air in syringe A can be passed into syringe B. Heat the copper turnings strongly and pass the air backwards and forwards between syringe A and syringe B. The hot copper reacts with the oxygen in the air to form black copper (II) oxide.

copper + oxygen → copper (II) oxide
2Cu + O_2 → 2CuO

When no more copper (II) oxide is being formed stop heating. Push the remaining air back into syringe A and let the apparatus cool. If you try this experiment you will most likely find that you are left with about 80 cm³ of air in syringe A.

So, 100 cm³ of air contains 100 − 80 = 20 cm³ of oxygen.

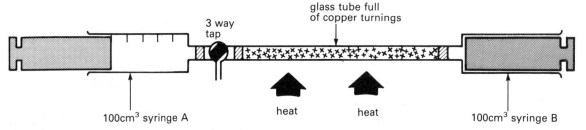

Fig 10.2 Finding out the percentage of oxygen in air

The percentage of oxygen in the air
$$= \frac{20}{100} \times 100 = 20\%$$

How would you change this experiment to show that the air you breathe out contains only 16% oxygen?

10.4 Making oxygen

We have seen that oxygen can be separated from the air. It can be bought compressed in cylinders. However, in schools, we often need a very small amount of oxygen for experiments. It is simpler to make some oxygen when it is needed rather than rent or buy a large cylinder. There are 2 common methods used to make oxygen in the laboratory.

1. *By breaking down hydrogen peroxide*

Hydrogen peroxide is a fairly unstable chemical. It easily breaks down to form water and oxygen:

hydrogen peroxide $\rightarrow$ water $+$ oxygen $\uparrow$
$$2H_2O_2 \quad \rightarrow 2H_2O + \quad O_2 \uparrow$$

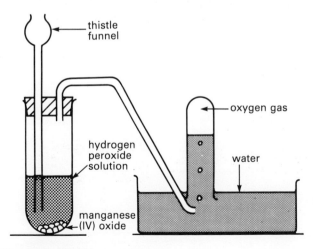

Fig 10.3 Making oxygen

The substance manganese (IV) oxide makes the hydrogen peroxide break down quickly at room temperature.

2. *By breaking down water*

Pure water does not conduct electricity. Water with a little dilute sulphuric acid added is a good conductor. If electricity is passed through acidified water it breaks down to form hydrogen and oxygen:

water $\rightarrow$ hydrogen $\uparrow$ $+$ oxygen $\uparrow$
$$2H_2O \rightarrow \quad 2H_2 \uparrow \quad + \quad O_2 \uparrow$$

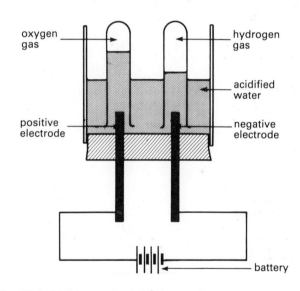

Fig 10.4 Making oxygen from water

10.5 Oxygen—the chemical

Oxygen exists as O_2 molecules. It is a colourless gas with no smell. It is not very soluble in water, so it is usually collected over water.

NAME OF ELEMENT	EXPERIMENT	REACTION
Phosphorus	If a small piece of white phosphorus is warmed very gently and then lowered into oxygen it bursts into flames. It burns with a white flame and makes a thick white smoke. After some time a fine white powder settles in the gas jar.	two different oxides are formed: phosphorus + oxygen → phosphorus (III) oxide $4P$ + $3O_2$ → $2P_2O_3$ phosphorus + oxygen → phosphorus (V) oxide $4P$ + $5O_2$ → $2P_2O_5$
Sulphur	If the sample of sulphur is heated until it just melts and is then lowered into oxygen it bursts into flames. It burns with a bright blue flame. A colourless gas with a choking smell is formed.	sulphur + oxygen → sulphur dioxide S + O_2 → SO_2
Carbon	If a sample of carbon is heated strongly (until just red hot) and then lowered into oxygen it *glows far more brightly*. A colourless gas is formed.	carbon + oxygen → carbon dioxide C + O_2 → CO_2
Magnesium	If a strip of magnesium ribbon is heated until it just starts to burn and is then lowered into oxygen it burns very strongly. A blinding white light is produced. A white powder is formed.	magnesium + oxygen → magnesium oxide $2Mg$ + O_2 → $2MgO$
Iron	If some iron wool is heated until red hot and then lowered into oxygen it glows white hot. Sparks fly in all directions. A brown powder is formed.	iron + oxygen → iron (III) oxide $4Fe$ + $3O_2$ → $2Fe_2O_3$

Table 4

Oxygen reacts with most other elements to form oxides. One method of reacting solid elements with oxygen is shown in Fig 10.5. A sample of the solid element is heated on a combustion spoon and the combustion spoon is then lowered into a gas jar of oxygen.

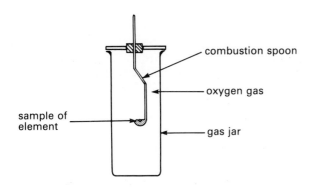

combustion spoon

oxygen gas

sample of element

gas jar

Fig 10.5 Burning Elements in oxygen

Table 4 shows what happens when a number of common elements react with oxygen in this way.

The elements in Table 4 also react with oxygen when heated in air, but the reactions are not as violent. When oxygen reacts with elements in this way, heat is always produced. The reactions are always *exothermic*.

The oxides of metal elements have different properties from the oxides of non metal elements.

Metal oxides

These are high melting point solids. They neutralise acids and are therefore known as *basic oxides*. Most do not dissolve in water. Metal oxides that dissolve in water form alkaline solutions.

Non metal oxides

These usually have low melting points. Many are gases. Most are soluble in water. They dissolve to form acidic solutions. These oxides are known as *acidic oxides*. There are a few non metal oxides that do not have acidic properties. These are known as *neutral oxides*. Nitrogen monoxide (NO) and carbon monoxide (CO) are examples of neutral oxides.

We have seen that oxygen reacts with many elements. It also reacts with many compounds. It is the element that is needed for burning. All fuels need a good supply of oxygen if they are to burn efficiently.

Example:

methane + oxygen →carbon dioxide + water
$$CH_4 + 2O_2 \rightarrow CO_2 + 2H_2O$$

Test for oxygen

If a glowing splint is placed in oxygen it will relight. This is the usual test for oxygen.

Uses of oxygen

The main use is in steel making (page 102). Large quantities of oxygen are needed. Many large steelworks have plants for making oxygen from air. Oxygen is used with ethyne (acetylene) for welding, brazing and metal cutting. The use of oxygen to help patient's breathing in hospitals has already been mentioned.

Questions

1.
a Name three gases present in normal air.
b Name three gases that pollute air.
c Give three reasons why air is a mixture and not a compound.

2. ARGON, CARBON DIOXIDE, CARBON MONOXIDE, HELIUM, OXYGEN, NITROGEN.

Choose from the above list:

a A gas used to make steel from molten iron.
b A gas used to fill light bulbs.
c A gas formed when wood burns.
d A gas which is more dense than air.
e 2 gases present in car exhaust fumes.
f The most plentiful gas in the Earth's atmosphere.
g A gas used up during breathing.
h A gas formed during breathing.

3. Draw a fully labelled diagram of the apparatus you would use to prepare a few test tubes of oxygen gas starting from hydrogen peroxide solution.

a How would you test the gas you collected to show it was oxygen?
b Write an equation for the reaction involved in this preparation.
c What mass of hydrogen peroxide would you need to use to prepare 1 mole of oxygen gas?

4. Oxygen is manufactured from air by making liquid air and then fractionally distilling it. Look up section **10.2** before answering these questions.

a Why is the air filtered before it is compressed?
b Why is the air dried before it is compressed to 200 atmospheres?
c Use the data on page 186 to find out which of the gases present in liquid air has the lowest boiling point.
d Suggest reasons why a chemical from air plant should be sited:
  (i) near a steel works.
  (ii) Near a factory making fertilisers.

5.
This is a diagram of a bunsen burner.

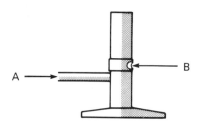

a What enters the bunsen burner at A?
b What is drawn into the bunsen burner at B?
c Name one gas *always* formed in a bunsen flame.
d Name the solid formed in the bunsen flame if the air supply is limited.
e What gas *can* be formed in a bunsen flame if the air supply is limited?
f Why is it important that the burners on gas fires are regularly checked and cleaned?

6.

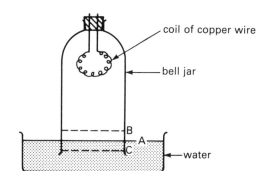

The apparatus in the diagram was set up with water in the bell jar up to level A. Electricity was passed through the copper wire for 2 minutes so that it glowed red hot. The electricity was then switched off. It was found that the water level in the bell jar went down to C but eventually ended up at B.

a   Why did the water level in the bell jar go down to C when electricity was passed through the copper wire?

b   Why did the water level slowly rise to B when the electricity was switched off?

c   Would you expect the copper wire to look different at the end of the experiment? Give a reason for your answer.

d   Name 1 gas used to fill light bulbs.

e   Why are light bulbs not filled with air?

11 Hydrogen

Each hydrogen atom contains only 1 proton, 1 electron and no neutrons. This means hydrogen is the element with the lightest atoms. Hydrogen gas exists as H_2 molecules by sharing electrons. It is the least dense of all gases.

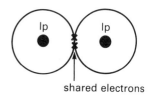

shared electrons

Fig 11.1 A hydrogen molecule

11.1 The uses of hydrogen

Hydrogen is a very important element. It has a large number of important industrial uses.

1. *Hydrogen is used to manufacture ammonia gas*

nitrogen + hydrogen $\rightleftharpoons$ ammonia

$$N_2 \quad + \quad 3H_2 \quad \rightleftharpoons \quad 2NH_3$$

This is the major use of hydrogen, as very large quantities of ammonia are needed to make fertilisers, dyes and plastics.

2. Hydrogen is used in the manufacture of margarine. It is used to change vegetable oils, such as palm oil or olive oil into solid fats.

3. Hydrogen is used to provide a reducing atmosphere in furnaces.

Most metals, when hot, react with oxygen in the air. They become tarnished with a layer of metal oxide. By having an atmosphere of hydrogen in the furnace, tarnishing can be prevented. In this way metals can be annealed (toughened) or brazed (heated) more efficiently.

4. Hydrogen is an important part of many fuels.

Water gas is a mixture of hydrogen and carbon monoxide. It contains 50% hydrogen.

Coal gas is a mixture of hydrogen, methane and carbon monoxide. It also contains about 50% hydrogen.

Town gas is a mixture of coal gas and methane, or natural gas. It also contains a large proportion of hydrogen.

5. Hydrogen can be burnt in oxygen to give a very hot flame, which is capable of cutting most metals.

6. Since hydrogen has such a low density it has been used for filling airships and balloons. It is no longer widely used for this as there have been a number of accidents because hydrogen is so inflammable (burns easily).

11.2 Making hydrogen for industry

Hydrogen has to be made on a large scale. Industry uses a number of methods to make the hydrogen it needs.

1. *From water using coke*

If steam is passed over white hot coke water gas is formed:

steam + coke → water gas

$$H_2O + C \rightarrow CO + H_2$$

If the water gas is mixed with more steam and passed over an iron catalyst, the carbon monoxide in the water gas is changed into carbon dioxide and more hydrogen is formed.

steam + water gas → hydrogen + carbon dioxide

$$H_2O + CO + H_2 \rightarrow 2H_2 + CO_2$$

The carbon dioxide can be removed by dissolving it in water under pressure. Hydrogen is left.

2. *From natural gas and water*

A mixture of carbon monoxide and hydrogen can be made by passing natural gas and steam over a nickel catalyst at very high temperatures. The main ingredient of natural gas is methane.

methane + steam $\xrightarrow[1000°C]{\text{nickel catalyst}}$ carbon monoxide + hydrogen

$$CH_4 + H_2O \rightarrow CO + 3H_2$$

You should see from the equation that the hydrogen has come from the methane *and* from the water.

The carbon monoxide is then changed into carbon dioxide and dissolved in water. The hydrogen is left. This is now the most common method used to make hydrogen industrially.

3. *Using electricity*

Hydrogen can be made by passing electricity through a number of solutions. Often hydrogen is formed as a by-product.

Sodium hydroxide is made by passing electricity through sodium chloride solution. Hydrogen is formed as a by-product in this process together with chlorine gas.

A number of small factories make the hydrogen they need by passing electricity through sodium hydroxide solution.

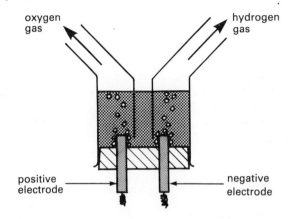

Fig 11.2 Making hydrogen from sodium hydroxide solution

The advantages of this method are:
1. The hydrogen made is pure.
2. Oxygen is formed as a by-product.
3. No sodium hydroxide is used up. Only the water is broken down.

There must be disadvantages to this method or every factory would use it to make its own hydrogen. What do you think the disadvantages are?

The hydrogen produced by industry is sold as compressed gas in cylinders and also as a liquid. Liquid hydrogen must be stored under great pressure at temperatures below −250°C.

11.3 Making hydrogen in schools

When we want to make small amounts of hydrogen gas in school laboratories, most of the industrial methods are not suitable. Hydrogen is usually made in laboratories by reacting zinc with dilute hydrochloric or sulphuric acid.

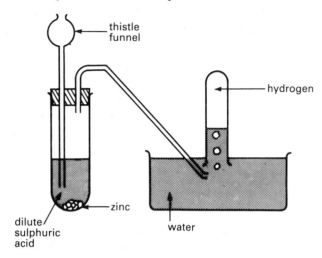

Fig 11.3 Making hydrogen in the laboratory

zinc + sulphuric acid → zinc sulphate + hydrogen
$$Zn + H_2SO_4 \rightarrow ZnSO_4 + H_2$$

Pure zinc reacts very slowly with dilute sulphuric acid. By adding a little copper (II) sulphate solution to the reaction mixture, hydrogen is produced much faster.

Hydrogen is only slightly soluble in water and so it is usually collected over water. Since it is far less dense than air it can be collected by upward delivery as shown in Fig 11.4.

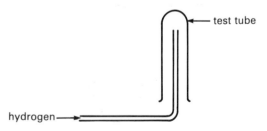

Fig 11.4 Collecting hydrogen by upward delivery

If a dry sample of hydrogen is needed it must be collected by upward delivery. Hydrogen gas can be dried by passing it through any drying agent, such as concentrated sulphuric acid, silica gel or anhydrous calcium chloride. The problem when collecting hydrogen by upward delivery is that you cannot tell when the test tube is full of hydrogen.

11.4 Hydrogen—the chemical

Hydrogen is a colourless, tasteless gas with no smell. It is the first element in the Periodic table. Hydrogen atoms are far too unstable to exist by themselves, so hydrogen is found as H_2 molecules.

Chemical properties of hydrogen

1. Mixtures of hydrogen and oxygen burn very readily to form water:

hydrogen + oxygen → water
$$2H_2 + O_2 \rightarrow 2H_2O$$

The reaction can often be explosive, so great care has to be taken when burning hydrogen gas. We use this burning reaction as a test for hydrogen.

Test for hydrogen: *mixtures of hydrogen and air burn, usually with a squeaky pop.*

Because of the risk of an explosion, you should *never* try lighting more than a test tube full of hydrogen.

2. Hydrogen will react with chlorine to form hydrogen chloride.

Hydrogen + chlorine → hydrogen chloride
$$H_2 + Cl_2 \rightarrow 2HCl$$

This reaction is best seen by lowering a jet of burning hydrogen into a gas jar of chlorine.

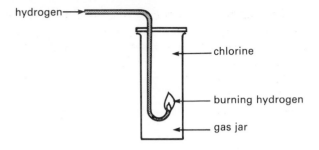

Fig 11.5 Burning hydrogen in chlorine

When burning hydrogen is lowered into a gas jar of chlorine the hydrogen continues to burn with a white flame. The green colour of the chlorine slowly disappears. When all the chlorine has reacted the hydrogen stops burning.

Note: The reaction between hydrogen and chlorine can sometimes be violently explosive. It should never be attempted by a pupil.

3. Hydrogen will take the oxygen from the oxides of some metals. The more unreactive metals such as iron, lead and copper can be obtained in this way.

Example:

copper (II) oxide + hydrogen → copper + water

$$CuO \quad + \quad H_2 \quad \rightarrow \quad Cu \quad + \quad H_2O$$

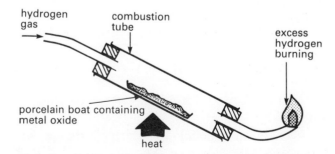

Fig 11.6 Reacting hydrogen with metal oxides

The combustion tube is sloped so that any water formed does not run back onto the hot parts of the tube, where it might cause the tube to crack.

4. Pure hydrogen is a neutral gas. It has no effect on litmus paper or universal indicator paper.

11.5 Hydrogen—the good mixer

The speed at which the particles of a gas move at depends on the mass of the particles. The lighter the particles the faster they move at any fixed temperature. Since hydrogen gas has the lightest particles they must be the fastest moving. This means that hydrogen will diffuse or mix faster than any other gas. You can show this by filling 2 balloons; one with hydrogen and the other with air. If these balloons are left, the one containing hydrogen will deflate faster than the one containing air. Hydrogen molecules diffuse out of the balloon faster than any of the molecules in air.

The problem with this simple experiment is that you have to wait a long time for the result. You could show that hydrogen diffuses faster than air more easily using the apparatus shown in Fig 11.7.

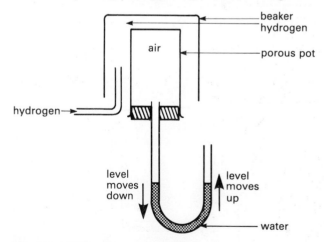

Fig 11.7 Diffusion of hydrogen

When the apparatus in Fig 11.7 is set up, some hydrogen molecules move into the porous pot and some air particles move out. Since hydrogen diffuses in faster than air diffuses out the number of particles in the porous pot increase. Therefore the pressure of gas in the porous pot increases. The water in the U tube moves because of this increase in pressure.

11.6 Oxidation and reduction

Oxidation and reduction are types of changes that happen during some chemical reactions. Oxidation and reduction are the reverse of each other.

Oxidation is to reduction what day is to night or what black is to white.

Chemists define oxidation in 3 different ways:

1. Oxidation is adding on oxygen to a substance.
2. Oxidation is removing hydrogen from a substance.
3. Oxidation is removing electrons from a substance.

Since reduction is the reverse of oxidation, it can also be defined in 3 ways:

1. Reduction is removing oxygen from a substance.
2. Reduction is adding on hydrogen to a substance.
3. Reduction is adding on electrons to a substance.

These ideas should become clearer if we look at a few reactions in which oxidation and reduction are taking place.

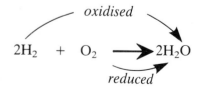

$$2H_2 \ + \ O_2 \ \longrightarrow \ 2H_2O$$

The hydrogen *adds on oxygen* to form water, so it is *oxidised.*
The oxygen *adds on hydrogen* to form water, so it is *reduced.*

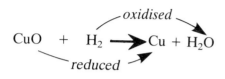

$$CuO \ + \ H_2 \ \longrightarrow \ Cu + H_2O$$

Oxygen is removed from the copper (II) oxide to form copper. Copper (II) oxide is *reduced.*
Oxygen is added on to the hydrogen to form water. Hydrogen is *oxidised.*

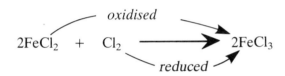

$$2FeCl_2 \ + \ Cl_2 \ \longrightarrow \ 2FeCl_3$$

The iron (II) chloride is oxidised, because the iron (II) ions are changed into iron (III) ions.

$$Fe^{2+} \ \longrightarrow \ Fe^{3+} \ + \ e$$
an electron

An electron has been *removed* from the iron (II) ion.
Chlorine is reduced because chlorine molecules are changed into chloride ions

$$Cl_2 \ + \ 2e \ \longrightarrow \ 2Cl^-$$
2 electrons

2 electrons have been *added onto* each chlorine molecule.

Any chemical reaction in which oxidation and reduction take place is known as a *REDOX* reaction.

In a REDOX reaction the substance which is reduced does the oxidising. It is known as the **oxidising agent.**

The substance which is oxidised does the reducing. It is known as the **reducing agent.**

In the reaction between hydrogen and oxygen to form water, the hydrogen is the reducing agent and the oxygen is the oxidising agent.

Table 1 shows some common oxidising and reducing agents.

OXIDISING AGENTS	REDUCING AGENTS
oxygen	hydrogen
nitric acid	carbon monoxide
concentrated sulphuric acid	sulphur dioxide
potassium permanganate	hydrogen sulphide

Table 1

Questions

1. Spot the mistakes in the following passage:
   A factory had a tank of liquid hydrogen that had been obtained by the fractional distillation of liquid air. One day the tank broke and hydrogen poured into the factory. The gas formed a thick blanket on the floor of the factory, which had to be evacuated. The corrosive gas did much damage to the metal equipment on the factory floor. Fortunately there were no naked lights and so the hydrogen did not burn. Firemen pumped water into the factory to dissolve the hydrogen and later disposed of the solution by burning it in an open space.

2.
   a When copper is heated in air, it tarnishes, and copper (II) oxide is formed. Write an equation for the reaction.
   b When copper (II) oxide is heated in hydrogen, copper and water are formed. Write an equation for the reaction.
   c When copper or brass components are brazed together in a furnace, an atmosphere of hydrogen is often kept in the furnace. Why is the hydrogen used?
   d What safety rules would be needed in a factory using hydrogen in this way?

3. Suggest reasons for the following:
   a A balloon filled with hydrogen rises.
   b A hydrogen filled balloon deflates faster than an air filled balloon.
   c Hydrogen can be made by reacting zinc with dilute sulphuric acid but this method is not used to make hydrogen industrially.

4. A student wanted to prepare a few test tubes of hydrogen gas. He drew the following diagram of the apparatus he intended to use:

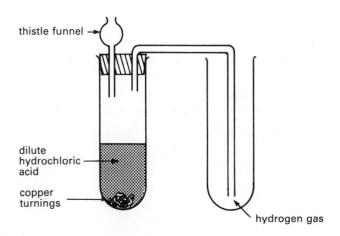

thistle funnel →

dilute hydrochloric acid

copper turnings

hydrogen gas

a Name three mistakes that the student made in his diagram.

b How would you prove that a test tube contained hydrogen gas?

5. Water and hydrogen chloride (HCl) are covalent gases. Draw diagrams to show how the electrons are arranged in molecules of these compounds.

6.

a When hydrogen burns in air, water is formed. Write an equation for the reaction.

b Draw a diagram of the apparatus you would use to collect some of the water formed when hydrogen burns. (You need not show how the hydrogen was prepared).

c How would you show that the liquid you collect is water?

7. In each of the following redox reactions identify:

　(i) the substance which is oxidised
　(ii) the substance which is reduced
　(iii) the oxidising agent

a　$PbO + H_2 \rightarrow Pb + H_2O$
b　$CH_4 + 2O_2 \rightarrow CO_2 + 2H_2O$
c　$2Na + Cl_2 \rightarrow 2NaCl$
d　$2Mg + CO_2 \rightarrow 2MgO + C$

12 The metal elements

When we first think of metals we may think of solids that conduct electricity, are strong and can be hammered into shape without shattering. In Chapter 4 we saw that to a chemist the word metal means much more than this. Metals have many properties in common. These common properties distinguish them from non metals.

Even though metals have many common properties they are different in many ways. *Example*: Potassium bursts into flames as soon as it is dropped into water, whereas gold can be recovered untarnished from the sea bed after hundreds of years. Chemists say that potassium is a very *reactive* metal and gold is a very *unreactive* metal.

12.1 The reactivity of metals

It is useful to arrange the metal elements in a reactivity series. This is a list of elements in which the most reactive element is at the top and the metals become less reactive as we go down the list. The reactivity series of common metals is shown in the following Table.

Some simple experiments can be performed in the laboratory to show that the above reactivity series is correct.

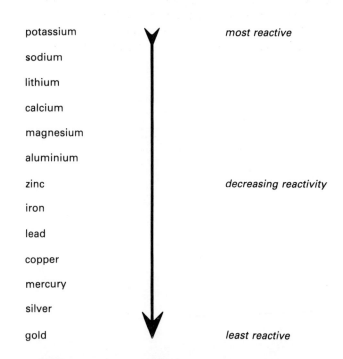

A. Reaction of metals with water, steam and dilute hydrochloric acid

1. *Water*

Table 1 shows what happens when a *small* piece of each metal is dropped into a trough of cold water.

METAL	REACTION	EQUATION					ORDER IN REACTIVITY SERIES
potassium	It reacts violently on the surface of the water. Enough heat is produced in the reaction to melt the potassium into a ball and to light the hydrogen gas formed. The hydrogen burns with a lilac flame. The remaining solution is alkaline.	potassium 2K	+ +	water $2H_2O$	$\rightarrow$ $\rightarrow$	potassium hydroxide 2KOH	+ +	hydrogen ↑ H_2 ↑	first
sodium	It reacts violently on the surface of the water. Enough heat is produced to melt the sodium, but not enough to ignite the hydrogen gas formed. The remaining solution is alkaline.	sodium 2Na	+ +	water $2H_2O$	$\rightarrow$ $\rightarrow$	sodium hydroxide 2NaOH	+ +	hydrogen ↑ H_2 ↑	second
lithium	The lithium floats on the surface of the water reacting vigorously to produce hydrogen gas and an alkaline solution. The reaction is not as violent as that of sodium. Not enough heat is produced to melt the lithium or to ignite the hydrogen gas.	lithium 2Li	+ +	water $2H_2O$	$\rightarrow$ $\rightarrow$	lithium hydroxide 2LiOH	+ +	hydrogen ↑ H_2	third
calcium	Calcium sinks and reacts steadily producing hydrogen gas and leaving an alkaline solution.	calcium Ca	+ +	water $2H_2O$	$\rightarrow$ $\rightarrow$	calcium hydroxide $Ca(OH)_2$	+ +	hydrogen ↑ H_2 ↑	fourth
magnesium	Magnesium turnings sink and a very slow reaction takes place, producing hydrogen gas.	magnesium Mg	+ +	water $2H_2O$	$\rightarrow$ $\rightarrow$	magnesium hydroxide $Mg(OH)_2$	+ +	hydrogen ↑ H_2 ↑	fifth

- hydrogen gas
- water
- magnesium turnings

The apparatus needs to be left for several days to collect a single test tube of hydrogen gas. The solution left is slightly alkaline.

Table 1

It can be seen that as we go down the reactivity series metals react less violently with water. Metals below magnesium in the reactivity series do not react with cold water.

2. Reaction of metals with steam

To investigate the reaction of metals with steam the apparatus in Fig 12.1 can be used:

The metal is strongly heated until it is very hot and then the mineral wool is heated so that steam passes over the hot metal. Table 2 shows what happens.

Note: Great care must be taken with this experiment to stop the water sucking back from the trough into the hot test tube.

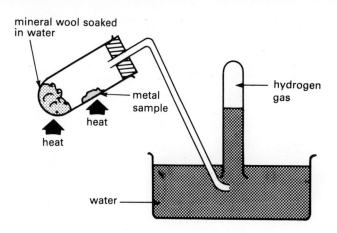

Fig 12.1

METAL	REACTION	EQUATION				ORDER IN REACTIVITY SERIES
magnesium	The hot magnesium reacts very violently with the steam. A bright white glow is produced and hydrogen gas is collected. White, powdery magnesium oxide is left in the tube.	magnesium + Mg +	steam → H_2O →	magnesium oxide MgO	+ hydrogen ↑ + H_2 ↑	*fifth*
zinc	When steam is passed over red hot zinc powder the zinc glows slightly more brightly and hydrogen gas is collected. Zinc oxide powder is left in the tube. It is yellow when hot and white when cold.	zinc + Zn +	steam → H_2O →	zinc oxide ZnO	+ hydrogen ↑ + H_2 ↑	*seventh*
iron	When steam is passed over red hot iron some hydrogen is formed. The iron cools and must be constantly heated while the steam is passed over it.	iron + 2Fe +	steam ⇌ $3H_2O$ ⇌	iron (III) oxide Fe_2O_3	+ hydrogen ↑ + $3H_2$ ↑	*eighth*

Table 2

As we go down the reactivity series metals react less violently with steam. Metals below iron in the reactivity series do not react with steam.

3. *Reaction of metals with dilute hydrochloric acid*

Potassium, sodium, lithium and calcium (the most reactive metals) should *never* be added to dilute acid as they react explosively.

Magnesium, zinc, iron and lead, from the middle of the reactivity series, react with dilute hydrochloric acid to form the metal chloride and hydrogen gas.

Example:

magnesium + hydrochloric → magnesium + hydrogen ↑
            acid   chloride

$$Mg \quad + \quad 2HCl \quad \rightarrow \quad MgCl_2 \quad + \quad H_2 \uparrow$$

The reaction of dilute hydrochloric acid on magnesium is fairly fast, but the *lower* the reactivity of the metal the slower the reaction becomes.

Lead reacts very, very slowly with dilute hydrochloric acid.

Copper, mercury, silver and gold (the least reactive metals) *do not* react with dilute hydrochloric acid.

Note: in the reactions of metals with water, steam, or dilute hydrochloric acid, the metal is always changed into an ionic compound.

Therefore metal atoms change into positively charged metal ions:

Example:

$Mg \quad \rightarrow \quad Mg^{2+} \quad + \quad 2e$
metal atom → metal ion + electrons
$Na \quad \rightarrow \quad Na^{+} \quad + \quad e$
metal atom → metal ion + electron

The reactivity of a metal depends on the ease with which it forms positive ions. The more reactive metals like sodium form positive ions far more easily than the less reactive metals such as copper.

B. Displacement of metals from solutions of salts

A more reactive metal will displace a less reactive metal from a solution of one of its salts.

Example: If a small piece of zinc is dropped into blue copper (II) sulphate solution, brown copper metal is formed and the zinc dissolves.

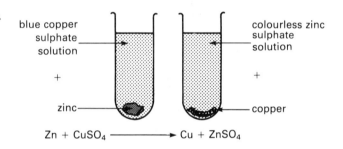

$$Zn + CuSO_4 \longrightarrow Cu + ZnSO_4$$

Fig 12.2

The more reactive metal (zinc) has displaced the less reactive metal (copper) from a solution of one of its salts (copper (II) sulphate).

Note: if copper is placed in zinc sulphate solution no reaction takes place.

In the displacement reactions of metals the more reactive metal changes into metal ions:

Example: $Zn \rightarrow Zn^{2+} + 2e$

The ions of the less reactive metal are changed into metal atoms.

Example: $Cu^{2+} + 2e \rightarrow Cu$

C. Competition of elements for oxygen

A more reactive metal will steal the oxygen from the oxide of a less reactive metal if heat energy is provided.

Example: If zinc powder is mixed with lead oxide powder on a tin lid, *no* reaction takes place. If the lid is heated a red glow starts to spread through the mixture. This glow continues to spread even if the heat is removed. Silvery beads of lead are formed. Therefore a chemical reaction takes place.

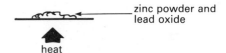
zinc powder and
lead oxide

heat

Fig 12.3

zinc + lead oxide → zinc oxide + lead
$$Zn + PbO → ZnO + Pb$$

The more reactive metal (zinc) has stolen the oxygen from the oxide of the less reactive metal (lead).

If zinc oxide and lead are heated together no reaction takes place.

It is sometimes difficult to think in terms of chemical reactions. You may find that this story helps you to understand the competition method of determining a reactivity series.

A jackel was sitting in its cage in a zoo, very happy, because it had just been given a juicy joint of meat. Just as the jackel was about to eat the meat, the cage door opened and in came a lion. The lion saw the meat, strolled over and ate it, knowing the jackel wasn't strong enough to object. The jackel feeling sad and hungry left the cage to look for some more meat. He followed his nose until he came to another cage which contained another juicy joint of meat. The jackels excitement was short lived: another lion was in the cage and at that moment started to eat the meat.

The motto of this story may well be 'Jackels can't win when there are lions about', but a chemist would see it slightly differently. We can write 2 equations:

lion + jackel with meat → lion with meat + jackel
lion with meat + jackel → no change

Wild animals often compete for food and the stronger animal usually wins. In much the same way we can consider that elements compete to combine with oxygen and the more reactive element wins the competition.

The competition of elements for oxygen may be used to place two important non-metals in the reactivity series.

1. *Carbon*

If burning magnesium is placed in a gas jar of carbon dioxide it continues to burn. White magnesium oxide is formed as well as black specks of carbon.

magnesium + carbon → magnesium + carbon
dioxide   oxide
$$2Mg + CO_2 → 2MgO + C$$

Magnesium steals the oxygen from carbon dioxide. Therefore magnesium is more reactive than carbon.

If zinc oxide powder is mixed with carbon and the mixture heated, a red glow spreads through the mixture and zinc metal is formed.

zinc oxide + carbon → zinc + carbon dioxide
$$ZnO + C → Zn + CO_2$$

Carbon steals the oxygen from zinc oxide. Therefore carbon is more reactive than zinc.

95

2. Hydrogen

If hydrogen is passed over heated lead oxide, lead and water are formed.

hydrogen + lead oxide → lead + water

$$H_2 + PbO \rightarrow Pb + H_2O$$

Hydrogen steals the oxygen, therefore it is more reactive than lead.

If steam is passed over heated iron, iron (III) oxide and hydrogen are formed.

iron + steam $\rightleftharpoons$ iron (III) oxide + hydrogen↑

$$2Fe + 3H_2O \rightleftharpoons Fe_2O_3 + H_2\uparrow$$

The iron steals the oxygen from water, therefore iron is more reactive than hydrogen.

A more complete reactivity series is therefore:

potassium sodium lithium calcium magnesium →

most reactive

aluminium carbon zinc iron hydrogen lead copper →

mercury silver gold →

least reactive

Aluminium: the peculiar one

Aluminium appears to be far less reactive than we would expect from its position in the reactivity series. Aluminium usually has a strongly held, thin film of oxide on the surface of the metal. This film stops it from reacting with water or air. If the oxide coating is removed, aluminium will corrode rapidly in air.

12.2 Uses of the reactivity series

If the position of a metal in the reactivity series is known, it is possible to predict a great deal about the properties of the metal and its compounds.

We can predict how the metal will react with various reagents.

Table 3 also tells us quite a lot about the uses of metals.

METAL	REACTION WITH WATER	REACTION WITH DILUTE HYDROCHLORIC ACID	REACTION WITH OXYGEN
potassium sodium lithium calcium magnesium	React with cold water	Explosive	Burns brightly when heated
aluminium	Protected by oxide film	React forming metal chloride and hydrogen	Reaction becomes less violent
zinc iron	Only react with steam		
lead	No reaction	Very slow	Tarnishes but does not burn
copper mercury silver		No reaction	
gold			No reaction

Table 3

Reactive metals like sodium and potassium are difficult to store. They are usually stored under oil to keep them out of contact with air and water. These metals are far too dangerous to find any uses in our homes. Fairly recently it has been found that, because they are good conductors of heat and have low melting points, they are suitable as coolants in nuclear reactors. In this very special case it is worth using them despite the enormous safety precautions needed.

The metal elements that we find in our homes tend to be the more unreactive ones. Make a list of all the different metals in your home and write down the use of each metal alongside. What fraction of the metals in your list come from the bottom half of the reactivity series?

We can also predict the reactions of some metal compounds. This can be seen in Table 4.

We can predict the solubility of some metal compounds in water:

METAL	SOLUBILITY OF CARBONATES	SOLUBILITY OF OXIDES
potassium sodium lithium	SOLUBLE	SOLUBLE
calcium magnesium aluminium zinc iron lead copper mercury silver gold	INSOLUBLE	INSOLUBLE

Table 5

METAL	HEAT ON CARBONATES	HEAT ON NITRATES	HEAT ON HYDROXIDES	HEATING CARBON WITH OXIDES
potassium sodium lithium	No reaction	Decompose producing oxygen gas as the only gas	Lose water and form oxide with greater ease ie at lower temperature ↓	No reaction
calcium magnesium aluminium zinc iron lead copper mercury silver	Decompose producing carbon dioxide	Decompose producing nitrogen dioxide and oxygen		Metal and carbon dioxide formed
			No hydroxide exists	
gold	No carbonate			No oxide exists

Table 4

Table 5 shows us that metals in the bottom half of the reactivity series form insoluble hydroxides. This information is used to help control industrial pollution. Many industries produce waste water which contains fairly high concentrations of transition metal compounds. If copper, nickel, chromium or mercury compounds were pumped into our rivers the pollution problems caused could be enormous. Strict regulations now control the waste that factories can put into rivers, and heavy metal compounds must be removed at the factory. Fortunately these polluting metals are in the lower part of the reactivity series.

Factories are able to add a cheap alkali, like lime (calcium hydroxide) to their waste water and precipitate the heavy metal hydroxides. The precipitate can then be filtered off, and safe water allowed to flow into rivers. Pollution is avoided, and the industry has the bonus that it can reclaim the heavy metals from the precipitated sludge.

We can also make predictions about how a sample of the metal could be extracted from its ore.

All metals are found in rocks. Only the very unreactive metals such as silver and gold can be found as elements. Most metals are found as metal compounds (oxides, sulphides, carbonates, sulphates etc). Rocks that contain metal compounds from which a *metal can* be extracted are known as *ores*. Ores are never pure compounds. To extract metals from their ores, the useless material in the ore has to be removed and the metal compound has to be chemically changed into the metal.

In the extraction of reactive metals such as aluminium, the ore is first treated to give a pure compound of the metal. The metal compound is *then* chemically changed into the metal. For metals in the middle of the reactivity series (like iron) the useless material in the ore is removed *at the same time* as the metal compound is changed into the metal.

Table 6 shows how the method of extraction of

METAL	NAME OF COMMON ORE	CHEMICAL NAME	FORMULA	METHOD OF EXTRACTION
potassium	Carnallite	Magnesium potassium chloride	$KCl.MgCl_2.6H_2O$	Pass electricity through molten metal chloride
sodium	Halite	Sodium chloride	$NaCl$	
calcium	Chalk, Limestone Marble	Calcium carbonate	$CaCO_3$	Convert to chloride then pass electricity through molten chloride
aluminium	Bauxite	Aluminium oxide	$Al_2O_3.2H_2O$	Pass electricity through molten oxide
zinc	Zinc blende	Zinc sulphide	ZnS	Convert to oxide by heating in air then reduce with carbon
iron	Haematite	Iron (III) oxide	Fe_2O_3	
lead	Galena	Lead sulphide	PbS	
copper	Pyrites	Copper iron(II)sulphide	$FeCuS_2$	
silver	found as			Merely separated from useless rock
gold	element			

Table 6

metals is linked to the position of the metal in the reactivity series.

It is an interesting fact that we could produce a fairly accurate reactivity series by finding out how long each metal element has been used by man. Silver and gold have been used for thousands of years whereas the most reactive metals were only extracted from their ores for the first time in the nineteenth century.

12.3 Metals and alloys

We have seen that metal elements have many useful properties, but pure metals are not widely used. The properties of metals such as strength and resistance to corrosion can be greatly improved by forming *alloys*.

An alloy is a mixture of one metal element with one or more other elements. The element mixed with the 'parent' metal is usually another metal or carbon.

How alloys are made

When alloys are made it is important that all the pure elements are completely mixed.

Some alloys are made directly by reducing mixed ores to form the alloy, but most alloys are made by mixing the pure elements in the correct proportions, when molten. The major ingredient is melted first and then the required quantities of the other elements are stirred in. The molten alloy formed is then poured into moulds to solidify.

By looking at a few common alloys the advantages of forming alloys can be seen.

Brass (Copper with zinc)
Brass is stronger than copper and yet more easily worked.

Duralumin (mainly aluminium with magnesium and copper)

Duralumin is much stronger than aluminium. Its combination of high strength, low density, and resistance to corrosion, make it ideal for pots and pans in kitchens and lightweight machinery.

Type metal (lead with antimony and tin)
Type metal is used to make type for printing. It has a low melting point which is convenient for casting. It expands when it solidifies, therefore tending to fill the mould and make sharp, clear type. It is far stronger than lead and therefore does not wear easily.

Stainless steel (iron with chromium and nickel and a little carbon)
It is extremely hard wearing and resistant to corrosion, even when heated. Its resistance to corrosion can be improved by increasing the chromium content.

Solder (lead with tin)
Solder is used for making electrical contacts. It has a very low melting point (less than 200°C) and therefore is not likely to do any damage even to sensitive electrical equipment.

A solder with 60% lead is known as plumber's solder. It has the advantage of becoming pasty as it solidifies. Therefore, extra solder can be easily removed leaving neat joints.

Bronze
Bronzes are alloys of copper with tin, but the 'bronze' with which we are most familiar contains a little tin and zinc in a copper base. This bronze is used to make ½p, 1p and 2p coins. It is hard wearing and resistant to corrosion.

Cupronickel (copper with nickel)
This alloy is used to make British 'silver' coins. The alloy is again hardwearing and resists tarnishing.

The following table gives some of the major uses of metals and their alloys.

METAL ELEMENTS	USE
sodium	A coolant in nuclear reactors
magnesium	Used to make duralumin alloy
aluminium	1. Used to make duralumin alloy
	2. Electrical cables
	3. Cooking foil.
zinc	1. Used to galvanise iron
	2. Dry battery cases
iron	Used to make steels.
lead	1. Used as a weather seal on buildings
	2. Radiation shields
copper	1. Used to make brass and bronze
	2. Electrical wiring
	3. Water piping
mercury	Thermometers
silver	Used to make silver salts for photography
gold	Jewellery when alloyed with copper

ALLOYS	USE
brass	1. Screws
	2. Light bulb caps.
bronze	Making 'copper' coins
duralumin	Pots and pans, lightweight machinery, window frames
cupronickel	Making 'silver' coins
steel	Car bodies, girders, railway lines
stainless steel	Cutlery, razor blades
solder	1. Making electrical contacts
	2. Joining piping

Table 7

12.4 Another look at some metals

Aluminium

Aluminium is a light metal. It has a density of about a third that of steel. The pure metal is not strong, but it forms a number of strong, low density alloys. Although it is a reactive metal it is more resistant to corrosion than a number of other metals. The firm oxide layer on its surface gives it protection against corrosion. It is also an excellent conductor of heat and electricity. These properties of aluminium make it a very important metal.

Aluminium is the most plentiful metal in the earth's crust. It is found in most rocks and clays, but not in a form that can easily be extracted. Aluminium is extracted from the ore bauxite ($Al_2O_3 . 2H_2O$).

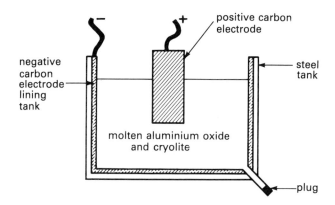

Fig 12.4

The stages are:
1. The bauxite is purified to make pure aluminium oxide.
2. The aluminium oxide is dissolved in molten cryolite.
3. Direct current electricity is passed through the molten mixture.

100

Aluminium is formed at the negative electrode:

aluminium ions + electrons →aluminium atoms
$$Al^{3+} + 3e \rightarrow Al$$

Oxygen is formed at the positive electrode.

4. Aluminium metal settles to the bottom of the tank and is run off as molten metal from time to time.

5. The molten metal is allowed to solidify in moulds.

Cryolite is a rock which is used in the extraction of aluminium for a number of reasons:

1. Aluminium oxide melts at about 2000°C. By using cryolite, a conducting solution of aluminium oxide can be made at 650°C. This saves energy.

2. The molten aluminium is more dense than the solution of aluminium oxide in cryolite, and does not mix with it. Therefore, the metal sinks to the bottom of the tank where it can easily be removed.

3. The cryolite itself is unaffected by the flow of electricity.

Anodising aluminium

We have already said that there is a thin film of aluminium oxide firmly held on the surface of the metal. It is possible to increase the thickness of this film—the process is called *anodising*.

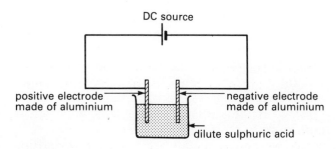

DC source

positive electrode made of aluminium

negative electrode made of aluminium

dilute sulphuric acid

Fig 12.5

As a current is passed through the dilute sulphuric acid, the oxide film on the positive aluminium electrode becomes thicker. The thicker oxide layer is porous and can absorb dyes. The metal can therefore be given an attractive colour. Since the colour is *in* the metal itself the colours are long lasting. Aluminium that has been anodised and dyed is widely used for cheap jewellery and other decorative uses.

Iron and steel

The importance of iron and steel to our lives can hardly be overestimated. Imagine the effect on a normal day if all the iron and steel suddenly disappeared: no cutlery, no cooker, no kettle, no water taps, no cars, no lorries, no trains. When we think of life without iron and steel we begin to realise how valuable iron is.

Fortunately, iron is the second most plentiful metal in the earth's crust. The main ores are haematite (Fe_2O_3) and magnetite (Fe_3O_4). It is from these ores that iron is extracted.

Iron is extracted from its ores as follows:

1. The iron ore is strongly heated in air. This removes moisture and some impurities.

2. The heated iron ore is fed into the top of a *blast furnace*, together with limestone and coke.

3. Hot air is blown into the furnace near the bottom. This blast of air allows coke to burn, making carbon dioxide and producing a very high temperature:

coke + air →carbon dioxide
$$C + O_2 \rightarrow CO_2$$

4. The carbon dioxide reacts with hot coke to form carbon monoxide:

coke + carbon dioxide→carbon monoxide
$$C + CO_2 \rightarrow 2CO$$

5. The carbon monoxide then reduces the *hot* iron ore to iron:

haematite + carbon → iron + carbon
        monoxide   dioxide

$$Fe_2O_3 + 3CO \rightarrow 2Fe + 3CO_2$$

6. The iron formed is molten and runs to the bottom of the furnace.

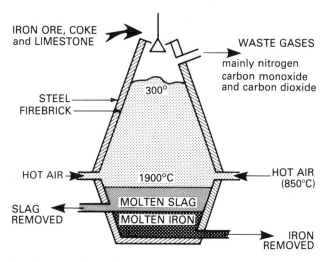

Fig 12.6 A Blast furnace

The iron formed in the blast furnace would be extremely impure if limestone *was not* used. The added limestone breaks down to form quicklime in the blast furnace because of the high temperature.

limestone → quicklime + carbon dioxide

$$CaCO_3 \rightarrow CaO + CO_2 \uparrow$$

The quicklime reacts with silica (sandy) impurities in the iron ore to form a molten slag:

quicklime + silica → slag (calcium silicate)

$$CaO + SiO_2 \rightarrow CaSiO_3$$

The slag does not mix with the iron but floats on top of it (like oil on water). Many of the impurities which would be in the iron, dissolve instead in the molten slag. The iron and slag are run off separately.

The iron run off from a blast furnace is known as pig iron, or cast iron. This iron contains 2–4% carbon as well as other impurities such as sulphur, phosphorus, and silicon. Cast iron is brittle and not strong. Most of the cast iron is changed into steel.

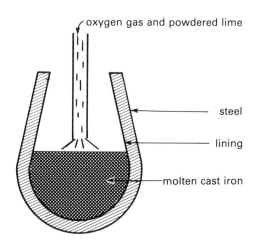

Fig 12.7

Steel making

Molten cast iron is poured into a large container. High pressure oxygen and powdered lime are then blown onto the surface of the molten iron. The blast of oxygen stirs the metal, and oxidises the impurities in the iron. The oxidised impurities either escape as gases or form a slag, which can be poured off the surface. The molten metal left is pure iron.

Carbon and/or metals are now stirred into the molten iron in the correct amounts to make the alloys required by various customers. The most common steel contains up to 0·5% carbon. It has many, many uses including car bodies, girders, screws and nails. Thousands of different steels have been made, all having slightly different properties. If the composition of a steel is changed slightly its properties may change greatly. This means that the steel industry must at all times carefully control its processes, if it is to meet the needs of its customers.

12.5 Rust

Iron and most steels have one big disadvantage: THEY RUST.

What is rust?

Rust is hydrated iron (III) oxide ($Fe_2O_3 . H_2O$)

How does rust form?

Rust forms whenever iron, oxygen, and water are present. Rusting is faster at high temperatures and when salt is dissolved in the water.

Why is rusting a problem?

Aluminium metal has a layer of oxide on its surface. This oxide layer is firmly held by the metal underneath and prevents the metal corroding. When iron rusts, iron (III) oxide is formed on the surface of the metal. This oxide layer is only weakly held by the metal underneath. It tends to flake off and then the fresh metal underneath starts to rust. In this way iron and steel objects can rust away completely.

How can we stop rusting?

Rusting can be prevented in a number of ways:

1. *Keeping the atmosphere dry*

If steel objects are kept in a dry atmo[sphere they] will not rust. This is not normally p[ossible but] some cameras are supplied with a s[mall bag of] silica gel (a drying agent). This pre[vents] rusting when stored in the case.

2. *By coating the iron or steel*

By covering the iron with a non porous coating, water and oxygen are kept away from the iron

Examples are:
Plastic coated steel as in wire fencing.
The painted steel in car bodies.
Grease coated iron and steel machinery.
Tin plating on steel in tin cans.
Chromium plating on steel bumpers of cars.

The disadvantage of these methods is that as soon as the coating is scratched the iron underneath starts to rust and continues to rust unless the coating is resealed.

3. *By sacrificing a more reactive metal*

If a more reactive metal is in firm contact with iron it will corrode instead of the iron rusting. Steel bottomed boats often have magnesium strips bolted to the hull below the water line. The magnesium slowly dissolves away. Only when the magnesium has all dissolved will the hull start to rust.

One of the most common ways of preventing iron and steel rusting is by *galvanising*. Iron and steel are galvanised by dipping the metal into molten zinc. A coating of zinc is formed on the surface of the iron or steel. The coating stops oxygen and water from reaching the metal underneath. If the coating is scratched, the iron *still does not rust* because zinc is more reactive than iron and therefore corrodes away first.

ions

. ALUMINIUM, BRASS, COPPER, IRON, POTASSIUM, MAGNESIUM, ZINC.

Choose from the above list:

a the most reactive metal
b the least reactive metal
c a metal which bursts into flames when dropped into water
d a metal that does not react with dilute hydrochloric acid
e an alloy
f the metal extracted from the ore bauxite
g the metal used to galvanise iron
h the most plentiful metal in the earth's crust
i a metal which forms a brown oxide
j a metal which forms a blue sulphate

2. Suggest reasons for the following:

a boats are never built of sodium
b saucepans are never made of lead
c mercury metal is used in thermometers
d tin cans are steel cans coated with tin
e lead is used as a weather seal on buildings
f aluminium is used for window frames
g copper is used for water pipes
h in high voltage electricity cables the current is carried by aluminium, but the cable has a core of steel

3. Decide if the following pairs of substances can react together. If they can, then write a word equation (or better still a balanced symbol equation) for the reaction:

a magnesium + oxygen
b copper + zinc nitrate solution
c iron (III) oxide + carbon monoxide
d lead oxide + carbon
e magnesium oxide + zinc
f zinc + lead nitrate solution
g copper (II) oxide and magnesium
h sodium + water
i copper + water
j silver + dilute hydrochloric acid
k magnesium + dilute hydrochloric acid
l lead + silver nitrate solution
m magnesium + carbon dioxide

4. In the extraction of iron in the Blast furnace:

a What 3 substances are added at the top of the furnace?
b What is the purpose of each of these substances?
c Why is air blown into the Blast furnace?
d Why is a high temperature needed in the Blast furnace?
e Write an equation (word or symbol) for the reaction that produces iron in the Blast furnace.
f Name *one* of the gases leaving the Blast furnace that is not present in the air that is blown *into* the furnace.
g What is the main impurity in the iron leaving the Blast furnace?
h Why is most of the iron produced in the Blast furnace changed into steel?

5.

a The uses of a metal are related to its properties. Study the properties of lead shown below:
   1. it is a very dense metal
   2. it has a low melting point
   3. it is a soft, easily bent metal
   4. it is resistant to corrosion
   5. it is a fairly weak metal
   6. its compounds are poisonous

Which of these properties is important for the uses listed below:

(i) lead is used as a radiation shield against

X-rays and radioactivity
 (ii) lead is used as a weather seal on buildings
 (iii) lead is used to make plumber's solder
 (iv) lead is used to make fishing weights
b (i) Why in the past was lead used for water pipes?
 (ii) Why is it no longer used for this purpose?

6. Use the following information to place the metals ABC and D in order of decreasing reactivity.
A does not react with dilute hydrochloric acid.
B forms a carbonate which does not decompose on heating.
C reacts with cold water, and forms a carbonate which loses carbon dioxide on heating.
D does not react with water, but does react when heated in steam.

7.
a What is an alloy?
b Why are alloys more widely used than pure metals?
c Name 3 alloys that can be found in your home. For each alloy:
 (i) name the elements it contains
 (ii) name the use to which it is put

8.
a From what ore is aluminium extracted?
b Why cannot aluminium be extracted by heating its ore with carbon?
c In the extraction of aluminium from its ore:
 (i) At which electrode is the aluminium produced?
 (ii) Why is it better for the aluminium produced to sink to the bottom of the molten solution, rather than float to the surface?
d Suggest a reason why aluminium was a rare and precious metal 100 years ago.
e Suggest a reason why tin cans and tin foil are being replaced by aluminium cans and foil.

9. COPPER, SODIUM, ZINC, CALCIUM, LEAD.

a Arrange the above metals in order of decreasing reactivity.
b Which of the above metals can be extracted from their ores by electrolysis?
c Which of the above metals have oxides which can be reduced by hydrogen gas?
d Which of the above metals react with cold water?
e Which of the above metals forms a soluble carbonate?
f Which of the above metals forms a positive ion most easily?

10. Two methods of preventing steel from rusting are:
 (i) to cover its surface with tin by plating
 (ii) to cover its surface with zinc by dipping (ie galvanising).

a Give an advantage of tinning over galvanising.
b Give 2 advantages of galvanising over tin plating.
c Give 2 reasons why it is more sensible to galvanise a steel dustbin rather than tin plate it.
d Explain why a can for storing apricots must be tinned and not galvanised.

11. Suppose you are given 2 unknown metals and solutions of their nitrates. Describe fully how you would find out which of the metals was the more reactive.

12. The following apparatus was used to pass hydrogen gas over heated copper (II) oxide in order to make copper.

a What is liquid Q? Why is it formed in the U tube?

b Write an equation for the reaction between hydrogen gas and copper (II) oxide.

c Why is the excess hydrogen burnt at X?

d When all the copper (II) oxide has been reduced to copper, the combustion tube is allowed to cool with the hydrogen still passing through it. Why is this?

e If 8·0 g of copper (II) oxide is used, what is the maximum amount of copper that can be formed?

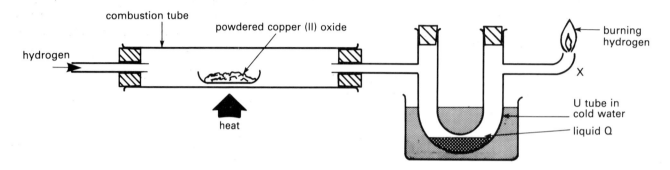

13 Carbon and its compounds

Suppose you saw the following advert in a local paper:

FOR SALE 100 g of pure carbon. £50 or nearest offer.

Would you think it was very cheap or very expensive? You could be right whichever you think, as there are two forms of pure carbon—*diamond* and *graphite*. 100 g of diamond for only £50 would be an amazing bargain. £50 for 100 g of graphite is far too expensive.

13.1 Allotropy of carbon

It seems very surprising that two substances as different as diamond and graphite can be different forms of the *same* element. Table 1 shows how different their properties are.

Properties of diamond	Properties of graphite
1. Diamond is a colourless, transparent, glass like solid.	**1.** Graphite is a dark grey, slightly shiny solid.
2. Diamond is a very hard substance that is used to cut glass.	**2.** Graphite is a soft substance with a slightly soapy feel.
3. Diamond does not conduct electricity.	**3.** Graphite conducts electricity and is unchanged by it.

Table 1

Even though diamond and graphite are so different, they can both be shown to be forms of pure carbon by burning. Both diamond and graphite will burn in oxygen to form carbon dioxide *only*.

carbon + oxygen→carbon dioxide

$$C \quad + \quad O_2 \quad \rightarrow \quad CO_2$$

Chemists say that diamond and graphite are *allotropes* of carbon.

Allotropes are different crystalline forms of the same element.

Diamond and graphite are so different because the carbon atoms are arranged differently in each form.

each carbon atom is held by 4 covalent bonds pointing towards the corners of a tetrahedron

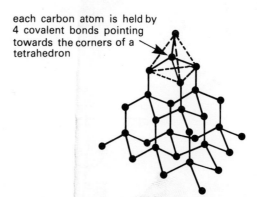

Fig 13.1 The arrangement of carbon atoms in diamond

In diamond each carbon atom is tied to 4 other

carbon atoms by *strong covalent bonds*. In this way a rigid, three dimensional structure is built up. This explains why diamond is such a hard substance. In the diamond structure all the outer shell electrons are used for bonding. There are no spare electrons, so diamond does not conduct electricity.

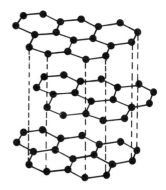

Fig 13.2 The arrangement of carbon atoms in graphite

In graphite, each carbon atom is tied to 3 other carbon atoms by *strong covalent bonds*. In this way, strong, rigid, flat layers are formed. Each carbon atom has one outer shell electron which is not used to form covalent bonds. These 'spare' electrons form an electron cloud between the layers. It is because of this electron cloud that graphite can conduct electricity.

In the graphite structure the carbon atoms are firmly held in each layer but there is little attraction between layers. The layers can easily slide over each other. When you write with a pencil, the pressure of your hand is enough to separate the layers in the graphite pencil lead. A trail of graphite layers is left on the paper recording what you write.

13.2 Making carbon for industry

Industry uses an enormous amount of carbon. It uses diamond for cutting and polishing. It uses graphite as a lubricant and an electrical conductor.

However, most of the carbon needed for industry is used in chemical reactions: reactions such as getting iron from iron ore in the Blast furnace. The carbon needed for large scale chemical reactions does not need to be completely pure, but it does need to be cheap and readily available. *Coke* is the form of impure carbon most widely used in industry.

Coke is made by heating coal strongly to about 1200°C in the absence of air. When coal is heated in this way, it cannot burn, but it does break down to form coke and a number of other useful products.

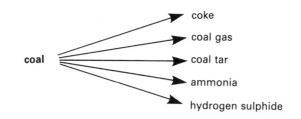

Coke

Coke is mainly made up of tiny graphite crystals. It burns without a smoke and so could be used as a smokeless fuel, but it does not burn well on domestic fires. Smokeless fuels for the home are made from coal in the same way as coke, but the coal is only heated to 600 – 700°C.

Coke is used industrially as a cheap reducing agent. It is used to produce metals from their oxide ores. Iron and zinc are produced in this way.

Coal gas

Coal gas is a mixture of hydrogen, carbon monoxide and hydrocarbons (mainly methane). It is used as a gaseous fuel, but has been largely replaced by natural gas in this country.

Coal tar

Coal tar is a mixture of hundreds of different substances. The tar can be fractionally distilled to give a wide range of products which include:
Solvents for paints.
Starting materials for making plastics.
Pitch for battery seals and weather seals.

Ammonia

The ammonia and ammonium compounds obtained from coal are usually converted into fertilisers such as ammonium sulphate.

The process of breaking down coal by heating in the absence of air is known as the *destructive distillation of coal*. It can be demonstrated in the laboratory using the apparatus in Fig 13.3.

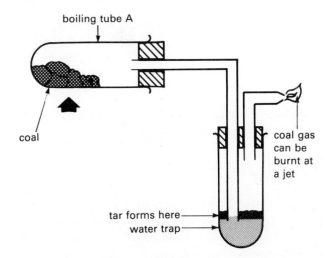

boiling tube A

coal

coal gas can be burnt at a jet

tar forms here
water trap

Fig 13.3 The destructive distillation of coal

As the coal is heated the air is driven out of the boiling tube A and the water trap prevents it re-entering. The water trap also dissolves any ammonia produced. To make a smokeless fuel like coke, the coal must be strongly heated until there is no further change.

This experiment should only be attempted in a fume cupboard and great care must be taken to ensure that the water in the trap does not suck back into the hot boiling tube A.

13.3 Carbon dioxide

One of the most important compounds of carbon is carbon dioxide. Normal air contains only 0.03% carbon dioxide but the air we breathe out contains far more; up to 4%. It is perhaps surprising that with so many animals breathing carbon dioxide into the atmosphere, its concentration does not build up. The main reason for this is *photosynthesis*.

Photosynthesis is the way green plants make their own food. They can combine carbon dioxide with water to form *glucose* (sugar). This glucose can then be converted into starch and other carbohydrates. To carry out this reaction plants need two things:

1. sunlight to provide the necessary energy
2. a chemical known as chlorophyll
We can write:

carbon + water $\xrightarrow[\text{and chlorophyll}]{\text{with sunlight}}$ glucose + oxygen ↑
dioxide

$$6CO_2 + 6H_2O \longrightarrow C_6H_{12}O_6 + 6O_2 \uparrow$$

You should now realise why carbon dioxide is important. Without it there would be no photosynthesis. Without photosynthesis, green plants could not grow. They could not provide the carbohydrate we need for energy. More than that photosynthesis replaces the oxygen that man uses up in so many ways.

Many people are concerned at the way in which the worlds' largest jungles and forests are being destroyed. Can you understand their concern?

Making carbon dioxide

Carbon dioxide is usually made in the laboratory by reacting calcium carbonate with dilute hydrochloric acid. Any carbonate could be used, but since calcium carbonate is so plentiful, it is the obvious choice. Calcium carbonate is found naturally as limestone, chalk and marble.

calcium + hydrochloric → calcium + carbon ↑ + water
carbonate   acid   chloride dioxide
$CaCO_3$ + $2HCl$ → $CaCl_2$ + CO_2↑ + H_2O

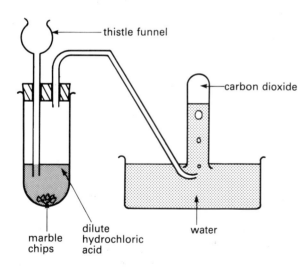

Fig 13.4 Preparation of carbon dioxide

Because carbon dioxide is only slightly soluble in water it can be collected over water. It is also far more dense than air and so can also be collected by downward delivery as shown in Fig 13.5.

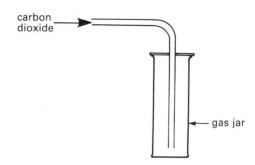

Fig 13.5 Collecting carbon dioxide by downward delivery

Physical properties of carbon dioxide

Carbon dioxide is a colourless gas with no smell. It is much more dense than air. If carbon dioxide gas is cooled down at atmospheric pressure it changes directly from a gas into a solid. This solid is known as *dry ice*. Dry ice has a number of interesting uses. It is used as a refrigerant. It is used by drama groups to produce 'mists' on stage. It is used by gardeners in greenhouses to increase the carbon dioxide content of the atmosphere. It has even been used to 'seed' clouds to make rain.

Chemical properties of carbon dioxide

1. *Carbon dioxide; the acid*

Carbon dioxide is not very soluble in water. 1000 cm^3 of water will only dissolve about 90 cm^3 of carbon dioxide at room temperature and atmospheric pressure. When carbon dioxide dissolves in water an acidic solution is formed. This solution is known as carbonic acid solution:

water + carbon dioxide ⇌ carbonic acid
H_2O + CO_2 ⇌ H_2CO_3

Carbonic acid is a very weak acid, but it will turn litmus paper red and universal indicator orange or yellow. Very often, distilled water kept in laboratories becomes acidic, because it dissolves carbon dioxide from the atmosphere. When this happens, the water has to be boiled to drive out all the carbon dioxide making neutral water once again.

Rain water is also acidic because it dissolves carbon dioxide from the atmosphere. This acidic rain water forms hard water when it passes over rocks containing calcium carbonate or magnesium carbonate.

Example:

calcium + carbonic → calcium hydrogen
carbonate   acid   carbonate
$$CaCO_3 + H_2CO_3 → Ca(HCO_3)_2$$

Calcium hydrogen carbonate solution is formed as the carbonate rock is dissolved away. This reaction helps to explain why caves are often found in limestone rocks.

If the calcium hydrogen carbonate solution is allowed to evaporate, calcium carbonate is again formed.

Example:

calcium hydrogen → calcium + carbon + water
    carbonate   carbonate ↓   dioxide ↑
$$Ca(HCO_3)_2 → CaCO_3↓ + CO_2↑ + H_2O$$

When this happens in limestone caves, stalagmites and stalactites can be formed (see Fig 13.6).

Because it is an acidic gas, carbon dioxide reacts with alkalis to form a salt and water only

Example:

sodium + carbon → sodium + water
hydroxide   dioxide   carbonate
$$2NaOH + CO_2 → Na_2CO_3 + H_2O$$

The similar reaction between carbon dioxide and lime water (calcium hydroxide) is used as a test for carbon dioxide. *Carbon dioxide will turn lime water milky.*

carbon + lime → calcium + water
dioxide   water   carbonate↓
$$CO_2 + Ca(OH)_2 → CaCO_3↓ + H_2O$$

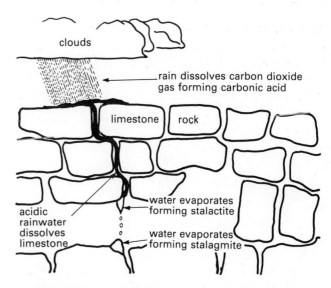

Fig 13.6 Forming stalagmites and stalactites

2. *Carbon dioxide and burning*

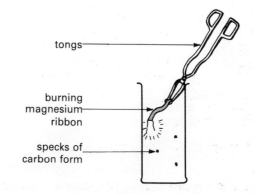

Fig 13.7 Burning magnesium in carbon dioxide

If burning magnesium is lowered into a gas jar of carbon dioxide gas it continues to burn. It steals the oxygen from the carbon dioxide forming magnesium oxide and black specks of carbon:

magnesium + carbon → magnesium + carbon
           dioxide   oxide
$$2Mg + CO_2 \rightarrow 2MgO + C$$

The behaviour of burning magnesium in carbon dioxide is exceptional. All other substances stop burning as soon as they are placed in an atmosphere of carbon dioxide. Because carbon dioxide does not allow other substances to burn in it, we say that carbon dioxide does not *support combustion*. Because of this property carbon dioxide is widely used in fire extinguishers.

13.4 Carbon monoxide

Carbon dioxide is a relatively harmless, even friendly gas. You do not need to take much care when you open a bottle of lemonade. You do not need to worry if you breathe in some of the carbon dioxide that escapes.

Carbon monoxide is far less friendly. It is poisonous and even breathing a very small amount can make you ill. Carbon monoxide reacts with haemoglobin in the blood and prevents it absorbing oxygen. Carbon monoxide is one of the main polluting gases as it is formed whenever any fuel burns in a limited supply of air. It is present in exhaust fumes and can be formed by oil or gas heaters unless the air supply is correctly adjusted. You may have heard people say "never reverse a car into a garage and leave the engine running." or "Make sure that you have your gas fire serviced regularly." You should now understand why these things are said.

Carbon monoxide is certainly not all bad. If the necessary safety precautions are taken it can be a very useful chemical. It burns to form carbon dioxide releasing a lot of energy:

carbon monoxide + oxygen → carbon dioxide
$$2CO + O_2 \rightarrow 2CO_2$$

It is therefore a useful *fuel*.

Because carbon monoxide has a strong tendency to form carbon dioxide it is a good *reducing agent*.

The oxides of iron, lead and copper can be changed into the metal by heating in an atmosphere of carbon monoxide. This reaction can be demonstrated in a fume cupboard using the apparatus shown in Fig 13.8.

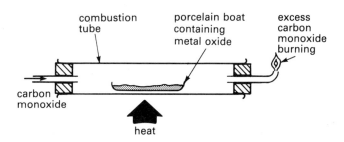

Fig 13.8 Reducing metal oxides with carbon monoxide

Example:

lead + carbon → lead + carbon
oxide monoxide   dioxide
$$PbO + CO \rightarrow Pb + CO_2$$

You may remember that in the Blast furnace iron ore is changed into iron by reacting with carbon monoxide.

Making carbon monoxide

Carbon monoxide is not usually prepared in laboratories, but the method shown in Fig 13.9 can be used. The gas should only be prepared in a fume cupboard; never in an open laboratory.

112

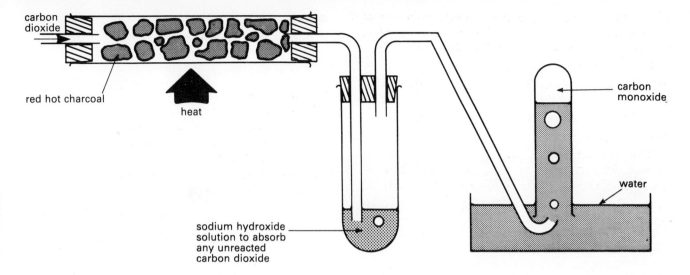

Fig 13.9 Preparing carbon monoxide in the laboratory

Carbon monoxide is almost insoluble in water and so is collected over water.

At the start of this chapter we saw that diamond and graphite, both forms of carbon, are very different. Now we have seen that the two oxides of carbon are also very different. You might try to make a table showing 4 differences between carbon monoxide and carbon dioxide. Then try to find 4 ways in which they are similar.

Questions

1. You have a supply of gas which contains hydrogen with a carbon dioxide impurity.

a How would you show that the gas contains carbon dioxide?

b What would you expect to see if the gas was bubbled through some distilled water containing universal indicator?

c How could you obtain a pure sample of hydrogen from this gas supply?

2. What is photosynthesis? Why is it so important?

3.

a Explain how rain water forms caves in limestone rock.

b Stalactites often form under concrete bridges. What substance in concrete makes it possible for them to form? Explain *how* these stalactites do form.

4. Diamond and graphite are the allotropes of carbon.

a What are allotropes?

b Give 2 uses of diamond. What property of diamond makes it suitable for each of these uses?

c Give 2 uses of graphite. What property of graphite makes it suitable for each of these uses?

d How would you show that diamond and graphite are both pure forms of carbon? (Assume expense is no problem in this experiment).

5.

a Carbon dioxide is used in fire extinguishers. What properties of carbon dioxide make it suitable for this use?

b Carbon dioxide cannot be used to extinguish burning magnesium. Why is this so?

6. How would you prepare a few test tubes of carbon dioxide gas in the laboratory?

When carbon dioxide is passed into lime water it first turns milky, but then the milkyness slowly disappears and a colourless solution reforms. What explanation can you offer for this?

7. Name 3 substances that can be obtained by the destructive distillation of coal. Give a major use for each of these substances.

8.

a What property of carbon monoxide makes it poisonous to man?

b What gas is formed when carbon monoxide burns in air? Write an equation for the reaction.

c Why does city air usually contain a lower concentration of carbon monoxide on Sundays?

d One suggestion for reducing the carbon monoxide content of car exhaust fumes is to fit an extra section onto the exhaust pipe containing copper (II) oxide.

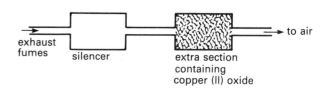

(i) How would this extra section reduce the carbon monoxide content of exhaust fumes?

(ii) Why do you think this method is not used? Give as many reasons as you can.

9. Why are 'fizzy drinks' made fizzy with carbon dioxide rather than air?

14 Organic chemistry

Think of fuels like methane, petrol and diesel oil. Think of plastics like nylon, polythene and perspex. Think of medicines like aspirin and penicillin. Think of the protein, fat and carbohydrate that we need for a healthy diet. All these substances have one thing in common. They are all made up of *covalent, carbon containing compounds*. These compounds are known as *organic chemicals*. The study of these compounds is known as *organic chemistry*.

14.1 Where do organic chemicals come from?

The most important source of organic chemicals is oil. Oil obtained from underground deposits is known as *crude oil* (petroleum). It is a mixture of many different organic compounds. Crude oil itself is of little use, but the chemicals it contains are extremely useful.

It is the job of oil refineries to separate crude oil into its components. The first stage in this separation is to fractionally distil the crude oil.

The crude oil is completely vaporised by a furnace and the vapour passes into a fractionating column. The fractionating column is a tall tower made up of a number of compartments. These get cooler going up the column. As the vapour rises up the column, different substances condense in different compartments and the liquids formed are drawn

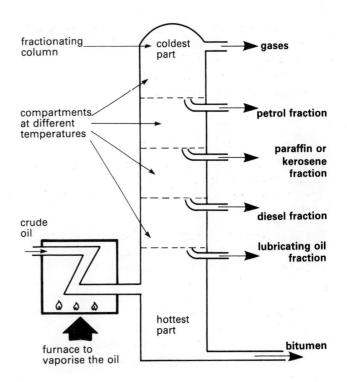

Fig 14.1 Fractional distillation of crude oil

off. The lower the boiling point of a substance the further it will travel up the column before condensing.

A number of methods have been used to allow the vapour to pass freely to a higher compartment and yet prevent the liquid formed running back down the column.

One of the simplest methods is shown in Fig 14.2.

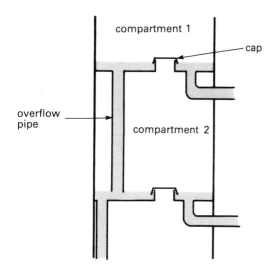

Fig 14.2 Detail of fractionating column

Vapour from compartment 2 passes into compartment 1 by lifting the small cap shown. In compartment 1 some of this vapour will condense, forming liquid, which is drawn off. Some of the liquid formed in compartment 1 is allowed to flow back into compartment 2, via the overflow pipe, where it is revaporised. This increases the efficiency of the distillation.

The fractional distillation of crude oil does not produce pure substances, but it does provide a number of fractions. Each fraction contains a large number of chemicals that boil at a similar temperature. Some of these fractions can be used directly, but usually each fraction is further distilled and treated by various chemical processes to produce purer organic chemicals.

Table 1 shows some of the uses of the fractions of crude oil.

Name of fraction	Use
Gases	Used as fuels such as bottled gas and lighter fuel
Petrol fraction	Used to make petrol for cars
Kerosene (Paraffin) fraction	Used for oil stoves and aircraft fuel
Diesel fraction	Used as a fuel for diesel engines
Lubricating oil fraction	Used as a lubricant and to make waxes and polishes
Bitumen	Used for road making and for sealing roofs

Table 1

14.2 Sorting out organic chemicals

Organic chemicals have a number of things in common:

They all contain carbon; most contain hydrogen.
They are nearly all covalent compounds.
They all burn or char when heated in air.

However, organic chemicals can be as different as TNT and candlewax. Because so many organic chemicals exist, we divide them up into groups or families of compounds with similar properties These families are known as *Homologous series*.

Compounds which are members of the same Homologous series have a number of things in common:
1. They can be represented by a general formula. *Example:* C_nH_{2n}.
2. They have similar chemical properties.
3. They have similar structures.
4. They have similar names.

5. The melting point, boiling point and density of members of the series increase steadily with increasing molecular mass (see page 51 for explanation of this).

We can understand the properties of an Homologous series more clearly if we consider a few examples.

The alkanes

The alkanes are *hydrocarbons*. This means that they are compounds that contain carbon and hydrogen only. Table 2 provides some information about the alkanes

Name of alkane	Formula	Molecular mass	Boiling point (°C)
methane	CH_4	16	−164
ethane	C_2H_6	30	−87
propane	C_3H_8	44	−42
butane	C_4H_{10}	58	0
pentane	C_5H_{12}	72	36
hexane	C_6H_{14}	86	69

Table 2 The alkanes

You should notice from Table 2 that:

1. All the alkanes have similar names. They all end in -ane.
The start of each name is different for each alkane. The start of the name tells us how many carbon atoms there are in one molecule of the alkane; meth means 1, eth means 2, prop means 3 and so on.
2. The alkanes can be represented by the general formula C_nH_{2n+2}, where n is the number of carbon atoms in a molecule of the alkane.
When $n = 1$, formula $= C_1H_{2+2} = CH_4$.
When $n = 4$, formula $= C_4H_{8+2} = C_4H_{10}$.

3. As the molecular mass increases the boiling point of the alkanes also increases.

We can see more similarities between the members of the alkane series if we consider the structures of the various compounds.

Name of Alkane	Molecular formula	Structural formula
methane	CH_4	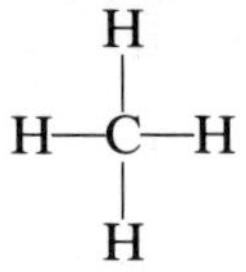
ethane	C_2H_6	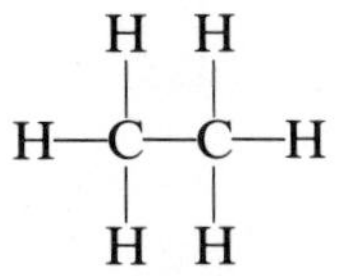
propane	C_3H_8	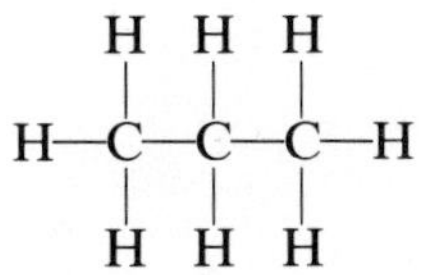
butane	C_4H_{10}	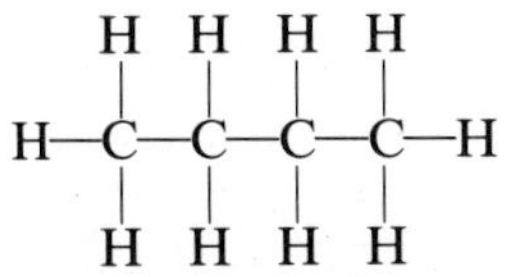 or 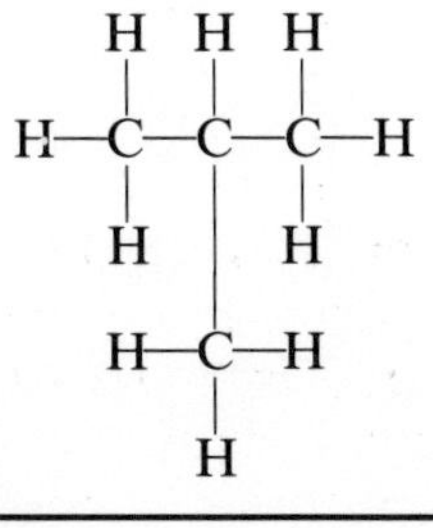

Table 3 Structure of the alkanes

Note The *molecular formula* shows how many atoms of each type there are in a molecule. *Example* 1 molecule of methane contains 1 carbon atom and 4 hydrogen atoms. It therefore has a molecular formula CH_4.

The *structural formula* shows how the atoms are arranged in the molecule.

Looking at Table 3 you should notice that:

1. The alkanes have similar structure. Each alkane (except methane) has a single bond between carbon atoms. Different Homologous series have other similarities in their structures. This is shown in Table 4.

2. There are 2 possible structural formulae for butane. One has the carbon atoms arranged in a row C—C—C—C, whereas the other has a branched arrangement of carbon atoms

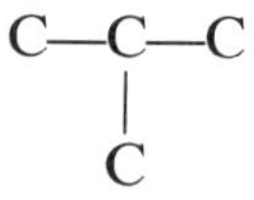

$$
\begin{array}{c}
\text{C—C—C} \\
| \\
\text{C}
\end{array}
$$

These different forms of butane are known as the *isomers* of butane. *Isomers are compounds with the same molecular formula but different structural formulae.*

NAME OF HOMOLOGOUS SERIES	GENERAL FORMULA	NAME OF A MEMBER OF THE SERIES	MOLECULAR FORMULA	STRUCTURAL FORMULA
alkene	C_nH_{2n}	ETHENE	C_2H_4	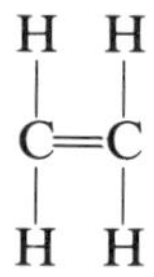
		PROPENE	C_3H_6	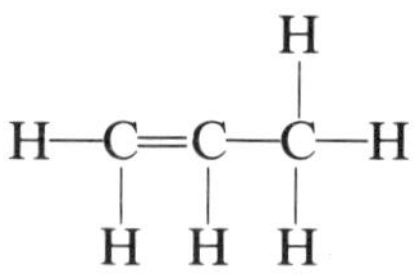
alkyne	C_nH_{2n-2}	ETHYNE	C_2H_2	$H—C{\equiv}C—H$
		PROPYNE	C_3H_4	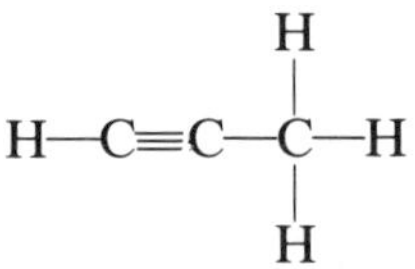

Table 4

NAME OF HOMOLOGOUS SERIES	GENERAL FORMULA	NAME OF A MEMBER OF THE SERIES	MOLECULAR FORMULA	STRUCTURAL FORMULA
alcohol	$C_nH_{2n+1}OH$	METHANOL	CH_3OH	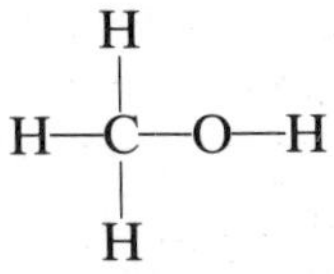 $H-\overset{\displaystyle H}{\underset{\displaystyle H}{C}}-O-H$
		ETHANOL	C_2H_5OH	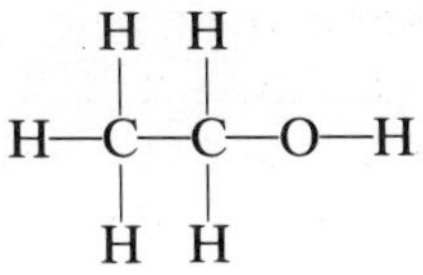 $H-\overset{\displaystyle H}{\underset{\displaystyle H}{C}}-\overset{\displaystyle H}{\underset{\displaystyle H}{C}}-O-H$
carboxylic acids	$C_nH_{2n+1}CO_2H$	METHANOIC ACID	HCO_2H	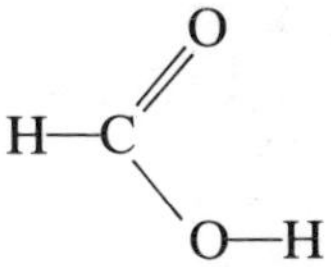 $H-C\overset{\displaystyle O}{\underset{\displaystyle O-H}{}}$
		ETHANOIC ACID	CH_3CO_2H	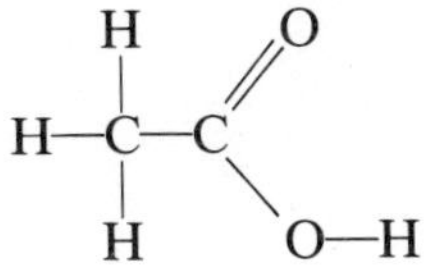 $H-\overset{\displaystyle H}{\underset{\displaystyle H}{C}}-C\overset{\displaystyle O}{\underset{\displaystyle O-H}{}}$

Table 4

Chemical properties of the alkanes

The alkanes are not a very reactive family of compounds. They do not take part in many chemical reactions, but they all react similarly when they do react.

1. All alkanes will burn in a plentiful supply of air to form carbon dioxide and water.

Example:

methane + oxygen→carbon dioxide + water

$$CH_4 + 2O_2 \rightarrow CO_2 + 2H_2O$$

2. The alkanes *do not* decolorise potassium permanganate solution and do not normally decolorise bromine water. However they will react with chlorine or bromine in the presence of sunlight or ultra violet light.

Example:

methane + chlorine $\xrightarrow{\text{sunlight}}$ chloro- + hydrogen methane chloride

$$CH_4 + Cl_2 \longrightarrow CH_3Cl + HCl$$

This is a *substitution* reaction in which one hydrogen atom in a methane molecule is substituted by a chlorine atom.

Uses of the alkanes

Because the alkanes take part in so few chemical reactions they are mainly used as fuels:
Methane is the main component of natural gas.
Butane is the main component of camping gas and lighter fuel.
Octane is a major component of petrol.
The heavier alkanes are used as waxes.

14.3 The Alkenes — a more reactive family

The alkenes are an Homologous series with the general formula C_nH_{2n}. All alkenes contain a *double bond* between two carbon atoms. This

Name of alkene	Molecular formula	Structural formula
ethene	C_2H_4	$\begin{array}{c} H \quad H \\ | \quad\; | \\ C = C \\ | \quad\; | \\ H \quad H \end{array}$
propene	C_3H_6	$\begin{array}{c} H \quad H \quad H \\ | \quad\; | \quad\; | \\ C = C - C - H \\ | \qquad\; | \\ H \qquad H \end{array}$
butene	C_4H_8	$\begin{array}{c} H \quad H \quad H \quad H \\ H - C = C - C - C - H \\ | \quad\; | \\ H \quad H \end{array}$ *or* $\begin{array}{c} H \qquad\qquad H \\ H - C - C = C - C - H \\ | \quad\; | \quad\; | \quad\; | \\ H \quad H \quad H \quad H \end{array}$ *or* $\begin{array}{c} H \\ | \\ H - C - C = C - H \\ | \qquad | \\ H \qquad H \\ H - C - H \\ | \\ H \end{array}$

Table 5 The alkenes

carbon-carbon double bond makes the alkenes far more reactive than the alkanes.

By looking at Table 5 you should notice that:

1. All alkenes have names ending in -ene.
2. All alkenes contain 1 carbon-carbon double bond per molecule.
3. Butene has 3 isomers. This is because the double bond can have different positions along the carbon chain and also the chain can be branched.

Chemical properties of alkenes

All alkenes burn in a plentiful supply of air to form carbon dioxide and water.

Example:

ethene + oxygen → carbon dioxide + water
$$C_2H_4 + 3O_2 \rightarrow 2CO_2 + 2H_2O$$

When the alkenes burn they release a large amount of energy. This would make them good fuels, but the alkenes have chemical properties that make them far too useful to burn.

Addition reactions of alkenes

Alkenes react with bromine or bromine water very rapidly. The bromine is decolorised and a colourless oil is formed:

ethene + bromine → 1,2-dibromoethane

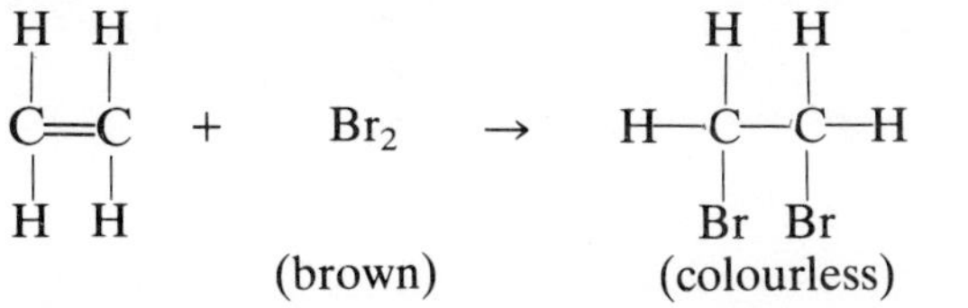

$$\begin{array}{ccc} \underset{\displaystyle H \quad H}{\overset{\displaystyle H \quad H}{C=C}} + Br_2 & \rightarrow & \underset{\displaystyle Br \quad Br}{\overset{\displaystyle H \quad H}{H-C-C-H}} \\ \text{(brown)} & & \text{(colourless)} \end{array}$$

It can be seen from the equation that the bromine molecule *adds* onto the alkene molecule to form a larger molecule. The carbon-carbon double bond allows the alkene to react by *addition*. Chemists say that alkenes are *unsaturated* substances because they can react by addition.

All unsaturated compounds will decolorise bromine. This is the usual test for an unsaturated compound.

We have seen that the alkenes can react by addition. What is really important is that they can react with themselves time and time again to form very large molecules. You may at some time have spent a summer afternoon making a daisy chain. We could describe the production of a daisy chain by using an equation.

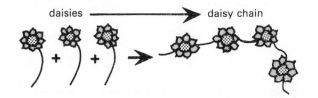

Ethene molecules can also add onto each other to form a kind of daisy chain. The 'daisy chain' formed when we start from ethene is a polyethene molecule or polythene (the plastic).

For ethene to form polythene, 1 bond in each ethene molecule must break, and new bonds must be formed, to hold the ethene molecules together. The arrows in the following equation show how this happens.

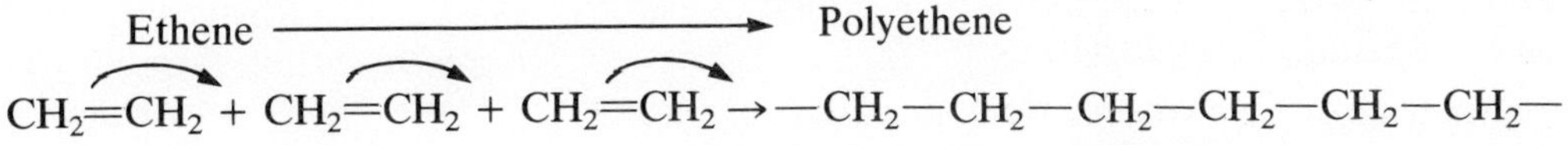

Ethene ⟶ Polyethene

$$CH_2{=}CH_2 + CH_2{=}CH_2 + CH_2{=}CH_2 \rightarrow -CH_2{-}CH_2{-}CH_2{-}CH_2{-}CH_2{-}CH_2{-}$$

The plastic polythene is made up of these very large *polyethene* molecules. Each polyethene molecule is made up of thousands of ethene molecules joined together.

The process in which a small molecule adds onto itself many times to form a large molecule, is known as *addition polymerisation*.

The starting small molecule is known as the *monomer*. The final large molecule is known as the *polymer*.

Any unsaturated compound should be capable of acting as a monomer for addition polymerisation. By varying the monomer, different polymers or plastics are formed with different properties.

Monomer	*Polymer*
vinyl chloride ⟶	polyvinyl chloride (PVC)

$$CH_2\!\!=\!\!CH + CH_2\!\!=\!\!CH \rightarrow -CH_2-CH-CH_2-CH-$$
$$\quad\;\; | \qquad\qquad | \qquad\qquad\quad | \qquad\qquad |$$
$$\quad\;\; Cl \qquad\qquad Cl \qquad\qquad\;\; Cl \qquad\qquad Cl$$

All plastics made by addition polymerisation are known as *thermosoftening* or *thermoplastic* substances. This means that they soften on warming. Because they soften on warming they can be moulded into different shapes. Table 6 shows the use made of some common plastics made by addition polymerisation.

14.4 Plastics — the rest of the story

We have seen that one method of making plastics is by a process known as addition polymerisation. Different plastics can be made by a process known as *condensation polymerisation*.

Condensation polymerisation is different from addition polymerisation in a number of ways:
1. In condensation polymerisation there are

Name of plastic	Use
polyethene	Wrapping foods, making bowls, buckets, watering cans, cold water pipes
polypropene	Moulded furniture. (It is more rigid than polyethene)
polystyrene	Making household goods like egg cups, and dishes. It is used for egg boxes. It is used to make synthetic rubber. Expanded polystyrene is used as a heat insulator and as a packaging material
perspex	Used instead of glass in windows and advertising signs

Table 6 Some thermosoftening plastics: their uses

usually 2 different monomers reacting together.
2. In condensation polymerisation a small molecule (usually water) is thrown out every time 2 monomer molecules react.

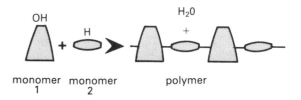

Examples of plastics formed by condensation are nylon, terylene, bakelite and the epoxy resins.

Plastics formed by condensation polymerisation can be either *thermosoftening* or *thermosetting*.

We have previously mentioned that thermosoftening plastics soften on heating and can therefore be moulded. Thermosetting plastics *do not* soften on heating. They cannot be moulded. They have to be made in the mould. Next time you use an Araldite type glue, or mend a rust hole with a plastic filler, it might be worth remembering that you are forming a thermosetting plastic by condensation polymerisation.

Why the difference?

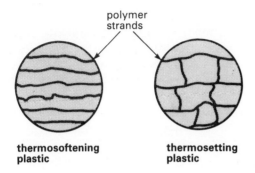

polymer strands

thermosoftening plastic

thermosetting plastic

Fig 14.3

In thermosoftening plastics the polymer molecules are long chains held together by weak attractive forces. On warming, these attractive forces between chains break down, and the chains are therefore free to move. The plastic can therefore be moulded. In thermosetting plastics the polymer molecule is a very large 3 dimensional structure. Individual parts of the structure cannot be separated. Therefore, it is a rigid material which does not soften on warming. Table 7 shows some uses of these plastics.

Plastics: friend or foe?

If one morning you woke to find that all the plastics in the world had disappeared, your life would change enormously. If you make a list of all the things made of plastic in your kitchen, or bathroom, or even garage, you will realise how

Name of plastic	Use
urea methanal	Light coloured electric fittings, plug tops, switch covers, adaptors
melamine methanal	Unbreakable table ware
phenol methanal (bakelite)	Saucepan handles, dark coloured plug tops, adaptors, switch covers
polyester resins	'Do it yourself' car body repair kits

Table 7 Some thermosetting plastics: their uses

useful plastics are. Life would be most unpleasant if they suddenly disappeared. On the other hand, you could then walk along a beach without being annoyed by plastic bottles or cups littering the beach. Also if your house caught fire there would be far less chance of you being overcome by poisonous fumes.

Plastics are not all good. They certainly pollute our environment and they can be extremely dangerous, as they produce highly poisonous fumes when they burn.

No one is going to pass a law banning plastic materials, but it is worth realising that they can be both friend and foe.

14.5 Ethene — the supply and demand problem

We have seen that ethene is used to make polyethene (polythene). It is also used to make the monomers for many other plastics. Millions of tons of ethene are required each year for the plastics industry.

Where does ethene come from?

Ethene is obtained from oil by a process known as *catalytic cracking*.

By passing the kerosene fraction of crude oil over a catalyst of silica and aluminium oxide at about 500°C, the hydrocarbon chains break down to form a mixture of unsaturated substances, together with hydrogen.

$$CH_3-CH_2-CH_2 \{ CH_2-CH_3 \rightarrow CH_3-CH=CH_2 \text{ propene}$$

cracks here

$$+ \quad CH_2=CH_2 \text{ ethene}$$

$$+ \quad H_2 \text{ hydrogen}$$

Catalytic cracking can be demonstrated in the laboratory using the apparatus in Fig 14.4.

The gas collected can be shown to contain unsaturated hydrocarbons by adding a few drops of bromine water.

What happens when the oil runs out?

There is no immediate danger of the world's oil supplies being used up, but oil will certainly be less available and more expensive in the future. Where will we get our organic chemicals from in the future? How will we manage to supply the plastics industry with the starting materials (monomers) it needs?

One possible answer to these questions lies in the process known as *fermentation*. In the absence of air, yeast will feed on sugar solution to produce ethanol and carbon dioxide (see Fig 14.5).

$$\text{sugar} \rightarrow \text{ethanol} + \text{carbon dioxide} \uparrow$$
$$C_6H_{12}O_6 \rightarrow 2C_2H_5OH + 2CO_2 \uparrow$$

The yeast contains an *enzyme*, or natural catalyst, called *zymase* which allows the reaction to take place.

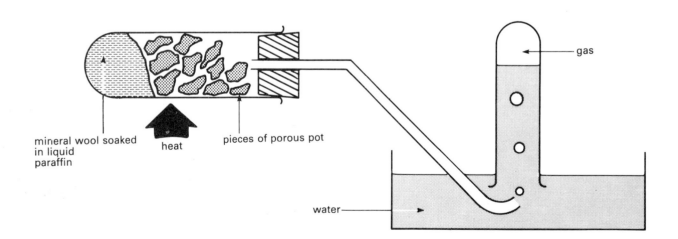

mineral wool soaked in liquid paraffin

heat

pieces of porous pot

gas

water

Fig 14.4 Catalytic cracking

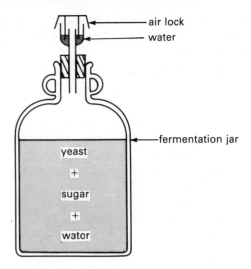

Fig 14.5 Fermenting sugar solution

Ethanol is a colourless inflammable (easily set on fire) liquid with a boiling point of 78°C. It is at present widely used as a fuel and as a solvent for cosmetics such as perfume. In the future, sugars extracted from vegetable matter may be fermented to form ethanol, and then this ethanol may be used to make the ethene the plastics industry needs.

Ethanol is easily changed into ethene by passing it over heated aluminium oxide.

$$\text{ethanol} \longrightarrow \text{ethene} + \text{water}$$

It is an interesting thought that the fermentation process that we use today to make wines and beers may one day save the plastics industry from extinction. Vegetables may be the main source of organic chemicals.

14.6 Organic chemicals and food

Before leaving organic chemistry we should realise that man himself is made up of many organic chemicals. Our bodies are very efficient chemical factories. They take in raw materials as food. Some is burnt to provide energy to run the factory. The rest is changed in some way or other to produce all the chemicals our bodies need. The organic chemicals that our bodies need to stay healthy can be divided into a number of groups: carbohydrates, fats, proteins, and vitamins.

Carbohydrates

Carbohydrates are polymers. They are made up of long chains of sugar units. The body breaks down these polymers to form smaller sugar molecules:

carbohydrate   *sugar*

A number of different sugar molecules exist but they all have the same general formula. ($C_xH_{2y}O_y$).

Example: Glucose $C_6H_{12}O_6$
Cane sugar $C_{12}H_{22}O_{11}$.

The small sugar molecules are soluble in water and can be carried to all parts of the body. Eventually, they are burnt to release energy:

$$\text{glucose} + \text{oxygen} \rightarrow \text{carbon dioxide} + \text{water} + \text{energy}$$
$$C_6H_{12}O_6 + 6O_2 \rightarrow 6CO_2 + 6H_2O$$

Fats

Fats, like sugars, are compounds which contain carbon, hydrogen and oxygen, but they do not have the same general formula. Fats are also used by our bodies to release energy. 1 g of fat will release twice as much energy as 1 g of carbohydrate when burnt. Our bodies can store large quantities of fat.

Protein

Protein is needed to make all body tissues: skin, hair, muscle and internal organs.

Proteins are polymers. They are made up of long chains of amino acids. Amino acids are simple molecules which contain an acid group (—COOH) and an amino group (—NH_2). The simplest amino acid is glycine.

glycine

Up to 23 different amino acids are used by our bodies to make the proteins it needs.

Our bodies take in protein, break it down into simple amino acids and then recombine these amino acids to make the different proteins it needs.

Vitamins

Vitamins are organic chemicals that our bodies need, but cannot make or store. They have to be supplied regularly.

Some vitamins are simple compounds (vitamin C has the chemical formula $C_6H_8O_6$). Other vitamins are far more complex (vitamin B12 has the formula $C_{63}H_{90}O_{14}N_{14}PCo$).

Questions

1. BAKELITE, BUTANE, ETHANOL, ETHENE, METHANE, POLYETHENE, SUGAR.

   Choosing from the above list, name:

   a 2 hydrocarbons which are in the same homologous series

   b a hydrocarbon that will react with bromine water

   c a thermosetting plastic

   d a thermosoftening plastic

   e an alkane

   f an alkene

   g an alcohol

   h a carbohydrate

   i a hydrocarbon with 4 carbon atoms per molecule

   j a substance formed by fermentation

2.

   a What name is given to organic compounds which contain carbon and hydrogen only?

   b Write the structural formulae of:
   (i) 2 compounds with the molecular formula C_4H_{10}

(ii) 3 compounds with the molecular formula C_5H_{12}.

c What name is given to substances with the same molecular formula but different structural formulae?

3.

a Ethene is an unsaturated compound. Which chemical reaction can be used to show that ethene is unsaturated?

b Draw the structural formula of ethene. What part of the structure shows that ethene is unsaturated?

c Ethene is the monomer from which the polymer polyethene is made. Draw a diagram to show the structure of part of a polyethene molecule.

d Polyethene is a thermosoftening plastic. What does this mean?

4.

a Name 3 important substances obtained from crude oil and give a major use of each.

b Name the process by which crude oil is separated into its components.

c What is the name of the process used to break down saturated hydrocarbon molecules into smaller unsaturated molecules? Why is this process so important?

d What is the name of the process by which small unsaturated hydrocarbon molecules add on to each other to form long chain saturated molecules?

e Give one example of:
(i) a thermosoftening plastic
(ii) a thermosetting plastic.

f Give one difference between the properties of a thermosoftening plastic and a thermosetting plastic.

5. Suggest reasons for the following:

a Drainpipes are now made of plastic rather than metal.

b Expanded polystyrene ceiling tiles are good heat insulators, but should not be used in kitchens.

c Most car seats are covered with a plastic coated cloth, rather than leather.

d Orange squash bottles are often made of plastic rather than glass.

6. Supermarkets often sell fresh food packed on an expanded polystyrene tray and covered with a thin polyethene film. What are the advantages and disadvantages of this:
(i) to the supermarket
(ii) to the customer?

7. Suppose you were making a wine by fermenting orange juice with yeast.

a What gas would be formed during the fermentation process?

b How could you tell when the fermentation was complete?

c How would you separate the yeast from the wine when the fermentation was complete?

d How could you get a sample of pure ethanol from the wine?

e Why is it dangerous to bottle a wine before the fermentation is complete?

8. FATS, CARBOHYDRATES, PROTEIN, VITAMINS.
Choosing from the above list, name:

a a type of food that burns to form carbon dioxide and water only

b a type of food that contains nitrogen

c a type of food with the general formula $C_xH_{2y}O_y$.

d a type of food which is digested to form amino acids

e a type of food that is made up of long chain molecules.

9.

a How would you show that an organic chemical forms carbon dioxide when it burns?

b How would you show that an organic compound forms water when it burns?

10. Give reasons why thermosetting plastics have the following uses:

a saucepan handles

b 'Do it yourself' car repair kits

c bread boards or vegetable chopping boards

11. Give reasons why thermosoftening plastics have the following uses:

a washing up liquid bottles

b climbing ropes

c insulating electrical wires

12. A friend has been away from school and has missed some work. Explain to him what an homologous series is and why the idea of homologous series makes organic chemistry simpler.

15 Nitrogen and its compounds

There is a lot of nitrogen about. 78% of the Earth's atmosphere is nitrogen. It exists as N_2 molecules. The two atoms in the molecule are very tightly held together. Because of this, nitrogen docs not take part in many chemical reactions. We say nitrogen is an *inert* substance. Many of the uses of nitrogen gas depend on it being inert. For example, nitrogen is used with argon to fill electric light bulbs. These gases are used because they do not react with the tungsten filament, even when it is white hot.

15.1 Nitrogen in compounds

Although nitrogen gas does not take part in many chemical reactions, a large number of very important compounds contain nitrogen. It is present in all protein. All plants and animals contain protein.

Animals get their protein by eating plants or other animals but plants make their own protein. For plants to make protein they need a supply of nitrogen. Any gardener will tell you that plants get their nitrogen from the soil. You might even hear a gardener say "There's plenty of nitrogen in that soil", as he looks affectionately at a nettle patch. Although plants do get their nitrogen from the soil, they cannot absorb nitrogen gas. They absorb water soluble compounds, which contain nitrogen. These compounds, usually nitrates, are absorbed through the roots.

As plants remove nitrates from the soil to make protein, the soil becomes less and less fertile. The nitrates have to be replaced. This happens naturally in a number of ways:

1. Some plants such as peas, beans and clover are known as *leguminous plants*. They have bacteria on their roots which change nitrogen gas into water soluble compounds of nitrogen. Other bacteria in the soil then change these compounds into nitrates.

2. During thunder storms some nitric acid is formed in the atmosphere. This nitric acid falls with the rain and reacts with the soil to form nitrates.

3. When plants and animals die, they decay. Their protein is changed into *ammonium salts*. Soil bacteria change these ammonium salts into nitrates.

Nitrogen is removed from the soil and nitrogen is returned to the soil. This natural circulation is known as *the nitrogen cycle*. It is shown in Fig 15.1 on page 130.

No farmer can rely on the nitrogen cycle to replace the nitrogen his crops remove from the soil. It would take far too long and would be uneconomic. Instead, farmers use nitrogen fertilisers to keep a high level of nitrates in the soil. The most common nitrogen fertilisers are ammonium sulphate and ammonium nitrate.

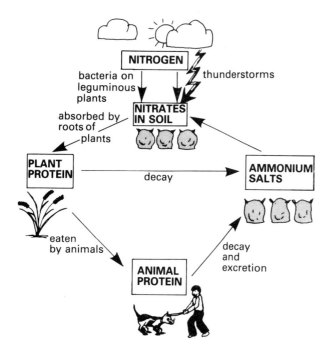

Fig 15.1 The nitrogen cycle

15.2 Making nitrogen gas more useful

There are natural deposits of substances such as sodium nitrate and potassium nitrate. These have been widely used as fertilisers in the past, but as farming became more intensive the demand for these substances outstripped the supply. There was a need to convert nitrogen gas into nitrogen fertilisers. Most nitrogen fertilisers are nowadays made from ammonia. The Haber process made it possible to manufacture ammonia from nitrogen gas.

The Haber process for manufacturing ammonia

In the Haber process nitrogen is made to react with hydrogen to form ammonia gas:

nitrogen + hydrogen $\rightleftharpoons$ ammonia

$$N_2 + 3H_2 \rightleftharpoons 2NH_3$$

Nitrogen is obtained from the air and hydrogen is obtained from natural gas or water.

To get the nitrogen and hydrogen to react together, the gases have to be compressed to 150 – 200 atmospheres pressure and passed over an *iron* catalyst at 380–400°C. Under these conditions about 25% of the nitrogen and hydrogen is changed into ammonia. This ammonia is separated from the nitrogen and hydrogen by liquifying the ammonia. The nitrogen and hydrogen are passed over the catalyst again.

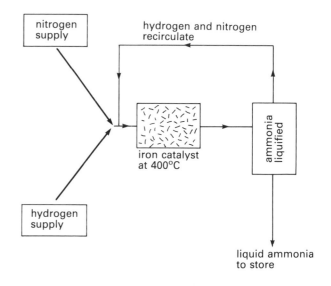

Fig 15.2 The Haber process

You will have seen from the equation that the reaction between nitrogen and hydrogen is reversible. At the same time as nitrogen and hydrogen are reacting to form ammonia, the ammonia is breaking up to reform nitrogen and hydrogen. A high pressure is used in the Haber process as this gives a greater amount of ammonia in the mixture leaving the catalyst chamber.

Uses of ammonia

The ammonia produced in the Haber process is sold either as a compressed gas or as a liquid. Most of this ammonia is used to make nitrogen fertilisers such as ammonium sulphate, ammonium nitrate, ammonium phosphate and urea. The other main use of ammonia gas are:

1. It is used to manufacture nitric acid.
2. It is used to manufacture nylon.
3. Solutions of ammonia in water are used to dissolve grease.
4. Ammonia can easily be stored as a liquid and it can easily be broken down to form nitrogen and hydrogen. For this reason ammonia is used industrially as a convenient source of hydrogen. Hydrogen is highly inflammable and has a very low boiling point. It is far more difficult to store than ammonia.

You should realise from its uses that ammonia is a very important chemical.

15.3 Ammonia — the chemical

We could not hope to make ammonia in the laboratory by a Haber process method. Instead it is prepared by heating an ammonium salt with an alkali. Ammonium chloride and calcium hydroxide are often used:

calcium + ammonium→ calcium + ammonia ↑ +water
hydroxide   chloride   chloride
$$Ca(OH)_2 + 2NH_4Cl \rightarrow CaCl_2 + 2NH_3\uparrow + 2H_2O$$

Flask A is sloped as shown in Fig 15.3 so that any water formed will run away from the hot flask.

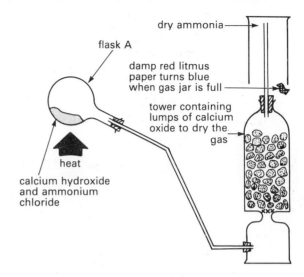

Fig 15.3 Making ammonia in the laboratory

Physical properties of ammonia

Ammonia is a colourless gas with a strong smell. It is less dense than air and is *very* soluble in water. Because of this ammonia has to be collected by upward delivery.

Chemical properties of ammonia

Ammonia is a very reactive gas. It takes part in a large number of chemical reactions.

1. *With water*

Ammonia is very soluble in water. Great care has to be taken when dissolving the gas in water. If the apparatus shown in Fig 15.4 page 132 was used, the ammonia would almost certainly dissolve so fast that cold water would be sucked up into the hot flask A. This could lead to an explosion.

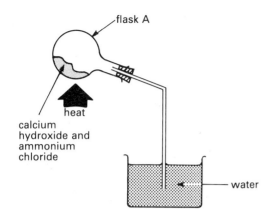

Fig 15.4 How **not** to dissolve ammonia in water!

If ammonia is to be safely dissolved in water some method must be used to prevent the water sucking back into the reaction flask. Fig 15.5 shows a simple method used to dissolve ammonia in water safely in the laboratory.

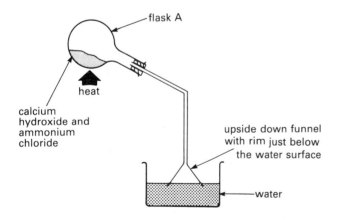

Fig 15.5 A safe method for dissolving ammonia in water

The funnel must be arranged with its rim just below the water surface. As the ammonia dissolves, the water starts to suck back in the funnel. As it does so the water level in the trough goes down. This leaves a plug of water in the wide part of the funnel. This plug cannot be supported and so it falls down. In this way suck back is prevented.

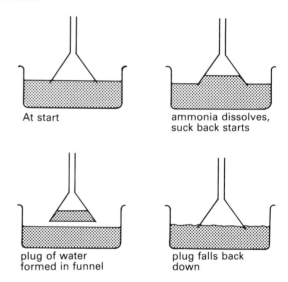

Fig 15.6

When ammonia dissolves in water it reacts with the water to form ammonium hydroxide which is a weak alkali:

ammonia + water ⇌ ammonium ⇌ ammonium + hydroxide
hydroxide   ions   ions

$$NH_3 + H_2O \rightleftharpoons NH_4OH \rightleftharpoons NH_4^+ + OH^-$$

2. *Ammonia as an alkali*

Ammonia is an alkaline gas. It will turn damp red litmus paper blue. *This can be used as a test for the gas.*

Because ammonia is an alkaline gas it will react with acids to form salts. This is the reason why ammonia cannot be dried using concentrated sulphuric acid. The acid would react violently with the ammonia:

ammonia + sulphuric acid → ammonium sulphate

$$2NH_3 + H_2SO_4 \rightarrow (NH_4)_2SO_4$$

When ammonia reacts with acids, ammonium salts are formed. One of these reactions is also used as a test for ammonia gas. If ammonia gas is brought into contact with hydrogen chloride gas, a thick white smoke of ammonium chloride is formed. A bottle of concentrated hydrochloric acid can be used as a source of hydrogen chloride:

ammonia + hydrogen → ammonium
        chloride   chloride ↓

$$NH_3 + HCl \rightarrow NH_4Cl \downarrow$$

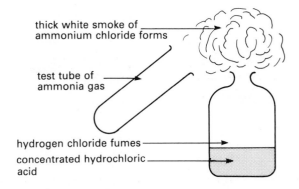

thick white smoke of ammonium chloride forms

test tube of ammonia gas

hydrogen chloride fumes

concentrated hydrochloric acid

Fig 15.7 Testing for ammonia gas

Solutions of ammonia in water, being alkaline, behave like solutions of sodium hydroxide in water. They can be used to precipitate metal hydroxides from solutions of metal salts:

Example:

iron (II) + ammonium → iron (II) ↓ + ammonium
sulphate   hydroxide   hydroxide   sulphate

$$FeSO_4 + 2NH_4OH \rightarrow Fe(OH)_2 \downarrow + (NH_4)_2SO_4$$
                                    dirty
                                  blue-green
                                  precipitate

Because solutions of ammonia in water also contain some free ammonia molecules, some differences are noticed. Both ammonium hydroxide solution and sodium hydroxide solution produce a pale blue precipitate with copper (II) sulphate solution. However, this precipitate dissolves in excess ammonium hydroxide solution, to form a dark blue solution. This does not happen with sodium hydroxide solution.

3. *Burning ammonia*

Ammonia will not burn in air, but it will burn in oxygen to form nitrogen and water.

ammonia + oxygen → nitrogen + water

$$4NH_3 + 3O_2 \rightarrow 2N_2 + 6H_2O$$

This is not an important reaction because the ammonia burnt is of far greater use than the nitrogen formed. However, when a platinum catalyst is present, ammonia and oxygen can be made to undergo a far more important and useful reaction.

ammonia + oxygen $\xrightarrow[\text{and heat}]{\substack{\text{platinum} \\ \text{catalyst}}}$ nitrogen monoxide + water

$$4NH_3 + 5O_2 \longrightarrow 4NO + 6H_2O$$

This reaction plays a very important part in the manufacture of nitric acid.

4. *Ammonia as a reducing agent*

If ammonia gas is passed over heated copper (II) oxide a reaction takes place. The copper (II) oxide

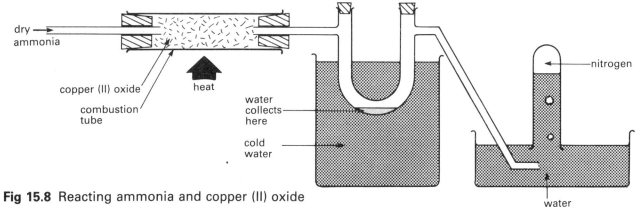

Fig 15.8 Reacting ammonia and copper (II) oxide

is reduced to copper by losing oxygen. Ammonia is changed into nitrogen and water. It is oxidised:

ammonia + copper (II) → copper + water + nitrogen ↑
                oxide

$$2NH_3 + 3CuO \rightarrow 3Cu + 3H_2O + N_2 \uparrow$$
oxidised   *reduced*

The ammonia is the reducing agent.

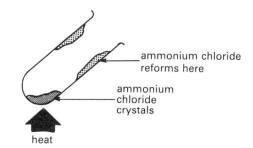

Fig 15.9 Thermal dissociation of ammonium chloride

15.4 Ammonium salts

Ammonium salts are the compounds formed when acids are neutralised by ammonia. They are ionic solids which are soluble in water. Some, like ammonium chloride, break down on heating and reform on cooling. They *thermally dissociate*.

When ammonium chloride is heated it does not melt, but changes directly into a colourless gas. It appears to sublime. Ammonium chloride is formed on the cooler parts of the test tube.

ammonium $\xrightarrow{\text{heat}}$ ammonia ↑ + hydrogen ↑ $\xrightarrow{\text{cool}}$ ammonium
chloride   chloride   chloride

$$NH_4Cl \xrightarrow{\text{heat}} NH_3 \uparrow + HCl \uparrow \xrightarrow{\text{cool}} NH_4Cl$$

134

Many ammonium salts are widely used. Table 1 shows the major uses of some ammonium salts.

Name of compound	Use
ammonium carbonate	1. Used as a raising agent in the food industry 2. Used in smelling salts
ammonium chloride	1. Used in dry batteries 2. Used as a flux in soldering
ammonium nitrate	1. Used as a fertiliser 2. Used in making explosives
ammonium phosphate	Used as a fertiliser to provide both nitrogen and phosphorus for the soil
ammonium sulphate	Used as a fertiliser

Table 1

15.5 Making nitric acid

Nitric acid (HNO_3), is another very important chemical which contains nitrogen. Millions of tons of nitric acid are made in Britain each year. Most of it is used to make ammonium nitrate, but large quantities are also used to make plastics, dyes and explosives.

Making nitric acid in the laboratory

Nitric acid can be made in the laboratory by warming any metal nitrate with concentrated sulphuric acid. Sodium nitrate is normally used:

sodium + sulphuric → sodium hydrogen + nitric ↑
nitrate   acid   sulphate   acid

$$NaNO_3 + H_2SO_4 \rightarrow NaHSO_4 + HNO_3 \uparrow$$

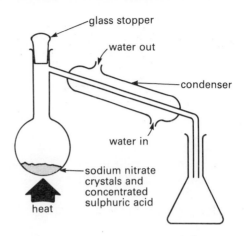

Fig 15.10 Making nitric acid in the laboratory

Nitric acid is formed as a vapour. This vapour is cooled in a condenser and condenses to a colourless liquid. This colourless liquid is pure nitric acid. The apparatus used has to be all made of glass, because nitric acid attacks rubber and cork.

If the reaction mixture is heated too strongly some of the nitric acid breaks down forming brown nitrogen dioxide gas:

nitric acid $\xrightarrow{\text{heat}}$ nitrogen ↑ + oxygen ↑ + water
    dioxide

$$4HNO_3 \longrightarrow 4NO_2 \uparrow + O_2 \uparrow + 2H_2O$$

This nitrogen dioxide dissolves in the nitric acid making it yellow. The yellow colour can be removed by blowing air through the nitric acid.

Making nitric acid in industry

In the past, nitric acid was manufactured by reacting sodium nitrate with concentrated sulphuric acid. This method is no longer used in Britain. All nitric acid is now manufactured from ammonia.

A mixture of ammonia and air is passed over a platinum catalyst at about 850°C. Ammonia reacts with oxygen in the air to form nitrogen monoxide and steam:

ammonia + oxygen → nitrogen + steam
                              monoxide

$$4NH_3 + 5O_2 \rightarrow 4NO + 6H_2O$$

The mixture leaving the catalyst chamber is then cooled, and mixed with more air so that the nitrogen monoxide is changed into nitrogen dioxide:

nitrogen monoxide + oxygen → nitrogen dioxide

$$2NO + O_2 \rightarrow 2NO_2$$

The nitrogen dioxide is then dissolved in water to form nitric acid:

nitrogen + water → nitric + nitrogen
dioxide   acid   monoxide

$$3NO_2 + 2H_2O \rightarrow 2HNO_3 + NO$$

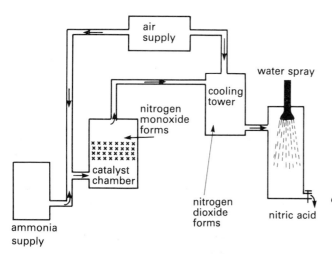

Fig 15.11 Manufacturing nitric acid

15.6 Nitric acid—the chemical

Nitric acid is normally used as a solution in water. Nitric acid solution behaves as an *acidic solution* and as an *oxidising agent*.

Nitric acid — the acid

Nitric acid solution shows most of the properties of acids:
It turns litmus paper red.
It reacts with carbonates forming carbon dioxide gas.
It reacts with bases forming salt and water only.

The only way in which nitric acid behaves differently from a normal acid is: *Nitric acid does not produce hydrogen gas with metals.* Dilute nitric acid reacts with metals to form the nitrate salt, water and an oxide of nitrogen.

Example:

nitric + zinc → zinc + water + nitrogen ↑
acid   nitrate   monoxide

$$8HNO_3 + 3Zn \rightarrow 3Zn(NO_3)_2 + 4H_2O + 2NO \uparrow$$

Nitric acid — the oxidising agent

Nitric acid, especially when concentrated, behaves as a powerful oxidising agent.

If carbon is warmed with concentrated nitric acid it gains oxygen and is oxidised to carbon dioxide.

carbon + nitric acid → carbon ↑ + nitrogen ↑ + water
                              dioxide   dioxide

$$\underset{oxidised}{C} + \underset{reduced}{4HNO_3} \rightarrow CO_2 \uparrow + 4NO_2 \uparrow + 2H_2O$$

Normal acids do not react with copper, because copper is below hydrogen in the reactivity series. Concentrated nitric acid reacts with copper because it is an oxidising agent.

copper + nitric → copper (II) + nitrogen ↑ + water
   acid   nitrate dioxide

$Cu + 4HNO_3 \rightarrow Cu(NO_3)_2 + 2NO_2 \uparrow + 2H_2O$

The nitrates

Nitric acid reacts with metals, bases and carbonates to form salts. These salts are known as nitrates. Nitrate salts have certain properties in common:

1. They all dissolve in water.
2. They are all decomposed when heated.

Although all nitrates decompose on heating, they do not decompose in the same way.

Most metal nitrates decompose on heating, producing brown nitrogen dioxide gas as well as oxygen.

METAL NITRATE → METAL OXIDE +
   NITROGEN DIOXIDE + OXYGEN

Example:

lead → lead + nitrogen + oxygen ↑
nitrate oxide dioxide ↑

$2Pb(NO_3)_2 \rightarrow 2PbO + 4NO_2 \uparrow + O_2$

However the nitrates of the very reactive metals found in group 1 of the Periodic Table decompose differently. They produce oxygen gas but no nitrogen dioxide on heating:

METAL → METAL + OXYGEN
NITRATE NITRITE

Example:

sodium nitrate → sodium nitrite + oxygen ↑

$2NaNO_3 \rightarrow 2NaNO_2 + O_2 \uparrow$

3. Many nitrates are *deliquescent*. They absorb water vapour from the atmosphere until they form a saturated solution. Care must be taken when storing nitrates. If copper (II) nitrate crystals are left in a bottle with a loose top, they may well turn to a solution before they are next used.

Questions

1. Suggest a method by which nitrogen in the air ends up as protein in animals.

2. Ammonia is manufactured by the Haber process.

a What are the raw materials used in this process? Where do they come from?
b What catalyst is used in the reaction?
c How is the ammonia separated from the unreacted gases?
d Give 2 major uses of the ammonia gas produced.

3. You are given supplies of dilute ammonium hydroxide, dilute sulphuric acid and litmus paper. Describe how you would prepare crystals of ammonium sulphate. What could you use your ammonium sulphate crystals for once they were made?

4. How would you obtain a sample of pure hydrogen from a mixture of hydrogen and ammonia?

5. You are given unlabelled bottles which contain ammonium chloride, lead nitrate and potassium nitrate, but you are not told which is which. They are all white solids. How could you identify which bottle is which by heating a small sample of each?

6. Ammonium sulphate $(NH_4)_2SO_4$, ammonium nitrate NH_4NO_3, and urea $CO(NH_2)_2$ are three commonly used nitrogen fertilisers.

a Calculate the mass of 1 mole of each substance.
b Calculate the mass of nitrogen in 1 mole of each substance.
c Which substance contains the greatest percentage by mass of nitrogen?
d What factors (apart from percentage nitrogen)

would you consider before deciding which was the best fertiliser?

7. Write word and symbol equations for the reactions of nitric acid with the following:

a copper (II) oxide
b sodium hydroxide
c calcium carbonate

8. AMMONIA, AMMONIUM CHLORIDE, AMMONIUM SULPHATE, CARBON DIOXIDE, IRON, LEAD NITRATE, NITRIC ACID, PLATINUM, SODIUM NITRATE, SULPHURIC ACID.

Choose from the above:

a An acid which will not produce hydrogen gas with zinc metal.
b A solid that produces brown fumes on heating.
c A gas which will reduce hot copper (II) oxide.
d A substance which will produce oxygen on heating.
e The substance used as the catalyst in the Haber process.
f An alkaline gas.
g A substance used as a nitrogen fertiliser.
h An acid formed in the atmosphere during thunder storms.
i A substance which thermally dissociates.

9. Spot the mistakes in the following passage taken from a student's note book.

Ammonia is a colourless gas with no smell. It is very soluble in water and turns damp blue litmus paper red. The gas is more dense than air and so is collected by downward delivery. Ammonia gas is usually prepared in the laboratory by heating ammonium chloride with calcium chloride. The gas can be dried by passing it through concentrated sulphuric acid.

One of the properties of ammonia is that it will form a thick white smoke with hydrogen chloride gas.

10. Suppose you were given a mixture of ammonium chloride, sodium chloride and sand. How would you get a pure sample of each?

11. How is nitric acid manufactured? In your account mention the raw materials used, the catalyst needed and the temperature at which this catalyst operates.
Give 2 major uses of nitric acid.

12. A friend shows you a stoppered test tube and says that it contains a mixture of ammonia and hydrogen chloride gas. Explain to him why this is impossible.

16 Sulphur and its compounds

Sulphur is a yellow solid element with a melting point of about 119°C. It can be found in nature as the element or as a wide range of sulphur containing compounds. Most supplies of sulphur are obtained from underground deposits of the element, but an increasing amount is now obtained from natural gas.

16.1 Obtaining sulphur

1. *From underground deposits*

Because sulphur has a low melting point, it can be obtained from underground deposits without mining it. The process by which sulphur is extracted is known as the Frasch process. It makes use of a Frasch pump as shown in Fig 16.1.

The Frasch pump is made up of three pipes with the same centre. These pipes are lowered into the sulphur deposit. Water at 160°C is passed down the outer pipe to melt the sulphur. The water is kept liquid at this temperature by keeping it under pressure. Hot compressed air is forced down the smallest pipe and this pushes the liquid sulphur up the middle pipe. The sulphur obtained by this method is over 99% pure.

Much of the sulphur obtained by the Frasch process is transported as a liquid in heated containers. The rest is allowed to solidify and needs to be broken up before it is sold.

2. *From natural gas*

Natural gas from the North Sea contains very little

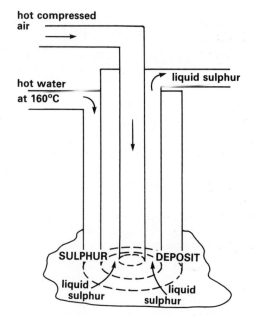

Fig 16.1 The Frasch pump

sulphur, but some natural gas deposits contain a sizeable amount of sulphur as hydrogen sulphide. This acidic gas can be separated from the natural gas by using an alkali. Once it has been separated it can be burnt in a limited supply of air to produce sulphur:

hydrogen sulphide + oxygen → water + sulphur ↓
$$2H_2S \quad + \quad O_2 \quad \rightarrow 2H_2O + \quad 2S \downarrow$$

16.2 Sulphur — the element

Solid sulphur is made up of molecules. There are 8 sulphur atoms in each sulphur molecule and they are arranged in a crown shaped ring.

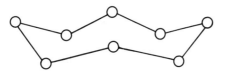

Fig 16.2 The sulphur molecule

Solid sulphur can exist in 2 different crystalline forms because the crown shaped molecules can pack together in 2 different ways. The 2 crystalline forms of sulphur are *rhombic sulphur* and *monoclinic sulphur*. They are known as the *allotropes* of sulphur and can be recognised by the shape of their crystals.

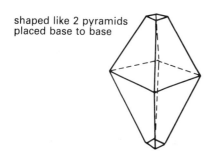

shaped like 2 pyramids placed base to base

Fig 16.3 Rhombic sulphur crystal

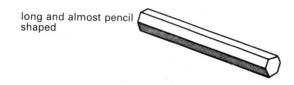

long and almost pencil shaped

Fig 16.4 Monoclinic sulphur crystal

You should remember that carbon can also exist as allotropes. Can you remember the names of the allotropes of carbon?

Making the sulphur allotropes

Rhombic sulphur: Crystals of rhombic sulphur can be made by dissolving sulphur in warm xylene (dimethylbenzene) at 40°C. After filtering off the excess sulphur, the solution can be left to cool in an evaporating basin.

Note: Since xylene is *both* poisonous and highly inflammable, this experiment must be carried out in a fume cupboard. Also, the xylene must be warmed on a water bath.

Monoclinic sulphur: Crystals of monoclinic sulphur can be made by *gently* heating sulphur until it *just* melts and then pouring the liquid sulphur into a double thickness cone of filter paper. When a skin first forms on the surface of the sulphur, the filter paper can be opened out. Needle shaped crystals of monoclinic sulphur will have formed.

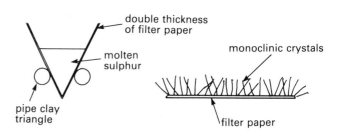

double thickness of filter paper

molten sulphur

monoclinic crystals

pipe clay triangle

filter paper

Fig 16.5 Making monoclinic sulphur

At room temperature rhombic sulphur is the more stable form. This means that any sample of monoclinic sulphur will gradually change to rhombic sulphur if left in the laboratory.

Heating sulphur: Sulphur behaves in a most odd way when it is heated. It melts at about 119°C to form a pale amber, runny liquid. As the liquid sulphur is heated it becomes darker and darker and less and less runny. At about 170°C it is dark brown and almost solid. It is like a syrup. When it is heated more it becomes more and more runny, until it boils at 445°C. The changes that take place are shown in Fig 16.6.

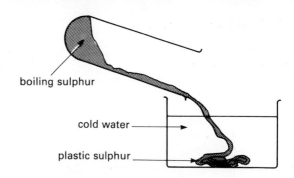

Fig 16.7 Making plastic sulphur

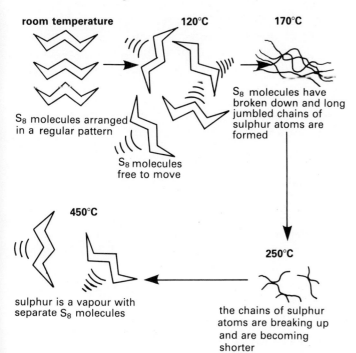

Fig 16.6 Heating sulphur

Plastic sulphur

If boiling sulphur is suddenly cooled by pouring it into cold water a dark solid which feels rubbery (like chewing gum) is formed. This solid is known as *plastic sulphur*. In plastic sulphur the sulphur atoms are arranged in long jumbled chains. If plastic sulphur is left it slowly changes back into hard, yellow, rhombic sulphur.

You should notice that while plastic sulphur is a different form of sulphur to monoclinic and rhombic, it is not an allotrope. *Allotropes must be crystalline.* Plastic sulphur is not.

Sulphur — the chemical

Sulphur is a fairly reactive element. It will burn in air or oxygen with a blue flame to form sulphur dioxide gas:

sulphur + oxygen → sulphur dioxide
$$S + O_2 \rightarrow SO_2$$

Sulphur is in the same group of the Periodic table as oxygen. It is therefore similar to oxygen in its chemical properties. Most metals when heated in oxygen form the metal oxide. Most metals when heated with sulphur form the metal sulphide.

Example: iron + sulphur → iron (II) sulphide
$$Fe + S \rightarrow FeS$$

Metal sulphides are used to produce hydrogen sulphide gas. Most metal sulphides will react with dilute acids to produce hydrogen sulphide gas.

Example:

iron (II) + hydrochloric $\rightarrow$ iron (II) + hydrogen
sulphide   acid   chloride   sulphide $\uparrow$
   FeS   +   2HCl $\rightarrow$ $FeCl_2$ + $H_2S \uparrow$

Uses of sulphur

Most sulphur is used to make sulphuric acid, but it does have other important uses. It can be used to harden rubber. This process is known as *vulcanising*. It is also used in matches and fireworks.

16.3 Sulphur dioxide (SO_2)

Sulphur dioxide is a colourless, poisonous gas with an irritating smell. It is more dense than air and dissolves in water forming an acidic solution.

Making sulphur dioxide

In the laboratory sulphur dioxide is made by warming dilute sulphuric acid with sodium sulphite:

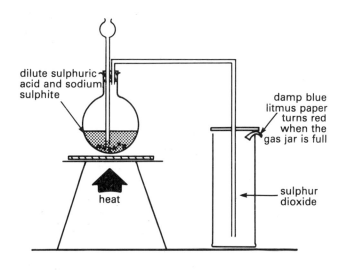

Fig 16.8 Making sulphur dioxide in the laboratory

sodium + sulphuric $\rightarrow$ sodium + sulphur + water
sulphite   acid   sulphate   dioxide $\uparrow$
Na_2SO_3 + H_2SO_4 $\rightarrow Na_2SO_4$+ $SO_2 \uparrow$ + H_2O

Because the gas is soluble in water it has to be collected by downward delivery.

Industrially, large quantities of sulphur dioxide are needed to manufacture sulphuric acid. It is made in a number of ways.

1. By burning sulphur in air. Molten sulphur is sprayed into a combustion furnace where it is burnt at a temperature of about 1000°C. This is the major source of sulphur dioxide at present.

2. By roasting sulphide ores. Metals such as zinc and lead are found as sulphides. These sulphides have to be changed into oxides, by heating in air, before the metal can be extracted. This reaction produces useful sulphur dioxide:

Example:

  zinc   + oxygen $\rightarrow$ zinc   + sulphur
sulphide   oxide   dioxide $\uparrow$
2ZnS   + $3O_2$ $\rightarrow$ 2ZnO + $2SO_2 \uparrow$

Sulphur dioxide — the chemical

Sulphur dioxide is an acidic gas. It dissolves in water to form sulphurous acid:

sulphur dioxide + water $\rightleftharpoons$ sulphurous acid
    SO_2 + H_2O $\rightleftharpoons$ H_2SO_3

Sulphur dioxide can behave both as an oxidising agent and as a reducing agent.

Sulphur dioxide as an oxidising agent

If sulphur dioxide is mixed with hydrogen sulphide an immediate reaction takes place and sulphur is formed:

hydrogen + sulphur $\rightarrow$ sulphur + water
sulphide   dioxide
  $2H_2S$ + SO_2 $\rightarrow$ $3S \downarrow$ + $2H_2O$
oxidised   *reduced*

Sulphur dioxide as a reducing agent

Sulphur dioxide, when dissolved in water, acts as a reducing agent because it is easily oxidised to sulphuric acid:

sulphurous +   oxygen   → sulphuric
  acid   (from a compound)   acid
$$H_2SO_3 \quad + \quad\quad [O] \quad\quad \rightarrow \quad H_2SO_4$$

Test for sulphur dioxide: it will turn potassium permanganate solution colourless. It will turn potassium dichromate solution dark green.

Sulphur dioxide — the polluter

Sulphur dioxide is one of the main polluting gases in industrial areas. It is formed whenever any fuel containing sulphur (coal, oil, gas) is burnt. Since it is an acidic gas it dissolves in rain water making an acidic solution. Acidic rainwater attacks limestone and many metals, causing them to corrode. Much of the recent decay of English churches and cathedrals has been blamed on acidic polluting gases like sulphur dioxide in the atmosphere.

Uses of sulphur dioxide

The main use of sulphur dioxide is to manufacture sulphuric acid, but it does have several other uses:
1. It is used to bleach wood pulp during paper making.
2. It is used as a food preservative.
3. It is used to fumigate greenhouses.

16.4 Sulphuric acid

You may know that sulphuric acid is used in car batteries, but did you know that sulphuric acid is one of the most important chemicals in the world? Millions and millions of tons of it are used by industry every year. It is used to make phosphate fertilisers, nitrogen fertilisers, paints, plastics, detergents, dyes and petrol. Almost every industry has some use for it.

Making sulphuric acid

Sulphuric acid is manufactured by *The Contact Process*. The raw materials are sulphur dioxide, air and water. In Britain most of the sulphur dioxide is produced by burning sulphur.

The sulphur dioxide is mixed with air and passed over a catalyst of vanadium (V) oxide at 450°C. The sulphur dioxide reacts with oxygen in the air to form sulphur trioxide:

sulphur + oxygen   **450°C**   sulphur
dioxide   **vanadium (V) oxide**   trioxide
$$2SO_2 \quad + \quad O_2 \quad \rightleftharpoons \quad 2SO_3$$

Sulphur trioxide reacts with water to form sulphuric acid:

sulphur trioxide + water → sulphuric acid
$$SO_3 \quad + \quad H_2O \quad \rightarrow \quad H_2SO_4$$

Unfortunately, if sulphur trioxide is passed into water the sulphuric acid is formed as a fine mist. This mist is difficult to condense. Instead, sulphur trioxide is dissolved in 98% sulphuric acid. A controlled amount of water is added at the same time so that the acid is kept at 98% sulphuric acid.

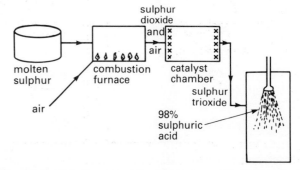

Fig 16.9 The Contact Process: the main stages

143

The burning of sulphur and the changing of sulphur dioxide into sulphur trioxide are exothermic reactions. They produce a great deal of heat. This heat is not wasted in a sulphuric acid plant. It is used to make steam to produce commercial electricity, which can be sold. It is largely because of the use of the energy produced in the Contact Process, that sulphuric acid is a fairly cheap chemical.

Sulphuric acid — the chemical

Dilute sulphuric acid behaves like a typical acid. It turns litmus paper red. It reacts with most metals producing hydrogen gas.

Example:

magnesium + sulphuric → magnesium + hydrogen ↑
          acid   sulphate

$$Mg + H_2SO_4 \rightarrow MgSO_4 + H_2 \uparrow$$

It also reacts with metal carbonates producing carbon dioxide gas.

Example:

copper (II) + sulphuric → copper (II) + carbon ↑ + water
carbonate   acid   sulphate   dioxide

$$CuCO_3 + H_2SO_4 \rightarrow CuSO_4 + CO_2 \uparrow + H_2O$$

And it also reacts with bases to form salt and water only.

Example:

magnesium + sulphuric → magnesium + water
  oxide   acid   sulphate

$$MgO + H_2SO_4 \rightarrow MgSO_4 + H_2O$$

While dilute sulphuric acid behaves as a typical acid, concentrated sulphuric acid has some very peculiar properties.

1. *As a drying agent*

Concentrated sulphuric acid has a very strong attraction for water. It is therefore used to dry many gases. The gases are dried by bubbling them through concentrated sulphuric acid. Ammonia and ethene are the only 2 common gases that cannot be dried using concentrated sulphuric acid. They react with it.

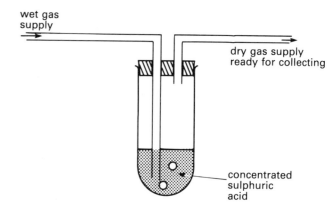

Fig 16.10 Using concentrated sulphuric acid to dry gases

2. *As a dehydrating agent*

So strong is the attraction of concentrated sulphuric acid for water that it will even remove water from some compounds.

If blue copper (II) sulphate crystals are dropped into concentrated sulphuric acid they turn white as they lose their water of crystallisation:

blue copper (II) → white anhydrous + water
sulphate crystals   copper (II) sulphate

$$CuSO_4.5H_2O \rightarrow CuSO_4 + 5H_2O$$

With some compounds such as sugar it will remove hydrogen and oxygen from the compound as water:

Sugar → carbon + water

$$C_6H_{12}O_6 \rightarrow 6C + 6H_2O$$

When concentrated sulphuric acid breaks down a compound, forming water, it is behaving as a *dehydrating* agent. The process is known as de-

hydration. Concentrated sulphuric acid also dehydrates skin and flesh. It can cause very serious and painful wounds.

3. *As an oxidising agent*

Concentrated sulphuric acid behaves as an *oxidising agent*. When it does, it is usually reduced to sulphur dioxide gas.

Copper and dilute sulphuric acid do not react because copper is too low in the reactivity series. However, concentrated sulphuric acid will react with copper because it is an oxidising agent:

copper + concentrated → copper (II) + sulphur + water
         sulphuric acid   sulphate   dioxide ↑

$$Cu + 2H_2SO_4 \rightarrow CuSO_4 + SO_2\uparrow + 2H_2O$$
oxidised   *reduced*

If carbon is warmed in concentrated sulphuric acid it is oxidised to carbon dioxide:

carbon + concentrated → carbon + sulphur + water
        sulphuric acid dioxide ↑ dioxide ↑

$$C + 2H_2SO_4 \rightarrow CO_2\uparrow + 2SO_2\uparrow + 2H_2O$$
oxidised   *reduced*

Questions

1. Sulphur and coal are both found in underground deposits. Coal has to be mined; sulphur can be extracted by using a Frasch pump.

a Why can't coal be obtained from underground deposits using a Frasch pump?
b Sulphur obtained by the Frasch process is often sold and transported as molten sulphur. What are the advantages and disadvantages of transporting it in this way?
c What is the major use of the element sulphur?

2. At room temperature sulphur exists as S_8 molecules. What shape are these molecules? How does the molecular structure of sulphur change as it is heated up to its boiling point?

3. Monoclinic sulphur and rhombic sulphur are the allotropes of sulphur.

a What are allotropes?
b Name another element that has allotropes.
c If you were shown crystals of rhombic sulphur and monoclinic sulphur how would you know which was which?
d Describe how you would make some plastic sulphur in the laboratory.
e Why is plastic sulphur not an allotrope of sulphur?
f What changes would you notice if a piece of plastic sulphur was left in the laboratory for 2 weeks?

4.
a How can sulphur be changed into sulphur dioxide? Write an equation for the reaction.
b Name two compounds which when mixed together at room temperature react to form sulphur dioxide. Write an equation for the reaction.
c How would you test a gas to show that it was sulphur dioxide?
d Sulphur dioxide is one of the main gases that pollute the atmosphere. It is responsible for much of the decay of limestone buildings. What property of sulphur dioxide makes it attack these buildings?

5. A friend tells you that he has a stoppered test tube containing a mixture of sulphur dioxide and hydrogen sulphide. Explain to him why this is not possible.

6. Write word equations and symbol equations for the reactions of dilute sulphuric acid with the following:

a copper (II) carbonate   c magnesium
b sodium hydroxide   d zinc oxide

7.

a When iron filings and sulphur powder are mixed at room temperature a mixture is formed. How would you separate this mixture?

b When iron filings and sulphur are heated together a compound forms:

  (i) name the compound formed
  (ii) write an equation for the reaction
  (iii) how does this compound react with dilute hydrochloric acid?

8. If burning magnesium is lowered into a gas jar of sulphur dioxide a white powder P and a pale yellow powder Q are formed. P reacts with dilute sulphuric acid to form R and water. Q does not react with dilute sulphuric acid. Q burns in air to reform sulphur dioxide.

a Identify P, Q and R.

b Write equations for the following reactions:

  (i) the reaction between sulphur dioxide and magnesium
  (ii) the reaction between P and dilute sulphuric acid
  (iii) the burning of Q.

9.

a Concentrated sulphuric acid is used to dry gases. Name one gas which cannot be dried using sulphuric acid.

b Give an example of a reaction in which concentrated sulphuric acid behaves as a dehydrating agent.

c What is the difference between drying and dehydrating?

10.

a Hydrogen sulphide burns in excess air to form water and sulphur dioxide. Write an equation for the reaction.

b Hydrogen sulphide burns in a limited supply of air to form water and sulphur. Write an equation for the reaction.

c What is the maximum amount of sulphur that you could get from 34 g of hydrogen sulphide by burning?

d Draw a diagram of the apparatus you would use to get sulphur from hydrogen sulphide.

11. Sulphuric acid is manufactured by the Contact process.

a What are the raw materials needed?

b Outline the different stages in the process.

c Name the catalyst used and the temperature at which it operates.

d Give 2 major uses of sulphuric acid.

17 Chlorine and its compounds

The element chlorine is a green gas. It is very reactive and even reacts with gold. Because it is so reactive, there is no free chlorine in the atmosphere. Instead, chlorine is found in compounds. The most plentiful compound of chlorine is sodium chloride. It is found in large underground deposits as rock salt and also dissolved in sea water. No wonder it is known as common salt. Sodium chloride is used to make a number of useful chemicals that are not found naturally.

17.1 Hydrogen chloride

If concentrated sulphuric acid is added to sodium chloride a reaction takes place and a colourless gas is formed. This gas has been known as salt gas, but its chemical name is hydrogen chloride:

sodium + concentrated → sodium + hydrogen ↑
chloride   sulphuric   hydrogen   chloride
              acid   sulphate

$$NaCl + H_2SO_4 \rightarrow NaHSO_4 + HCl \uparrow$$

Hydrogen chloride can be made in the laboratory using the apparatus shown in Fig 17.1. The gas has to be collected by downward delivery as it is more dense than air and very soluble in water.

Hydrogen chloride — the chemical

Hydrogen chloride is a colourless gas with a sharp irritating smell. It does not burn and it does not allow other substances to burn in it. Hydrogen

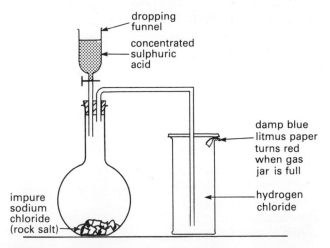

Fig 17.1 Making hydrogen chloride in the laboratory

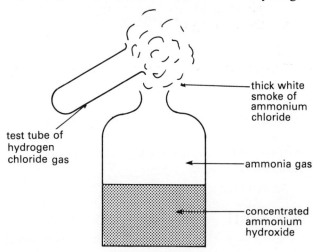

Fig 17.2 Testing for hydrogen chloride

chloride reacts with ammonia gas to form a thick white smoke of ammonium chloride:

$$\text{ammonia} + \text{hydrogen} \rightarrow \text{ammonium}$$
$$\text{chloride} \qquad \text{chloride}$$
$$NH_3 \ + \ HCl \ \rightarrow \ NH_4Cl$$

This reaction is often used as a test for hydrogen chloride. A bottle of concentrated ammonium hydroxide can be used as a source of ammonia.

When hydrogen chloride comes into contact with moist air it forms a white mist. We say that hydrogen chloride fumes in moist air. Hydrogen chloride is in fact very soluble in water. Special precautions have to be taken when making a solution of hydrogen chloride in water.

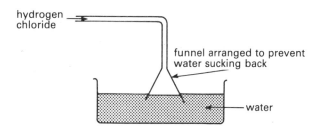

Fig 17.3 Making a solution of hydrogen chloride in water

Hydrogen chloride is a covalent substance, but when it dissolves in water it reacts with the water forming ions. The solution formed is known as *hydrochloric acid*.

$$\text{hydrogen} + \text{water} \rightarrow \text{hydrochloric}$$
$$\text{chloride} \qquad\qquad \text{acid}$$
$$HCl \ + \ H_2O \rightarrow H_3O^+ + Cl^-$$

Dry hydrogen chloride does not have the properties of an acid. It does not affect *dry* litmus paper and does not produce carbon dioxide from carbonates. However, hydrogen chloride will react with some metals producing hydrogen gas. This can be demonstrated using the apparatus shown in Fig 17.4.

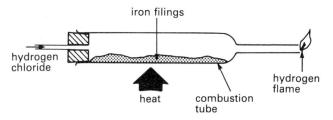

Fig 17.4 Reacting iron with hydrogen chloride

$$\text{iron} + \text{hydrogen} \rightarrow \text{iron (II)} + \text{hydrogen}$$
$$\text{chloride} \qquad \text{chloride}$$
$$Fe \ + \ 2HCl \ \rightarrow \ FeCl_2 \ + \ H_2$$

The hydrogen formed can be burnt at the end of the combustion tube.

17.2 Hydrochloric acid

We have seen that hydrochloric acid is a solution of hydrogen chloride in water. If the solution is saturated with hydrogen chloride it is known as concentrated hydrochloric acid. Concentrated hydrochloric acid contains about 36% hydrogen chloride by weight.

Manufacturing hydrochloric acid

Hydrochloric acid is made industrially by dissolving hydrogen chloride in water. The hydrogen chloride is not made by reacting salt with concentrated sulphuric acid; it is made by burning hydrogen in chlorine gas:

$$\text{hydrogen} + \text{chlorine} \rightarrow \text{hydrogen chloride}$$
$$H_2 \ + \ Cl_2 \ \rightarrow \qquad 2HCl$$

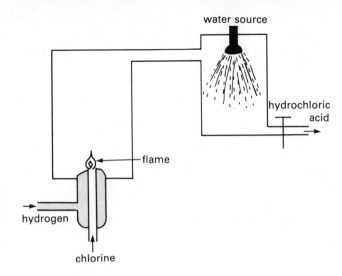

Fig 17.5 Manufacturing hydrochloric acid

Hydrochloric acid — the chemical

Hydrochloric acid behaves as a typical acid when concentrated and when dilute. It turns blue litmus paper red. It reacts with most metals producing hydrogen gas:

Example:

magnesium + hydrochloric → magnesium + hydrogen ↑
             acid   chloride

$$Mg + 2\,HCl \rightarrow MgCl_2 + H_2\uparrow$$

It reacts with carbonates producing carbon dioxide gas.

Example:

calcium + hydrochloric → calcium + carbon ↑ + water
carbonate   acid   chloride   dioxide

$$CaCO_3 + 2HCl \rightarrow CaCl_2 + CO_2\uparrow + H_2O$$

It also reacts with bases to form salts and water only.

Example:

copper (II) + hydrochloric → copper (II) + water
  oxide   acid   chloride

$$CuO + 2HCl \rightarrow CuCl_2 + H_2O$$

Apart from its acidic properties, hydrochloric acid can be oxidised to chlorine using manganese (IV) oxide.

Example:

concentrated + manganese → manganese
hydrochloric (IV) oxide   (II) chloride
  acid

                            + water + chlorine ↑

$$4HCl + MnO_2 \rightarrow MnCl_2$$
$$+ 2H_2O + Cl_2\uparrow$$

17.3 Chlorine

Chlorine is made in the laboratory by oxidising hydrochloric acid (see page 150).

Alternatively, chlorine can be made by reacting concentrated hydrochloric acid with potassium permanganate. If potassium permanganate is used no heat is needed.

Chlorine is collected by downward delivery because it is soluble in water and more dense than air.

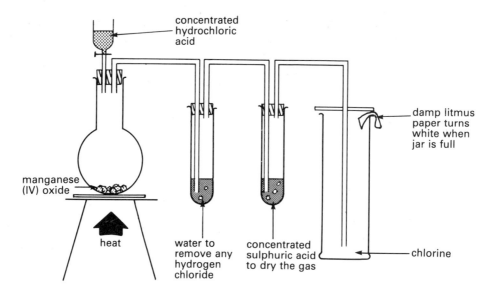

Fig 17.6 Making chlorine in the laboratory

Manufacturing chlorine

In industry chlorine is made from salt water by passing electricity through it. Hydrogen and sodium hydroxide are formed at the same time.

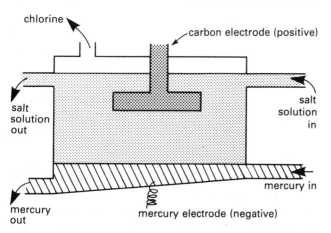

Fig 17.7 Cell for manufacturing chlorine

In this process, chlorine is formed at the positive electrode. Sodium hydroxide and hydrogen are formed when the spent mercury is poured into water. The gas chlorine is liquified before it is sold.

Chlorine — the chemical

The element chlorine exists as Cl_2 molecules. Each chlorine atom has seven electrons in its outermost shell. By 2 atoms sharing electrons the chlorine molecule is formed

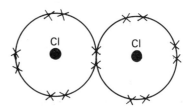

Fig 17.8 The chlorine molecule

Chlorine has a choking, irritating smell and is extremely poisonous. Its poisonous nature and the fact that it is more than twice as dense as air help to explain why it was used as a weapon during World War 1.

Chlorine does not burn and does not allow most substances to burn in it, but it is a very reactive element. It reacts with most elements, except carbon, to form the chloride of that element.

Example: zinc + chlorine → zinc chloride
$$Zn + Cl_2 \rightarrow ZnCl_2$$

Chlorine is moderately soluble in water. It dissolves to form a solution which is known as *chlorine water*. Chlorine water is in fact a mixture of hydrochloric and hypochlorous acids.

chlorine + water $\rightleftharpoons$ hydrochloric + hypochlorous
$$\text{acid} \qquad \text{acid}$$
$$Cl_2 + H_2O \rightleftharpoons HCl + HOCl$$

Chlorine water is unstable and is decomposed by sunlight. Sunlight causes the hypochlorous acid to break down to hydrochloric acid and oxygen.

hypochlorous $\xrightarrow{\textbf{sunlight}}$ hydrochloric + oxygen ↑
$$\text{acid} \qquad \text{acid}$$
$$2HOCl \longrightarrow 2HCl + O_2 \uparrow$$

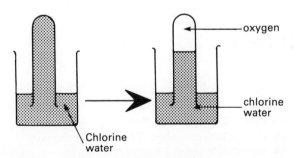

Fig 17.9 Changes in chlorine water on leaving in sunlight

Because chlorine water decomposes in this way it has to be kept in dark bottles in the laboratory.

Testing for chlorine

Chlorine gas will turn damp blue litmus paper red and then bleach it. This is the usual test for chlorine.

Chlorine is a bleach in the presence of water. The oxygen from the hypochlorous acid formed is easily lost and this oxidises most dyes to colourless compounds:

Hypochlorous + dye › colourless + hydrochloric
$$\text{acid} \qquad\qquad \text{compound} \qquad \text{acid}$$

Uses of chlorine

1. Chlorine is used to sterilise domestic water supplies. After water from reservoirs has been filtered to remove any solids, it may still contain harmful germs. These are killed by passing chlorine into our water supply before it reaches our homes. The amount of chlorine used must be very carefully controlled. It must be enough to kill all the germs and yet not enough to give the water an unpleasant taste. Certainly there must not be enough chlorine in the water to harm the people using it.

2. Chlorine is used in swimming pools to kill harmful germs. It is used in much higher concentrations than in domestic water supplies. The chlorine taste makes the water most unpleasant if you swallow some while swimming.

3. Chlorine is used in the manufacture of plastics. The main plastic which contains chlorine is polyvinylchloride (PVC).

4. Chlorine is used to make a number of industrial solvents such as trichloroethane, which is widely used for degreasing metals.

5. Chlorine is used to make domestic bleaches. Most domestic bleaches are made by dissolving chlorine gas in sodium hydroxide solution:

sodium + chlorine → sodium + sodium + water
hydroxide   chloride   hypo-
                                  chlorite

$$2NaOH + Cl_2 \rightarrow NaCl + NaOCl + H_2O$$

17.4 The Halogens

The halogens are the elements in group 7 of the Periodic Table. They include fluorine, chlorine, bromine and iodine.

Name of halogen	Formula	Appearance at room temperature
fluorine	F_2	pale yellow gas
chlorine	Cl_2	green gas
bromine	Br_2	brown liquid (easily vaporised)
iodine	I_2	shiny grey solid (easily vaporised)

Table 1 The Halogens

All the halogens exist as *diatomic molecules*. This means that there are 2 atoms in each molecule of the element. They have similar chemical properties even though they differ greatly in appearance. Fluorine is the most reactive and they become less reactive going down the group:

Fluorine	Chlorine	Bromine	Iodine
most			**least**
reactive	decreasing reactivity →		**reactive**

You may remember that a more reactive metal will displace a less reactive metal from a solution of one of its salts. In the same way, a more reactive halogen will displace a less reactive halogen from a solution of one of its salts.

If chlorine is bubbled into a solution of potassium bromide, bromine is formed:

Example:

chlorine + potassium → bromine + potassium
           bromide   chloride

$$Cl_2 + 2KBr \rightarrow Br_2 + 2KCl$$

Uses of the halogens and their compounds

Fluorine is used in the manufacture of inert plastics such as Teflon which is used for non stick saucepans.

Bromine is used to manufacture silver bromide which is light sensitive and used in photographic films (see section 18.5).

Iodine is used as a mild antiseptic when dissolved in potassium iodide solution. Silver iodide is used in high speed films as it is more light sensitive than silver bromide.

Questions

1. BROMINE, CHLORINE, HYDROGEN CHLORIDE, IODINE, SILVER BROMIDE, SODIUM CHLORIDE.

Choose from the above list:

a A halogen which is a liquid at room temperature.
b A green gas.
c A chemical found in sea water but not in fresh water.
d A substance decomposed by sunlight.
e A colourless gas that fumes in damp air.
f A substance used to preserve food.
g A gas that dissolves in water to form 2 different acids.

152

h A solid element in group 7 of the Periodic table.

i A substance that bleaches damp litmus paper.

2. Fluorine, atomic number 9, exists as F_2 molecules. Draw a diagram to show the arrangement of electrons in a fluorine molecule.

3. Write word equations and symbol equations for the reactions of dilute hydrochloric acid with the following:

a calcium carbonate
b magnesium
c sodium hydroxide
d copper (II) oxide

4. A white crystalline solid K reacts with concentrated sulphuric acid to form a colourless gas L. L is an acidic gas and forms white fumes in moist air. A concentrated solution of L in water reacts with manganese (IV) oxide to form a green gas M.

When a piece of hot sodium metal is placed in gas M the white solid K is reformed.

Identify K, L and M giving your reasons.

5. The following apparatus was set up. The white deposit started to form after about 4 minutes.

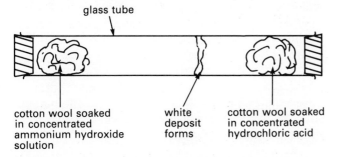

glass tube

cotton wool soaked in concentrated ammonium hydroxide solution

white deposit forms

cotton wool soaked in concentrated hydrochloric acid

a What gas escapes from the concentrated ammonium hydroxide solution?

b What gas escapes from the concentrated hydrochloric acid?

c Name the white deposit formed.

d Why is the white deposit not formed immediately the apparatus is set up?

e Why is the white deposit not formed halfway between the 2 plugs of cotton wool?

6. Silver nitrate solution reacts with calcium chloride solution as shown in the following equation:

$$CaCl_2 + 2AgNO_3 \rightarrow 2AgCl\downarrow + Ca(NO_3)_2$$

What mass of silver chloride could be obtained from 11·1 g of calcium chloride?

7. Chlorine is a poisonous gas. Why is it safe to:

a add chlorine to all domestic water supplies
b season food with sodium chloride?

8. Hydrogen burns in chlorine to form hydrogen chloride.

a Write an equation for the reaction.

b Hydrogen chloride is extremely soluble in water. Explain how you would safely make a solution of hydrogen chloride in water in the laboratory. Include a diagram of the apparatus you would use.

c How would you show that a solution of hydrogen chloride in water:

(i) was acidic.
(ii) contained ions.

d What is the usual name for a solution of hydrogen chloride in water?

18 The speed of chemical reactions

The chemical changes that take place when an apple ripens are very slow. We do not blink and find that an apple has ripened; blink again and find it over ripe. In fact the changes are so slow that we cannot see them happening. On the other hand, if a match is put to a mixture of natural gas and oxygen it might explode. The reaction may be complete in a fraction of a second; so fast that we cannot see it happening. Chemical reactions vary from very fast to very slow.

This can give problems to chemists in industry. They obviously do not want reactions to take place at an explosive rate, but they do want them to take place fast enough to make the best use of their chemical plant. Chemists want to be able to control the speed of chemical reactions. They want to be able to speed them up or slow them down.

Before chemists could hope to *control* the speed of chemical reactions they had to find out what factors affect the speeds of reactions.

18.1 The size of particles

When a solid reacts with a liquid or a gas, the size of the solid particles affects the speed of the reaction.

The smaller the solid particles, the faster the rate of the reaction.

This can be shown in the laboratory by the following simple experiment.

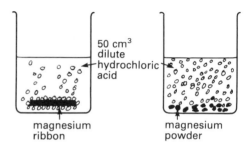

Fig 18.1 The reaction of magnesium and acid

Using a measuring cylinder carefully place 50 cm^3 of dilute hydrochloric acid into each of two small beakers. Take a 10 cm length of magnesium ribbon and weigh it. Then weigh an equal amount of magnesium powder. Drop the piece of magnesium ribbon into one beaker of acid, starting a stopwatch as you do so. Note how long it takes for the magnesium to completely react. Repeat the experiment by putting the magnesium powder in the second beaker of acid.

If you try this experiment you will find that the powder reacts in a shorter time. It must therefore have reacted faster. Would you expect the magnesium ribbon to react faster or slower if it had been rolled up into a tight reel?

Explanation

You should see from Fig 18.2 that if a block of magnesium is placed in acid, the acid can only react with the magnesium on the surface of the block. The speed of the reaction depends on the surface area of the block.

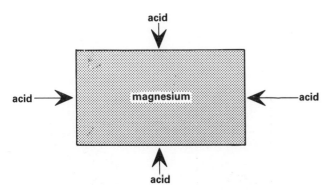

Fig 18.2

If the block of magnesium is cut into smaller pieces extra surfaces are made available for the acid to attack. This is shown in Fig 18.3.

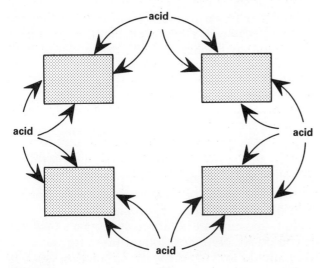

Fig 18.3

The acid can react with more magnesium at any one time, so the speed of the reaction increases. The more the magnesium is broken down into smaller particles, the larger its surface area becomes and therefore the faster it reacts.

It is worth realising that some solids, which we think of as harmless, can be very dangerous as fine powders. We store coal in sheds or bunkers near our homes. We do not think of bags of flour as a fire hazard in our kitchens. However, coal dust and finely powdered flour can burn explosively in air. Great care has to be taken in coal mines and in flour mills to control dust and sparks. Insufficient control has led to a number of disasters.

18.2 Concentration

The concentration of reacting substances is a second factor that affects the speed of chemical reactions.

If the concentration of a reagent increases, the rate at which it reacts increases.

This can once again be shown in the laboratory by using the reaction between magnesium and hydrochloric acid.

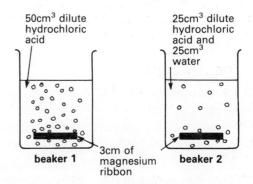

Fig 18.4

Place 50 cm³ of dilute hydrochloric acid into a small beaker. Into a second small beaker place 25 cm³ of dilute hydrochloric acid and 25 cm³ of water. Both beakers now contain 50 cm³ of acid solution, but the acid will be twice as concentrated in the first beaker. Cut 2 pieces of magnesium ribbon exactly 3 cm long. Drop one piece of magnesium into the first beaker starting a stopwatch as you do so. Note how long it takes for the magnesium to completely react. Repeat the experiment by dropping the other piece of magnesium into the second beaker.

You will find that the magnesium completely reacts in a shorter time in the more concentrated acid. This means that it reacts faster in the more concentrated acid.

Explanation

dilute   more concentrated   even more concentrated

Fig 18.5

As a substance becomes more concentrated there are more particles of that substance in a given space. This is shown in Fig 18.5. The greater the concentration of particles the greater the chance they have of colliding with each other.

When particles collide they can either bounce apart or they can react to form a new substance. One way in which this can happen is shown in Fig 18.6.

If particles collide more often they will react more often. Therefore increasing the concentration of a substance increases the rate at which it will react.

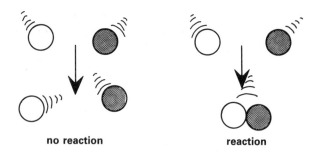

no reaction   reaction

Fig 18.6

18.3 Temperature

Temperature can have a very large effect on the speed of a chemical reaction.

If the temperature of the reagents is increased, they will react faster.

For many reactions increasing the temperature by 10°C makes the reaction take place twice as fast.

We can show the effect of temperature on the rate of a reaction in the laboratory by using the reaction between sodium thiosulphate solution and dilute hydrochloric acid. When dilute hydrochloric acid is added to sodium thiosulphate solution, a fine deposit of sulphur is formed. This makes the solution cloudy. As more and more sulphur is formed the solution becomes more and more cloudy. Eventually it is impossible to see through the solution.

Place 50 cm³ of sodium thiosulphate solution in a small beaker and note its temperature. Place the beaker on a piece of paper marked with a cross. Add 10 cm³ of dilute hydrochloric acid to the sodium thiosulphate solution, starting a stopwatch as you do so. Note how long it takes for the cross to disappear looking through the solution (see Fig 18.7).

Repeat the experiment, but heat the sodium thiosulphate solution to 40°C before adding the acid. You will find that the cross disappears in a shorter time. The reaction is faster at the higher temperature.

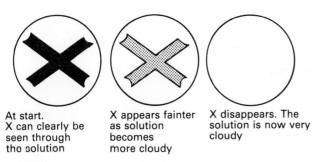

At start.
X can clearly be seen through the solution

X appears fainter as solution becomes more cloudy

X disappears. The solution is now very cloudy

Fig 18.7

Explanation

There are 2 reasons why a higher temperature causes a faster speed of reaction:
1. Particles move faster when hot.

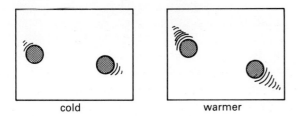

cold   warmer

Fig 18.8

As the temperature increases, the particles of the reacting substances move faster. They collide with each other more often, and therefore react more often. The rate of reaction therefore increases. However, this does not explain why temperature has such a large effect on the rate of some reactions.

2. More collisions lead to reaction. As the temperature increases, the particles of the reacting substances get more energy. They become less stable. This means that they are more likely to react when they collide. If a greater proportion of the collisions between reagent particles lead to a reaction, then obviously the rate of reaction must increase.

18.4 Catalysts

Catalysts are substances that speed up chemical reactions but are chemically unchanged at the end of the reaction.

It is quite difficult showing that a substance is a catalyst in the laboratory. You have to show that:
1. It does speed up the chemical reaction.
2. It is the same chemical at the end of the reaction.

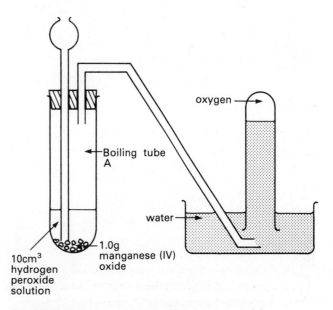

oxygen

Boiling tube A

water

10cm³ hydrogen peroxide solution

1.0g manganese (IV) oxide

Fig 18.9 Decomposing hydrogen peroxide

It can be demonstrated by using the decomposition of hydrogen peroxide. Hydrogen peroxide decomposes to form water and oxygen. The usual catalyst is manganese (IV) oxide (see Fig 18.9, page 157):

hydrogen peroxide → water + oxygen ↑
$$2H_2O_2 \rightarrow 2H_2O + O_2 \uparrow$$

Weigh out 1·0 g of manganese (IV) oxide and place it in the boiling tube A as shown in Fig 18.9. Manganese (IV) oxide is a black powder. Pour 10 cm^3 of hydrogen peroxide solution down the thistle funnel and start a stopwatch. Note how long it takes to collect a test tube full of oxygen. When the reaction *stops* filter the mixture through a *previously weighed* filter paper. Allow the filter paper with black solid on it to dry. While it is drying, repeat the experiment but without using any manganese (IV) oxide.

You will find that the reaction is *far slower*. When the filter paper is dry, reweigh it, and show that it contains 1·0 g of a black powder. This black powder has to be shown to be manganese (IV) oxide. Manganese (IV) oxide produces chlorine gas with concentrated hydrochloric acid. The black powder left at the end of this experiment also does this, so it must be manganese (IV) oxide.

So manganese (IV) oxide is a catalyst for this reaction.

Catalysts are of great importance in the chemical industry. They allow reactions to take place at a reasonable rate at a fairly low temperature. They allow a great deal of heat energy to be saved. Many catalysts used in industry are transition metals or transition metal compounds.
Examples: vanadium (V) oxide is used to make sulphuric acid. Platinum is used to make nitric acid. Iron is used to make ammonia. Nickel is used in the manufacture of margarine.

It would be wrong to think of catalysts as lumps of pure substances. A great deal of research has been done to increase the efficiency of catalysts. They often contain definite impurities to increase their efficiency. Their particle size and surface area are carefully controlled.

Nature has her own catalysts. They are called *enzymes*. You may remember that the enzyme *zymase* is present in yeast. It is this enzyme that enables yeast to convert sugar into ethanol.

18.5 Light

We have considered most of the factors which affect the speed of chemical reactions. However, some reactions are speeded up considerably by the presence of light. One of the best known of these reactions is the decomposition of silver bromide into silver and bromine:

silver bromide → silver + bromine ↑
$$2AgBr \rightarrow 2Ag + Br_2 \uparrow$$

This reaction is the basis of modern photography. In a photographic film tiny silver bromide crystals are placed in a gelatin layer. The silver bromide crystals are quite stable in the absence of light, but when they are exposed to light they immediately start to decompose forming black silver and bromine vapour which escapes.

Questions

1. When zinc reacts with dilute sulphuric acid hydrogen gas is formed.

a Draw a diagram of the apparatus you would use to measure how much hydrogen had been formed at various times in this reaction.

In such an experiment the following results were obtained.

Volume of hydrogen(cm³)	21	38	51	58	60	60
Time (minutes)	2	4	6	8	10	12

All the zinc was eventually used up.

b Plot a graph of the volume of hydrogen formed against time. From your graph calculate:
(i) the volume of hydrogen formed after 1 minute
(ii) the volume of hydrogen formed after 5 minutes
(iii) the time taken to collect 45 cm³ of hydrogen gas

c How long does it take for all the zinc metal to be used up?

2.

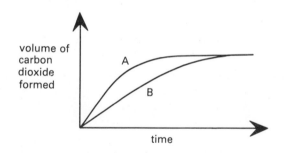

Calcium carbonate reacts with dilute hydrochloric acid to form carbon dioxide gas.

In *experiment* 1 a lump of calcium carbonate was allowed to react with 50 cm³ of dilute hydrochloric acid. The volume of carbon dioxide formed at various times was noted.

Experiment 2 was a repeat of experiment 1. The *only* difference was that powdered calcium carbonate was used in experiment 2.

The results of experiments 1 and 2 were plotted as the graph shows.

a Which of the curves (A or B) shows the results of experiment 1? Give a reason for your answer.

b Assuming that there is calcium carbonate left at the end of both experiments explain:
(i) why the speed of the reaction gets slower and slower
(ii) how you can tell from the graph that the same amount of hydrochloric acid was used in experiment 1 and in experiment 2.

3. "As energy becomes more and more expensive, industry will need to make its catalysts more and more efficient"
Explain why this is so.

4. Suggest reasons for the following:

a Magnesium ribbon reacts faster with concentrated hydrochloric acid than with dilute hydrochloric acid.

b Magnesium powder reacts with hydrochloric acid faster than magnesium ribbon.

c Most chemical reactions take place faster at higher temperatures.

5.

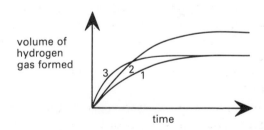

Three separate experiments were performed in which magnesium ribbon was allowed to react with *excess* hydrochloric acid. The amounts of hydrogen formed at different times were noted. The results of these experiments are shown in the graph.

a In which experiment was the most concentrated hydrochloric acid used? Give a reason for your answer.

b In which experiment was the greatest amount of magnesium ribbon used? Give a reason for your answer.

6. Hydrogen peroxide decomposes to form water and oxygen gas. Manganese (IV) oxide and cobalt (III) oxide are both catalysts for the decomposition.

a How would you show that manganese (IV) oxide speeds up the rate at which hydrogen peroxide decomposes?

b How would you find out which of the 2 substances mentioned is a better catalyst for the decomposition of hydrogen peroxide?

19 Electricity and matter

Electricity is a very convenient form of energy. We use it in our homes for lighting, heating, cooking, washing clothes and for many other things. One of the big advantages of electricity is that it can easily be controlled. It can be turned on or off at the flick of a switch.

Electricity can be easily controlled because it passes through some materials but not through others.

A substance that allows electricity to pass through it is called a *conductor* of electricity.

A substance that does not allow electricity to pass through it is called a non conductor or *insulator*.

19.1 Conductors and insulators

If you were given a selection of substances in the laboratory and asked to divide them into conductors and insulators it would be a fairly easy job. All you would need to do is to connect up the apparatus shown in Fig 19.1.

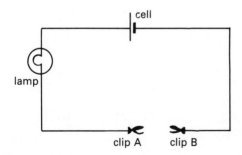

Fig 19.1

You would connect clips A and B to the substances you were testing. If the substance was a conductor the lamp would glow. If it was an insulator the lamp would not light up.

Table 1 shows some conductors and insulators that you might find in the laboratory.

CONDUCTORS	INSULATORS
Copper, aluminium, zinc, iron, steel, graphite, salt water, aqueous copper (II) sulphate, dilute hydrochloric acid, dilute sulphuric acid, aqueous sodium hydroxide	Sulphur, oxygen, iodine, carbon dioxide, ethanol, water, wax, polythene, PVC, copper (II) sulphate crystals, sodium chloride crystals, sugar, any pure acids, a solution of sugar in water

Table 1

Insulators

Looking at the insulators in Table 1 you will see they can be divided into a number of groups.

1. *Non metal elements*: all non metal elements except graphite are insulators. They will not conduct electricity in any state; solid, liquid or gas.

2. *Covalent compounds*: all covalent compounds are insulators. It does not matter whether they are solids like wax and sugar, liquids like ethanol and water, or gases like carbon dioxide. Pure acids fit into this group. So do the plastics, such as PVC, which are so widely used as insulators.

3. *Ionic solids*: ionic substances like sodium chloride and copper (II) sulphate are insulators, but only when they are solids.

Conductors

Looking at the conductors in Table 1 you will see they can also be divided up into a number of groups.

1. *Metals*: all metals conduct electricity when solid or molten. Some metals are better conductors than others.

Aluminium and copper are two of the best conductors. This is why they are so widely used for electrical wiring.

2. *Acidic solutions*: pure acids are covalent but when they dissolve in water they form ions and become conductors.

3. *Ionic compounds*: ionic compounds like sodium chloride conduct electricity when they are molten, or dissolved in water, but not when they are solid.

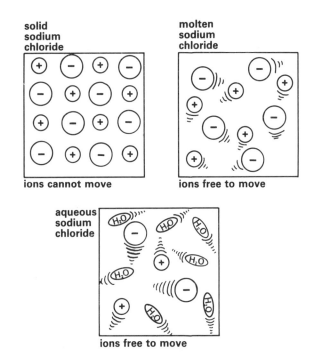

Fig 19.2

19.2 How do conductors conduct?

For a substance to conduct electricity, it must contain charged particles which are free to move. In metals (and graphite) the charged particles are electrons. The electrons that are free to move are the outer shell electrons or valence electrons. It is these valence electrons that carry an electric current through metals.

Apart from metals (and graphite) all other conductors contain ions. It is these ions that carry the electric current through the substance. Ionic solids such as sodium chloride do not conduct electricity because the ions are firmly held and cannot move. Only when molten or dissolved in water are the ions free to move.

When electricity passes through a metal, the metal is not affected. However, when electricity passes through an ionic substance (either molten or in solution) the substance is broken down in some way.

A substance that conducts electricity but is decomposed by the electricity is known as an *electrolyte*.

19.3 Passing electricity through electrolytes

Fig 19.3 shows an apparatus suitable for passing electricity through an electrolyte.

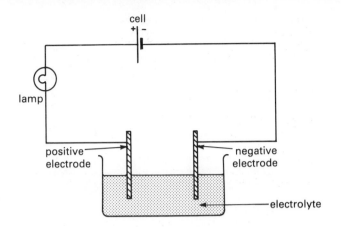

Fig 19.3

When electricity is passed through an electrolyte, the electricity enters and leaves the electrolyte via electrical contacts. These contacts are known as *electrodes*.

The positive electrode is known as the *anode*.
The negative electrode is known as the *cathode*.

The ions in the electrolyte are attracted towards the electrodes.

Negative ions (called *anions*) are attracted towards the anode.
Positive ions (called *cations*) are attracted towards the cathode.

When electricity is passed through an electrolyte, chemical reactions take place at the electrodes, and the electrolyte is broken down. This process is known as electrolysis.

Electrolysis is the process in which a substance conducts electricity and is decomposed by it.

Many substances can be broken down or decomposed by heating. You may remember that limestone (calcium carbonate) can be changed into quicklime (calcium oxide) in this way:

$$
\begin{array}{ccccc}
\text{calcium} & \rightarrow & \text{calcium} & + & \text{carbon} \\
\text{carbonate} & & \text{oxide} & & \text{dioxide} \uparrow \\
CaCO_3 & \rightarrow & CaO & + & CO_2 \uparrow
\end{array}
$$

Electrolysis is also a way of breaking down substances. It uses electrical energy instead of heat energy. Consider some of the ways in which electrolysis can be used.

1. Electrolysis of molten lead bromide

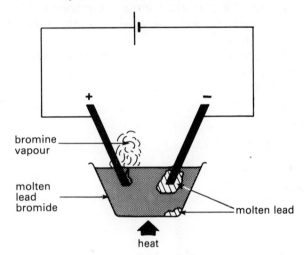

Fig 19.4

When electricity is passed through molten lead bromide, it is broken down to form lead metal and bromine vapour:

$$
\begin{array}{ccccc}
\text{lead bromide} & \rightarrow & \text{lead} & + & \text{bromine} \uparrow \\
PbBr_2 & \rightarrow & Pb & + & Br_2 \uparrow
\end{array}
$$

The lead is formed at the cathode and the bromine is formed at the anode.

We can consider the reactions at the anode and at the cathode separately.

At the anode

Negative bromide ions are attracted towards the

positive anode. At the anode they lose electrons and form bromine molecules:

bromide ions → bromine molecules ↑ + electrons

$$2Br^- \rightarrow Br_2 \uparrow + 2e$$

At the cathode

Positive lead ions are attracted towards the negative cathode. At the cathode they gain electrons and form lead atoms:

lead ions + electrons → lead atoms

$$Pb^{2+} + 2e \rightarrow Pb$$

2. Electrolysis of copper (II) sulphate solution

The way in which copper (II) sulphate solution conducts electricity depends on the electrode material.

(i) *With platinum electrodes*

Copper metal is formed at the cathode and oxygen gas is formed at the anode.

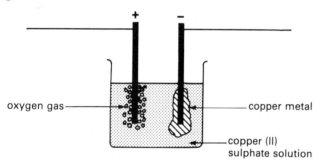

Fig 19.5

The solution contains copper (II) ions (Cu^{2+}) and sulphate ions (SO_4^{2-}) from the ionic copper (II) sulphate. It also contains some hydrogen ions (H^+) and hydroxide ions (OH^-) because water is slightly ionised.

At the anode

Hydroxide ions lose electrons forming water molecules and oxygen molecules:

hydroxide → water + oxygen ↑ + electrons
ions   molecules   molecules

$$4OH^- \rightarrow 2H_2O + O_2 \uparrow + 4e$$

The sulphate ions are unchanged

At the cathode

Copper (II) ions gain electrons to form copper atoms.

copper (II) ions + electrons → copper atoms

$$Cu^{2+} + 2e \rightarrow Cu$$

(ii) *With copper electrodes*

Copper is still formed on the cathode, but the reaction at the anode is different. Instead of oxygen gas being formed, the anode dissolves.

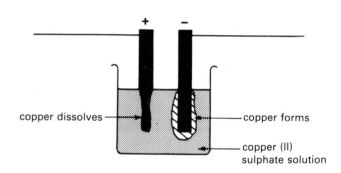

Fig 19.6

At the anode

Copper atoms from the anode lose electrons to form copper (II) ions. These ions pass into the solution.

copper atoms → copper (II) ions + electrons

$$Cu \rightarrow Cu^{2+} + 2e$$

The overall change is that copper is moved from the anode to the cathode. This makes the process suitable for copper plating. For copper plating, the object to be plated is made the cathode and a piece of pure copper is used as the anode.

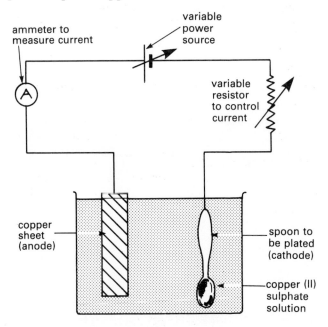

Fig 19.7 Copper plating a spoon

For successful copper plating the current, temperature and concentration of the electrolyte must be carefully controlled. The anode is sometimes arranged as a cylinder around the object to be plated. This gives a more even plating.

3. Electrolysis of dilute sulphuric acid

Pure water is a very poor conductor of electricity because it is mainly covalent. In pure water less than one molecule in one million is split into ions:

water $\rightleftharpoons$ hydrogen ions + hydroxide ions
$$H_2O \rightleftharpoons H^+ + OH^-$$

If a little sulphuric acid is added to water it becomes a good conductor of electricity. The

electrolysis of water containing a little sulphuric acid (dilute sulphuric acid) can be shown in the laboratory using the apparatus shown in Fig 19.8.

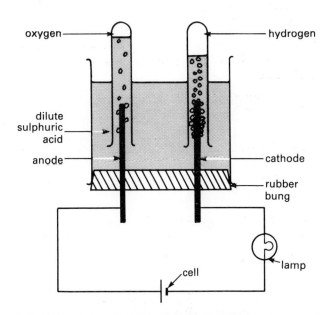

Fig 19.8 Electrolysis of acidified water

The electrolyte contains hydrogen ions (H^+) and sulphate ions (SO_4^{2-}) from the sulphuric acid. It also contains hydrogen ions (H^+) and hydroxide ions (OH^-) from the slightly ionised water.

At the anode

The hydroxide ions lose electrons forming water molecules and oxygen molecules:

hydroxide $\rightarrow$ water + oxygen $\uparrow$ + electrons
ions   molecules   molecules
$$4OH^- \rightarrow 2H_2O + O_2\uparrow + 4e$$

The sulphate ions are unchanged.

At the cathode

Hydrogen ions gain electrons to form hydrogen molecules:

hydrogen ions + electrons → hydrogen
$$\qquad\qquad\qquad\qquad\qquad\text{molecules} \uparrow$$
$$2H^+ \quad + \quad 2e \quad \rightarrow \quad H_2 \uparrow$$

The overall change is that water is split up into its elements.

water → hydrogen ↑ + oxygen ↑
$$2H_2O \rightarrow \quad 2H_2 \uparrow \quad + \quad O_2 \uparrow$$

This is a very convenient way of producing hydrogen gas. However, it is not used on a large scale in most parts of the World because of the high cost of electricity.

19.4 Making use of electrolysis

Electrolysis is of benefit to man in a number of ways:

1. It has allowed him to produce large quantities of the more reactive metals such as aluminium. Before the discovery of electricity aluminium was a very rare and precious metal. Many aluminium compounds existed, but it was difficult to extract aluminium from them. Nowadays, vast quantities of aluminium are made by the electrolysis of molten aluminium oxide (see page 100). It is used in so many ways that hardly a day goes by without

us using the metal in some way or other. Think how many ways you have used aluminium today.

2. Electrolysis allows us to easily purify some metals. Copper can be purified in this way.

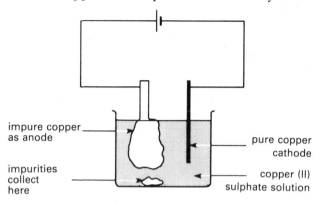

Fig 19.9 Purifying copper

When the current flows copper is dissolved from the impure anode and transferred to the pure cathode. The impurities are left behind.

3. The discovery of electrolysis allowed the modern electroplating industry to develop. Metals like steel are often plated. Car bumpers are chromium plated because it makes them look more attractive and it prevents the steel underneath from rusting. By tin plating steel cans, a container seeming to be

Name of substance	Electrolyte	Other substances formed at the same time
aluminium	molten alumina in cryolite	oxygen
sodium hydroxide	sodium chloride solution	hydrogen and chlorine
magnesium	molten Carnallite	chlorine
sodium	molten sodium chloride	chlorine
hydrogen	sodium hydroxide solution	oxygen

Table 2

made of pure unreactive tin is produced. A can made of pure tin would be very much more expensive and certainly not as strong.

Table 2 shows some substances manufactured by electrolysis.

19.5 Making electricity from chemical reactions

We have already seen that electricity can cause chemical reactions to take place. The opposite is also possible. Chemical reactions can be used to produce electricity. This is what happens in a car or torch battery.

When magnesium is dropped into dilute hydrochloric acid, it reacts to produce hydrogen gas. The reaction is exothermic. Energy is given out as heat. When copper is placed in dilute hydrochloric acid there is no reaction.

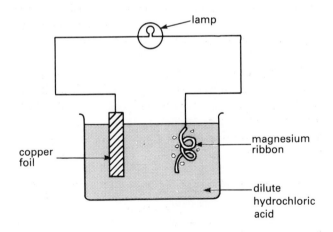

Fig 19.10 Making a battery

Using the apparatus shown in Fig 19.10, some of the energy released when magnesium reacts with acid is released as electrical energy rather than

heat energy. The electricity produced flows round the circuit and lights the lamp.

Whenever two different metals are placed in an electrolyte, electricity is produced. All cells or batteries work on this principle.

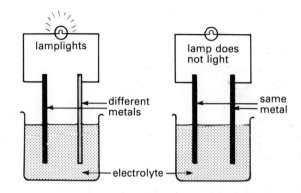

Fig 19.11 A cell or no cell

In dry cells the electrolyte is made into a paste so that it will not spill.

You should note that the electricity produced by cells is direct current electricity (DC). The alternating current electricity (AC) that is supplied to our homes is produced by a different method.

Questions

1. ALUMINIUM, GRAPHITE, OXYGEN, SALT, SUGAR, SULPHUR, ZINC.
   Choose from the above list:

a 2 elements which conduct electricity at room temperature.

b 2 elements which do not conduct electricity at room temperature.

c An element extracted from its ore by electrolysis.

d A substance which conducts electricity when molten but not when solid.

e A substance which conducts electricity when solid or molten.

f A non metal which conducts electricity when solid.

g A substance made up of ions.

h A compound made up of molecules.

2.

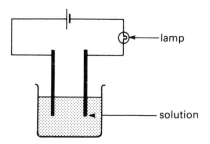

In turn, 4 different solutions were placed in the circuit shown in the diagram.

The solutions were: (i) copper (II) sulphate solution; (ii) sodium chloride solution; (iii) sugar solution; (iv) dilute sulphuric acid.

Decide which solution was in the circuit when the following results were obtained. Give reasons for your choice:

a The lamp lights; a colourless gas is formed at both electrodes.

b The lamp lights; a pinky brown solid is formed on the negative electrode.

c The lamp lights; a green gas is formed at the positive electrode.

d The lamp does not light.

3. Electricity is passed through molten calcium chloride. It decomposes to form calcium, and chlorine gas.

a Why will molten calcium chloride conduct elec-tricity whereas solid calcium chloride will not?

b At which electrode is the calcium metal formed? Write an equation for the reaction that takes place at this electrode.

c At which electrode is chlorine gas formed? Write an equation for the reaction that takes place at this electrode.

4. Imagine you are stranded on a small island. You find a portable radio but the battery is dead. You also find some copper wire and some iron nails. Explain how you could use these with sea water to make a battery suitable for the radio.

5. A small leaf was painted with a graphite paste and then made the cathode in the circuit shown in the diagram. The leaf became coated with copper metal.

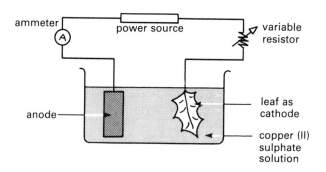

a Why must the leaf be painted with graphite paste before it is plated?

b Why is the leaf made the cathode rather than the anode?

c What material is suitable for the anode?

d What is the purpose of the ammeter?

e What is the purpose of the variable resistor?

f Why cannot an alternating current be used to copper plate the leaf?

6. Write sentences to show that you understand the meaning of the following words:

anode, cathode, anion, cation, electrode, electrolyte, electrolysis.

7.

a Draw a fully labelled diagram of the apparatus you would use to electrolyse acidified water and collect the gases formed at the electrodes.

b Name the gas formed on the cathode. How would you test for this gas?

c Name the gas formed at the anode. How would you test for this gas?

8. Aluminium is manufactured by the electrolysis of a molten mixture of alumina (Al_2O_3) in cryolite.

a What material is used for: (i) the anode, (ii) the cathode in this process?

b Why is cryolite used as part of the electrolyte?

c At which electrode is the aluminium formed?

d Write an equation for the formation of aluminium metal from aluminium ions.

e What is formed at the other electrode?

f Why was aluminium a very rare metal 150 years ago?

20 Energy from chemicals

We use energy to provide heat and light for our homes, offices, shops and factories. We use energy to power our cars, lorries, trains, boats and planes. We use energy in our factories to make the things we need, and the things that just make life more comfortable. We use an enormous amount of energy. In Britain it costs many thousands of millions of pounds each year to provide the energy we need. Most of our energy is obtained from chemicals known as *fuels*. In this chapter we are going to study some of these fuels.

20.1 The fossil fuels

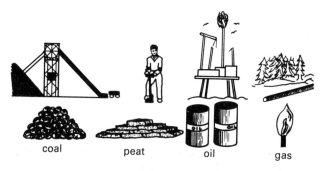

Fig 20.1 The fossil fuels

The fossil fuels are coal, peat, oil and gas. They were formed by nature millions of years ago.

The formation of coal and peat

Coal was formed about 200 – 300 million years ago. Plants in great forests died and fell to the ground. They were covered by other plants and were gradually changed by bacteria. The lower layers of plant matter were changed into peat. Over a long period of time layers of mud, sand and rock formed over the layers of plant matter. They were pushed down deeper and deeper into the Earth's crust. Heat and pressure gradually changed the peat into coal. The deeper the coal was pushed the more it was compressed into harder and harder coal. The hardest type of coal is known as anthracite and this is usually found at the deepest levels. However, a very long time has passed since coal was formed. Major upheavals have taken place in the Earth's crust since that time. These have brought some anthracite deposits near the surface.

Britain has large deposits of coal in Scotland, South Wales, the North of England and the Midlands, but there is little peat. However, in Eire there is not much coal, but there are large deposits of peat.

The formation of oil and gas

Oil and gas were also formed many millions of years ago. Shallow coastal seas existed at that time, that were rich in animal life. As tiny creatures in these seas died they sank to the bottom and started to decay. Gradually rivers washed mud, sand and rock down into the seas and the deposits of dead creatures were buried. They were changed by bacteria, heat and pressure to produce oil and gas. As layers of rock formed on top of the oil and gas, it was squeezed and forced through any porous rock. Only when it came in contact with a hard non porous rock was the oil and gas trapped.

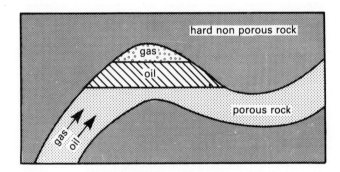

Fig 20.2 An example of an oil trap

Sometimes oil and gas deposits are not found together. Can you work out how this is possible? Slowly turning Fig 20.2 may help.

How good are fossil fuels?

We use coal, oil, and gas as fuels because they release a large amount of energy when they are burnt. Table 1 shows the approximate amounts of energy released when 1 tonne of different fuels are burnt.

Name of fuel	Number of energy units released on burning 1 tonne of fuel
coal	27
peat	9
oil	45

Table 1

1 energy unit = 1 million KJ. 1 energy unit will produce as much heat as a 1 bar electric fire does in nearly 12 days.

TNT isn't a good fuel. There must be more to a fuel than the ability to produce large amounts of energy. Think of the qualities that a good fuel should have:

1. It should release large amounts of energy at a controllable rate.

2. It should be safe to store and use.

3. It should be easily obtained.

4. It should be safe and easy to transport.

5. It should not cause pollution.

6. It should be cheap and plentiful.

I'm sure that you can think of many other qualities that a good fuel should have.

If we use these qualities we can make a balance sheet for coal, oil, and gas. We can compare their good qualities with their disadvantages.

Coal

For	Against
1. It is easily burnt and easily controlled. It is just as suitable for domestic fires as industrial furnaces.	1 It has to be mined. This requires large amounts of manpower and machinery. Both are likely to become more and more expensive.
2. It is easily stored. It is safe to store. It does not suddenly explode.	2. It is fairly difficult to transport. It cannot be pumped like oil. It has to be loaded and unloaded.
3. There is sufficient coal to last well into the 21st century.	3. If it was not burnt it would be a useful source of organic chemicals, such as those needed to make plastics.
4. The major products formed when it burns are carbon dioxide and water. These are harmless.	4. Coal can cause pollution when it burns, especially if it has a high sulphur content. Fortunately it can be fairly easily changed into a smokeless fuel.
	5. Mining operations can scar the countryside.

Table 2

Oil

For	Against
1. It is adaptable. It can be used for domestic heating and industrial furnaces.	1. It has to be obtained from underground deposits. These are often in inaccessible places: under the sea, in jungles, within the Arctic circle.
2. It is fairly easily transported in bulk, because it can be pumped.	2. It is the most important source of organic chemicals. In a way it is too precious to burn.
3. The major products formed when it burns are carbon dioxide and water. These are harmless.	3. If we continue to use oil at present rates, there is unlikely to be enough at the end of the 20th century.
4. It is reasonably safe and easy to store.	4. It can cause major pollution. 'Oil hits tourist beach.' and 'Oil slick kills sea birds.' are not uncommon headlines.
	5. Because it is not evenly spread throughout the world it can be used as a political weapon.

Table 3

Gas

For	Against
1. It is adaptable. It can be used for domestic heating and industrial furnaces.	**1.** It has to be won from underground deposits in the same way as oil.
2. It is easily controlled as it burns.	**2.** A gas is far more difficult to store than a solid or a liquid.
3. Gas reserves are about the same as those of oil. However, since gas can be made from both coal and oil, gas could be used as a fuel well into the 21st century.	**3.** It can burn explosively. Very careful maintenance if gas burning equipment is needed.

Table 4

The fact that we use coal, oil, and gas so widely means that society believes that the advantages of these fuels outweigh the disadvantages. However it may well be that in 10 or 20 years the balance will have swayed against these fuels. Some people say that hydrogen will be the fuel of the future. Try making a balance sheet for hydrogen as a fuel.

20.2 Energy from the nucleus

For about 80 years it has been known that some elements such as uranium are unstable. Atoms of these elements spontaneously break down to form atoms of different elements. These unstable elements are known as *radioactive* elements. The spontaneous breaking down of their atoms is known as *radioactivity*.

Radioactive elements can breakdown in a number of ways.

1. *By losing alpha (α) particles*

Some radioactive elements break down by throwing alpha particles out of their nuclei at great speed. An alpha particle is the nucleus of a helium atom; it is a cluster of 2 protons and 2 neutrons.

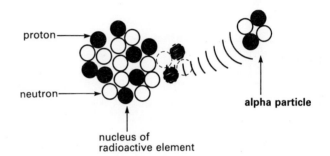

Fig 20.3 Losing an alpha particle

2. *By losing beta (β) particles*

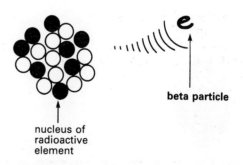

Fig 20.4 Losing a beta particle

Another way in which radioactive elements break down is by throwing beta particles out of their nuclei at high speed. Beta particles are high speed electrons. You may wonder how electrons can be lost from the nucleus of an atom. What happens is that a neutron changes into a proton and an electron.

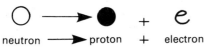

neutron ⟶ proton + electron

The proton stays in the nucleus, but the electron is thrown out.

3. By producing gamma (γ) radiation

When a radioactive element breaks down it often produces radiation known as gamma radiation. Gamma radiation is similar to light or X-rays but it is far more penetrating. Suppose different types of radiation are aimed at photographic plates partly covered with a hand. When the plates are developed, we would expect the results shown in Fig 20.5.

visible light:

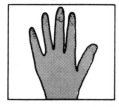

a complete shadow showing the outline of the hand. The light cannot pass through flesh or bone.

X-rays:

shadow shows position of bone only. The X-rays pass through the flesh, but not through the bone

Fig 20.5 The penetrating power of different radiations

gamma radiation:

little or no shadow. The gamma radiation is able to pass through flesh and bone

Fig 20.5

When a radioactive element breaks down by producing alpha particles, beta paricles or gamma radiation, energy is released. Unfortunately this energy cannot be used, because the rate at which atoms break up cannot be controlled. The rate at which radioactive substances decay is not affected by temperature, pressure or any of the things that affect the rate of chemical reactions.

Nuclear fission

If slow neutrons are fired at the nuclei of some atoms, the atoms split into 2 lighter atoms. A large

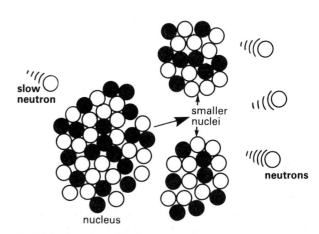

Fig 20.6 Nuclear fission

amount of energy is released at the same time. This process is known as nuclear fission.

You will see from Fig 20.6 that when nuclear fission takes place, extra neutrons are produced. These neutrons can be used to cause further fission. By controlling the numbers of neutrons we can control the rate of fission reactions. It is because of this that fission reactions are used to produce energy in nuclear power stations.

The nuclear reactor

The fuel used in nuclear reactors is the isotope of uranium of mass number 235, ie $^{235}_{92}U$.

The other isotope of uranium does not take part in fission reactions.

neutrons. As more neutrons are absorbed, there are less available to cause fission of the $^{235}_{92}U$ therefore the rate of fission decreases.

The fission of $^{235}_{92}U$ releases very large amounts of energy as heat. This heat is transferred away from the core by pumping a coolant through the core. Carbon dioxide, water and liquid sodium are 3 coolants that have been used in different types of reactor. The heat produced is then used to produce electricity.

The fission reaction is not the only one that takes place in the nuclear reactor. A large number of highly radioactive substances are formed. The reactor core must be very carefully shielded to prevent harmful radiation escaping. Several metres of concrete are used for this shielding.

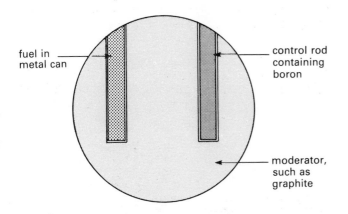

Fig 20.7 Part of a reactor core

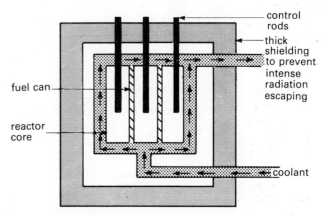

Fig 20.8 Simplified diagram of a nuclear reactor

Fission takes place in the fuel, and very fast neutrons are produced. These neutrons are slowed down by the moderator. The neutrons have to be slowed down in order to cause further fission. The rate at which fission takes place is controlled by control rods. These rods absorb

We can now make a balance sheet for $^{235}_{92}U$ as a fuel in nuclear reactors (see page 176).

With uranium-235 the balance sheet is far more even than in the case of coal, oil or gas. Most industrialised countries will use nuclear power in

For	Against
1. Nuclear energy is the only new, large, energy source that will be available at the beginning of the next century.	**1.** Less than 1% of any uranium sample is $^{235}_{92}$U. The rest is $^{238}_{92}$U. The 2 isotopes have to be at least partially separated.
2. Although expensive to build, once in operation nuclear power stations have low running costs and make electricity cheaply.	**2.** The possibility of a major disaster always exists when using fission reactions.
3. Extremely strict regulations control the use of nuclear fuels. Therefore, nuclear power stations are largely pollution free.	**3.** There is a limited amount of uranium in the world. Like oil it will soon be used up if $^{235}_{92}$U becomes a major energy source.
4. Uranium-235 can be changed into plutonium. This can be used in fast breeder reactors to produce even more energy.	**4.** Plutonium (if that were used) is a highly toxic and dangerous element.
	5. Highly radioactive waste is produced. It is difficult to get rid of it safely.

Table 5

the future, but the extent to which they use it will vary a great deal.

20.3 What about electricity?

No Chapter on energy would be complete without some mention of electricity. We use electricity in so many ways. However, electricity is a *secondary fuel*. It has to be made. You will never find an electricity mine. Not only do we have to make our electricity but we have to make it as we need it. There is no efficient way of storing large quantities of electrical energy.

Electricity is made from heat energy which can be released from other fuels. The heat energy is used to heat water. This produces steam which drives turbines producing electricity.

This process is very inefficient. Only $\frac{1}{3}$ of the heat energy is converted into electrical energy. It is only because the electrical energy can be used so efficiently that the process is justified.

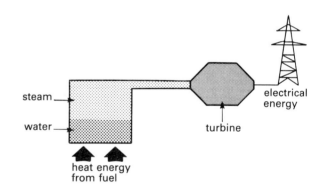

Fig 20.9 Making electricity

You may remember that in Chapter 19 we saw that it was possible to produce electrical energy directly from chemical reactions. However it is not possible to do this on a large scale. The small amounts of electricity that can be produced in this way are only suitable for portable objects like torches, radios or calculators.

Questions

1. ALPHA, BETA, GAMMA, PROTON, NEUTRON, ELECTRON.

   Choose from the above list, words suitable to complete the spaces in the following passage:

   When radioactive substances decay they produce (1) _____ and (2) _____ particles and (3) _____ radiation. (4) _____ particles consist of 2 protons and 2 neutrons, whereas (5) _____ particles are high energy electrons. A (6) _____ particle is lost from the nucleus by a neutron changing into a (7) _____ and a (8) _____ . The (9) _____ stays in the nucleus but the (10) _____ is thrown out.

2.
   a Explain briefly how coal was formed.
   b Why is the hardest coal usually found at great depths in the Earth's crust?
   c Why is some hard coal found close to the Earth's surface?

3. The Table shows the amount of heat produced when 1 mole of various alkanes are burnt.

Name of alkane	Formula	Mass of 1 mole (g)	Number of units of heat energy produced per mole of alkane
methane	CH_4	16	89
ethane	C_2H_6	30	156
butane	C_4H_{10}	58	287
pentane	C_5H_{12}	72	351
hexane	C_6H_{14}	86	419

   Plot a graph of mass of 1 mole of alkane against the number of units of heat energy produced when 1 mole of the alkane burns.

   Use your graph to work out how many units of heat energy are produced when 1 mole of propane (C_3H_8) burns.

   Is it possible to tell which of the alkanes is the best fuel from the above results? Give a reason for your answer.

4. You are going to put a central heating system into your home. You will use coal or oil or gas to fuel the central heating system.
   a How will your choice of fuel be affected by:
      (i) where you live.
      (ii) the size of your home?
   b What other factors will affect your choice of fuel?

5. Name: (i) 2 gaseous fuels (ii) 2 liquid fuels (iii) 2 solid fuels.
   Give an example of where each of these fuels is used.

6. As coal, oil and gas become more expensive people look for alternative fuels. What are the advantages and disadvantages of wood as a fuel?

7. "The destructive distillation of coal produces a better solid fuel than coal *and* a range of useful by-products."
   a In which ways is the solid fuel produced by the destructive distillation of coal better than coal?
   b Name 2 of the useful by-products formed by the destructive distillation of coal. Give a major use for both of them.

21 Qualitative analysis

Newspaper Tuesday 24th November

"A number of dark blue canisters have been found on North Cornish beaches. Police believe that they may contain highly toxic potassium cyanide. They are thought to have been washed from the decks of the Greek freighter *Alpha-Omega* during last weekends' violent storms. Anyone finding similar canisters is advised not to touch them, but to inform the police immediately".

Newspaper Friday 27th November

"Police scientists report that the canisters found on North Cornish beaches earlier this week did not contain potassium cyanide as feared. They did in fact contain coconut oil."

When stories like this appear in our newspapers, it means that somewhere a chemist has been busy finding out what was in those canisters. It is important that chemists know how to identify unknown substances. It is important that you know how to decide safely whether an unlabelled bottle in your laboratory contains distilled water or concentrated nitric acid. It is useful for you to know how to find out if some white crystals are sodium chloride or lead nitrate. *Qualitative analysis is the name that chemists give to identifying unknown substances.* This chapter is concerned with the qualitative analysis of substances that you find in the laboratory. Most of these substances are ionic. You will need to carry out separate tests to identify the positive ions (cations) and negative ions (anions).

21.1 Starting analysis

When you are attempting to identify an unknown substance you will need to use much the same skills as a detective investigating a crime. You must be *organised* and *alert*. There are three main ways in which you will get information about an unknown substance:

1. A colour change may provide information. *Example:* If a substance is yellow when hot and white when cold it is likely to contain zinc ions (Zn^{2+}).

2. Forming a gas may provide information. *Example:* If hydrogen sulphide gas (rotten egg gas) is formed, the unknown substance most likely contains sulphide ions (S^{2-}).

3. Forming a precipitate may provide information. *Example:* If sodium hydroxide solution forms a brown jelly like precipitate when added to an unknown solution, that solution must contain iron (III) ions (Fe^{3+}).

Be organised

Often when testing an unknown substance a gas is formed. It is of little use watching bubbles of gas escaping from a test tube and then thinking that you need to test the gas. You must be organised: you must be prepared! You must have all the chemicals you need for testing gases ready at the start of your analysis.

Table 1 shows some of the tests used to identify gases.

Name of gas	Tests for the gas
ammonia	**1.** Characteristic smell **2.** Turns damp red litmus paper blue **3.** Forms a thick white smoke with hydrogen chloride
carbon dioxide	Turns lime water milky
chlorine	**1.** Choking irritating smell **2.** Turns damp blue litmus paper red then white
hydrogen	Burns, often with a pop, putting out a lighted splint
hydrogen chloride	**1.** Sharp stinging smell **2.** Turns damp blue litmus paper red and forms a thick white smoke with ammonia
hydrogen sulphide	**1.** Smells of rotten eggs **2.** Turns colourless lead nitrate solution black
nitrogen dioxide	A brown gas that turns damp blue litmus paper red
oxygen	Relights a glowing splint
sulphur dioxide	**1.** Characteristic unpleasant smell **2.** Turns orange potassium dichromate solution to a *clear* green colour
water vapour	**1.** Turns blue cobalt chloride paper pink **2.** Turns anhydrous copper (II) sulphate from white to blue

Table 1

If a gas is formed when you are testing an unknown substance you should first *carefully* smell the gas. This may give you a clue as to which gas it is. However, **it is safe to assume that a gas with an unpleasant smell is a poisonous gas.** It is much better to identify a gas by using chemicals. Chemicals can't be poisoned. Fig 21.1 shows some of the ways in which gases can be tested.

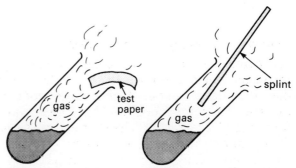

1. Test the gas with litmus, cobalt chloride paper etc as it is formed

2. Test the gas with a glowing or lighted splint as it is formed

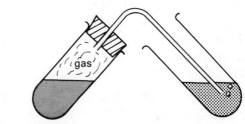

3. Pass the gas into a test solution, e.g. lime water

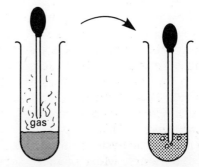

4. Collect some of the gas in a teat pipette as it forms and pass it into a test solution, eg lime water

Fig 21.1 Testing gases

Be alert

When you are given an unknown substance for the first time look at it carefully. Its appearance may give you a number of clues. Table 2 shows some of the deductions that you could make from the colour of an unknown substance.

Colour of substance	Deduction
grey	it may be a metal
blue	it may contain copper (II) ions (Cu^{2+})
green	it may contain copper (II) ions (Cu^{2+}) it may contain iron (II) ions (Fe^{2+})
yellow	it might contain iron (III) ions (Fe^{3+})
white	it is most likely not a transition metal compound

Table 2

21.2 Testing for cations

1. *The flame test*

Some cations colour a bunsen flame. These ions can be identified by the flame test.

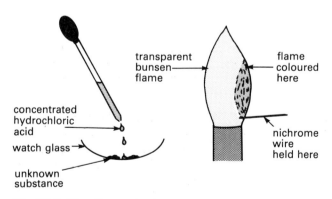

Fig 21.2 The flame test

Place a few crystals of the unknown substance on a watch glass and then add a few drops of concentrated hydrochloric acid. Dip the end of a piece of nichrome wire into this mixture. Then hold the nichrome wire near the base of a transparent bunsen flame as shown in Fig 21.2.

The nichrome wire can be cleaned by dipping it in concentrated hydrochloric acid and then heating it strongly in a bunsen flame. Table 3 shows some of the results that can be obtained in the flame test.

Ion Present	Formula of ion	Colour of flame
sodium	Na^+	bright orange (Street light colour)
potassium	K^+	pale purple
calcium	Ca^{2+}	red
copper (II)	Cu^{2+}	dark green

Table 3

2. *Reaction with sodium hydroxide*

The cations of many compounds are identified by testing with sodium hydroxide solution as shown in Fig 21.3.

In this test the precipitates formed are insoluble metal hydroxides. They are formed by metal ions from the unknown substance reacting with hydroxide ions from the sodium hydroxide solution:

Example:

$$\text{copper (II) ions} + \text{hydroxide ions} \rightarrow \text{copper (II) hydroxide} \downarrow$$

$$Cu^{2+} + 2OH^- \rightarrow Cu(OH)_2 \downarrow$$

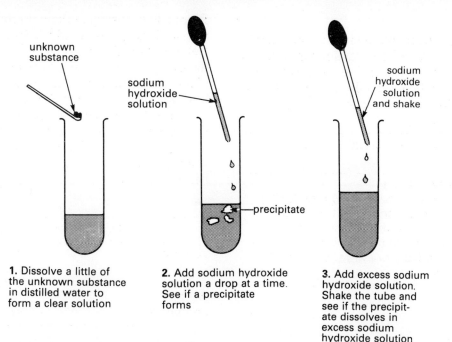

unknown substance

sodium hydroxide solution

sodium hydroxide solution and shake

precipitate

1. Dissolve a little of the unknown substance in distilled water to form a clear solution

2. Add sodium hydroxide solution a drop at a time. See if a precipitate forms

3. Add excess sodium hydroxide solution. Shake the tube and see if the precipit- ate dissolves in excess sodium hydroxide solution

Fig 21.3

Cation present in unknown substance	Formula of cation	Observation on adding a few drops of sodium hydroxide solution	Observation on adding an excess of sodium hydroxide solution
calcium	Ca^{2+}	Faint white ppt forms	No change
copper (II)	Cu^{2+}	Pale blue ppt forms	No change
iron (II)	Fe^{2+}	Dirty blue-green ppt forms	No change
iron (III)	Fe^{3+}	Brown ppt forms	No change
lead	Pb^{2+}	White ppt forms	Ppt dissolves to form a colourless solution
zinc	Zn^{2+}	White ppt forms	Ppt dissolves to form a colourless solution

Table 4

Table 4 shows the results that can be expected if the unknown substance contains certain cations.

3. *Reaction with ammonium hydroxide solution (aqueous ammonia)*

Solutions of ammonia in water can also be used to test for cations in solutions. The reactions are very similar to those with sodium hydroxide solution. Precipitates of the metal hydroxide are formed. However, there are some important differences.

Cation present in unknown substance	Formula of cation	Observation on adding a few drops of ammonium hydroxide solution	Observation on adding an excess of ammonium hydroxide solution
calcium	Ca^{2+}	No ppt	No change
copper (II)	Cu^{2+}	Pale blue ppt forms	Ppt dissolves to form a dark blue solution
iron (II)	Fe^{2+}	Dirty blue-green ppt forms	No change
iron (III)	Fe^{3+}	Brown ppt forms	No change
lead	Pb^{2+}	White ppt forms	No change
zinc	Zn^{2+}	White ppt forms	Ppt dissolves to form a colourless solution

Table 5

Table 5 shows the results that can be expected when certain cations are present.

You should realise by looking at Tables 4 and 5 that some cations like copper (II) or iron (III) can be identified using either sodium hydroxide solution or ammonium hydroxide solution. However to identify zinc ions or lead ions both sodium hydroxide solution and ammonium hydroxide solution must be used.

Identifying the peculiar cations

Most cations are metal ions, but there are 2 exceptions. These are the hydrogen ion (H^+) and the ammonium ion (NH_4^+).

Testing for hydrogen ions

The hydrogen ion is the ion responsible for acidity. A solution must therefore contain hydrogen ions if:
1. It turns litmus paper red.
2. It turns universal indicator red, orange or yellow.
3. It reacts with any carbonate producing carbon dioxide gas.

Testing for ammonium ions

Any compound containing ammonium ions will react with sodium hydroxide solution to form ammonia gas. This reaction is used as a test for ammonium ions. The unknown substance is warmed with sodium hydroxide solution and any gas formed is tested with damp red litmus paper.

21.3 Testing for anions

1. *Heating the solid*

Name of anion	Formula of anion	Possible observations on heating
Carbonate	CO_3^{2-}	Carbon dioxide gas may be produced
Sulphite	SO_3^{2-}	Sulphur dioxide gas may be produced
Nitrate	NO_3^-	Oxygen gas may be produced *or* oxygen gas and nitrogen dioxide gas may be produced

Table 6

A lot of information about the anions present in

an unknown substance can be obtained just by heating it.

Table 6 shows some of the results that can be expected if certain anions are present in the unknown substance.

2. *Reaction with hydrochloric acid*

By adding dilute hydrochloric acid to an unknown substance you can find out if it contains *carbonate* or *sulphite* ions.

Carbonates produce carbon dioxide gas. This can be detected using lime water.

Sulphites produce sulphur dioxide gas. This can be detected using potassium dichromate solution. It may be necessary to warm the mixture to free the sulphur dioxide gas.

3. *Reaction with silver nitrate solution*

Silver nitrate solution is used to test *solutions* of unknown substances. It enables *carbonate* ions and *chloride* ions to be identified, as shown in Fig 21.4.

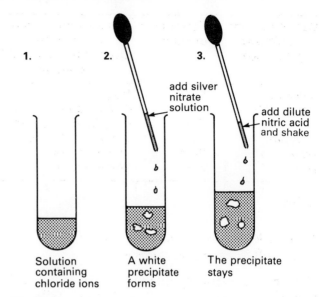

Fig 21.4

4. *Reaction with barium nitrate solution*

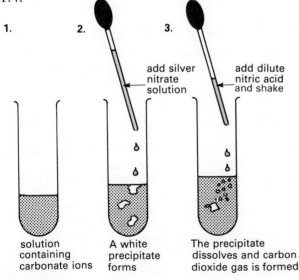

Fig 21.4

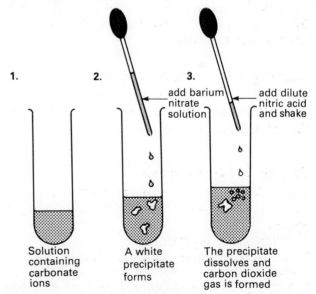

Fig 21.5

183

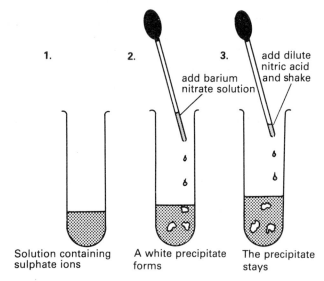

Fig 21.5

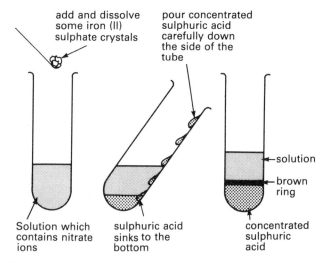

Fig 21.6

Barium nitrate (or barium chloride), like silver nitrate, can be used to test for anions in *solutions*. Barium nitrate solution can be used to identify *carbonate* ions and *sulphate* ions as shown in Fig 21.5.

5. *The Brown ring test*

All nitrates dissolve in water, but it is not easy to show that a solution contains nitrate ions. A special test known as the brown ring test has to be performed. This is explained in Fig 21.6.

A dark brown ring is formed between the sulphuric acid layer and the solution if nitrate ions are present in the solution.

Note: Concentrated sulphuric acid is an extremely dangerous liquid. Very great care must be taken with this test.

Questions

1. An unlabelled bottle contains a white powder. It is thought to be potassium carbonate.
a How would you show that the white powder contains potassium ions?
b How would you show that the white powder contains carbonate ions?

2. AMMONIA, CARBON DIOXIDE, CHLORINE, HYDROGEN, HYDROGEN CHLORIDE, OXYGEN, SULPHUR DIOXIDE.
From the above list of gases choose 1 which:
a is less dense than air
b turns acidified potassium dichromate solution green
c relights a glowing splint
d burns in air
e dissolves in water to form an acidic solution
f dissolves in water to form an alkaline solution
g turns lime water milky
h fumes in damp air

i bleaches damp litmus paper
j is formed when sulphur burns.

3. Name:
a 2 metal carbonates which are insoluble in water
b a metal chloride which is insoluble in water
c a metal sulphate which is insoluble in water
d a metal hydroxide which is soluble in water
e a red brown metal hydroxide
f a metal which colours a bunsen flame red
g a blue metal hydroxide
h a metal nitrate which forms brown fumes on heating
i a metal nitrate which does not form brown fumes on heating

4. You have three unlabelled bottles. One contains sodium chloride, one contains sodium carbonate and the third contains a mixture of sodium chloride and sodium carbonate. How would you find out which is which?

5. Suppose you are given a solution of copper (II) chloride in water.

a What colour would you expect the solution to be?

b Describe what you would expect to observe when the following are added to separate samples of the copper (II) chloride solution:
   (i)   silver nitrate solution
   (ii) sodium hydroxide solution
   (iii) dilute hydrochloric acid
   (iv) ammonium hydroxide solution.

6.
a Name the 2 metals present in brass.
b If a piece of brass was completely dissolved in nitric acid:
   (i) What colour would you expect the solution formed to be?
   (ii) How would you show that the solution formed contains the ions of ONE of the metals present in brass? (Name the metal you choose.)

7. A farmer has a sack of ammonium nitrate fertiliser, but he thinks it may contain lime (calcium hydroxide) instead:

a How would you prove that it was not lime?
b How would you prove that it was ammonium nitrate?

Data page

Element	Symbol	Atomic number	Relative atomic mass	Density at 20°C (g/cm^3)	Good or bad conductor of electricity	Melting point °C	Boiling point °C
Aluminium	Al	13	27	2·7	Good	660	2450
Argon	Ar	18	40	1·7 g/dm^3	Bad	−189	−186
Arsenic	As	33	75	5·7	Good	sublimes at 610	
Barium	Ba	56	137	3·5	Good	710	1770
Bromine	Br	35	80	3·1	Bad	−7	58
Calcium	Ca	20	40	1·5	Good	850	1440
Carbon	C	6	12	2·3	Good (graphite) Bad (diamond)	3500	3900
Chlorine	Cl	17	35·5	1·5 g/dm^3	Bad	−101	−34
Chromium	Cr	24	52	7·1	Good	1900	2600
Cobalt	Co	27	59	8·9	Good	1492	2900
Copper	Cu	29	64	9·0	Good	1083	2580
Fluorine	F	9	19	0·8 g/dm^3	Bad	−220	−188
Gallium	Ga	31	70	6·0	Good	30	2250
Germanium	Ge	32	73	5·3	Good	958	2880
Gold	Au	79	197	19·3	Good	1063	2660
Helium	He	2	4	0·2 g/dm^3	Bad	−270	−269
Hydrogen	H	1	1	0·1 g/dm^3	Bad	−259	−253
Iodine	I	53	127	4·9	Bad	114	183
Iron	Fe	26	56	7·9	Good	1539	2900
Krypton	Kr	36	84	3·5 g/dm^3	Bad	−157	−153
Lead	Pb	82	207	11·3	Good	327	1750
Lithium	Li	3	7	0·5	Good	180	1330
Magnesium	Mg	12	24	1·7	Good	650	1100
Manganese	Mn	25	55	7·4	Good	1250	2100
Mercury	Hg	80	201	13·6	Good	−39	357
Neon	Ne	10	20	0·8 g/dm^3	Bad	−249	−246
Nickel	Ni	28	59	8·9	Good	1453	2820
Nitrogen	N	7	14	1·2 g/dm^3	Bad	−210	−196

Element	Symbol	Atomic number	Relative atomic mass	Density at 20°C (g/cm³)	Good or bad conductor of electricity	Melting point °C	Boiling point °C
Oxygen	O	8	16	1·3 g/dm³	Bad	−219	−183
Phosphorus	P	15	31	1·8	Bad	44	280
Platinum	Pt	78	195	21·4	Good	1769	3800
Potassium	K	19	39	0·9	Good	63	760
Scandium	Sc	21	45	3·0	Good	1400	2500
Selenium	Se	34	79	4·8	Good	217	685
Silicon	Si	14	28	2·4	Good	1410	2480
Silver	Ag	47	108	10·5	Good	961	2180
Sodium	Na	11	23	1·0	Good	98	883
Strontium	Sr	38	88	2·6	Good	770	1460
Sulphur	S	16	32	2·1	Bad	119	445
Tin	Sn	50	119	7·3	Good	232	2600
Titanium	Ti	22	48	4·5	Good	1680	3300
Vanadium	V	23	51	6·1	Good	1920	3400
Uranium	U	92	238	19·0	Good	1133	3800
Zinc	Zn	30	65	7·1	Good	419	907

Additional exercises

1. You will need to use the data page for this exercise.

a Name three elements which are liquids at 1000°C.

b Name three elements which are solids at 1500°C.

c Name three elements which are gases at −200°C.

d Which element has a relative atomic mass of 55?

e Which elements have a relative atomic mass of 40?

f Which element is four times more dense than calcium?

g Which element is three times as dense as scandium?

h Which element has the same density as chromium?

i Which element has atoms twice as heavy as sulphur atoms?

j Which element has atoms twice as heavy as silicon atoms?

k Which element has atoms four times as heavy as neon atoms?

l Which element has the highest boiling point?

m Which element has the lowest melting point?

n Which element has the lowest density?

o Which element has the highest density?

p Name a good conductor of electricity which is a liquid at 100°C.

q Name an element which does not conduct electricity and is a liquid at 100°C.

r Name two elements which are liquids at room temperature (20°C).

s Which element is a liquid over the smallest temperature range?

t Which element has a relative atomic mass equal to its atomic number?

2. 10 changes have been made to diagram A in order to produce diagram B. Write the changes in the space provided.

Diagram A

ammonium chloride
and calcium hydroxide

nitrogen

water

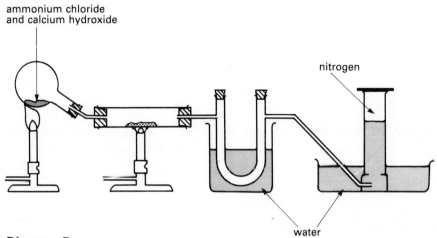

Diagram B

ammonium chloride
and calcium hydroxide

nitrogen

water

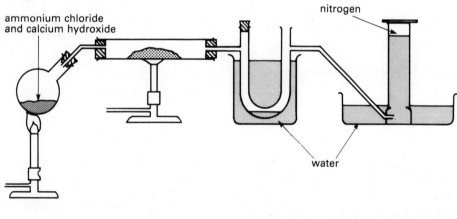

a	b	c
d	e	f
g	h	i
j		

189

3. 10 changes have been made to diagram A in order to produce diagram B. Write the changes in the space provided.

Diagram B

Diagram A

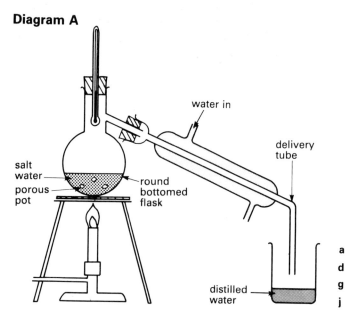

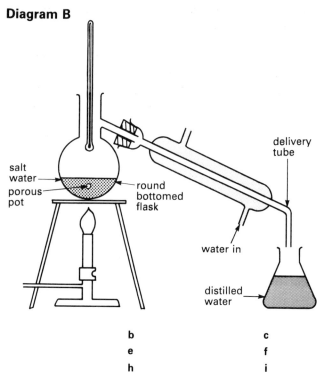

a

b

c

d

e

f

g

h

i

j

4. Read the following passage very carefully.

Think of the last time you used toothpaste. Was the toothpaste a dirty grey colour? Did it taste of garlic or soap? Did the toothpaste shoot across the bathroom as soon as you squeezed the tube, or did you have to struggle to force any out of the tube? Does your toothpaste dry out if you leave the top off? Does it grow a mould on it? Does your toothpaste appear to react with the toothpaste tube? The answer to all these questions is almost certainly no.

You should now realise that toothpaste is not the simple mixture we might expect it to be. Most toothpastes contain over twenty different ingredients. They contain abrasives, such as silica and diatomaceous earth, binding agents to keep the paste together, moisturising agents to keep it moist, detergents, flavourings and colourings. All these as well as the active ingredient which is normally there to prevent tooth decay or to provide healthy gums. Even so the main ingredient in all toothpastes is water.

a Suppose you were going to manufacture a toothpaste. Name 7 important properties your toothpaste should have.

b Many people like garlic flavoured food, but no-one has ever manufactured a garlic flavoured toothpaste. Suggests a reason for this.

c Why is a good standard of cleanliness important in a toothpaste factory?

d Name two substances which are used as abrasives in toothpaste.

e Not all toothpastes contain the same active ingredients. Make a list of those which are used and try to find out why each of them is used.

f Carry out a survey to find out which is the most commonly used toothpaste in your school. Also find out why people use a particular brand of toothpaste. Is it habit, cost, taste, colour or some other reason?

Modern names

Throughout this book the names of chemicals have been kept as simple as possible. However, some of the chemicals mentioned have more modern names which are gradually being introduced. You may meet these modern names in other books. The following table shows the modern names of some common chemicals.

Common name	Modern name
Potassium permanganate	Potassium manganate (VII)
Potassium dichromate	Potassium dichromate (VI)
Hypochlorous acid	Chloric (I) acid
Nitric acid	Nitric (V) acid
Nitrous acid	Nitric (III) acid
Sulphuric acid	Sulphuric (VI) acid
Sulphurous acid	Sulphuric (IV) acid
Sodium hypochlorite	Sodium chlorate (I)
Sodium nitrate	Sodium nitrate (V)
Sodium nitrite	Sodium nitrate (III)
Sodium sulphate	Sodium sulphate (VI)
Sodium sulphite	Sodium sulphate (IV)
Sodium thiosulphate	Sodium thiosulphate (VI)

Appendix of units

Scientists often have to make measurements. When they make these measurements it is important that they state the units they are using. This appendix is concerned with the units that you may meet in your chemistry course.

Density
The density of a substance is its mass divided by its volume. Density is usually measured in grammes per cm^3. The density of iron is 7·9 grammes per cm^3. The density of sulphur is 2·1 grammes per cm^3.

Mass
The mass of a substance tells us how much matter it contains. Scientists usually measure mass in grammes (g) or kilogrammes (Kg). 1Kg = 1000 g. Sometimes tonnes are used. (1 tonne = 1000 Kg) Grammes, kilogrammes and tonnes are metric units. Some non metric units of mass are still used. We buy vegetables by the pound (lb) 1 lb = 454 g. We buy sweets by the ounce (oz). 1 oz = 28·53 g.

Solubility
The solubility of a substance tells us how much of that substance will dissolve in a fixed amount of solvent. Solubility is usually measured in grammes per 100 g of solvent. The solubility of sodium chloride in water at 20°C is 36 g per 100 g of water. This means that at 20°C the maximum amount of sodium chloride that can be dissolved in 100 g of water is 36 g.

Temperature
The temperature of a substance tells us how hot that substance is. Most temperatures are now measured in degrees Celcius (°C). Water freezes at 0°C and boils at 100°C. However, many cooking recipes still mention temperature in degrees Farenheit (°F). Water freezes at 32°F and boils at 212°F.

Volume
The volume of a substance tells us how much space it fills. Scientists measure volume in cm^3, dm^3 and litres. One cm^3 is the space occupied by a box 1 cm long, 1 cm wide and 1 cm deep.

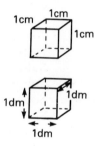

One dm^3 is the space occupied by a box 1 dm long, 1 dm wide and 1 dm deep.

Since 1 dm = 10 cm, then 1 dm^3 = 1000 cm^3. One litre is the same volume as 1 dm^3 or 1000 cm^3.

In everyday life we also use some different units of volume. Milk is delivered in pints (1 pint = 568 cm^3).

Gas meters measure the number of cubic feet of gas we use (1 cubic foot = 28·31 litres).

Index

All major references are shown in *italics* in this index.

2s 2+5
3? 4+5

$$K_2CO_3 + 2HNO_3 \rightarrow 2KNO_3 + CO_2 + H_2O$$

$$K_2CO_3 + 2HNO_3 \rightarrow 2KNO_3 + CO_2 + H_2O$$

9

$$2NaOH + H_2SO_4 \rightarrow Na_2SO_4 + 2H_2O$$

Na	O	H	S	→	Na	S	O	H
2	6	3	1		2	1	8	3 4
							6	

$$2NaOH + H_2SO_4 \rightarrow Na_2SO_4 + 2H_2O$$